THE CHURCH IN THE NEW TESTAMENT

THE CHURCH
IN THE
NEW TESTAMENT

RUDOLF SCHNACKENBURG

BURNS & OATES
LONDON AND TUNBRIDGE WELLS

Original edition "Die Kirche im Neuen Testament",
Herder, Freiburg. Translated by W. J. O'Hara.
First published in Federal Germany.
This translation © Herder KG and
Search Press 1965, 1974.

This edition published 1974
by Burns & Oates
Wellwood, North Farm Road, Tunbridge Wells, Kent TN2 3DR

Reprinted 1981

ISBN 0 86012 002 3

Printed in Great Britain by
Biddles Ltd, Guildford, Surrey

CONTENTS

Preface

I was guided in the construction of the present work by the point of view which I had expressed at the end of my earlier book, *God's Rule and Kingdom* (1963), 355 f.: "To do justice to every aspect of the Church ... it would be advisable to complement this approach from above from the concepts of the reign of God and Christ with another approach from below: that of the earthly existence and constitution of the Church, its relation to the cosmos and its heavenly 'presence'." A much more extensive work might be written on the Church in the New Testament, but perhaps concentration on certain questions can itself be of service.

The various aspects of the New Testament conception of the Church which are discussed here make it impossible to avoid a certain amount of repetition in different sections. New Testament theology requires several starting points on account of the position between historical and systematic theology that is proper to it. Not only has the historical development of theological ideas within the New Testament to be dealt with, but as far as possible a methodical survey and synthesis has to be provided. The reader's indulgence is therefore requested for overlapping in various parts of this essay. What is offered is an attempt to throw light on as many aspects of the New

Testament idea of the Church as possible with the means that are available to the exegete.

Like my earlier work on the idea of the *basileia*, this study is intended to promote mutual discussion. It is not meant as the last word on any of the questions touched upon, some of which are still vigorously disputed. Yet I should consider myself fortunate if I could make a modest contribution to a discussion so prominent at the Second Vatican Council.

As regards the abundant literature of the subject, some limitation was inevitable. Regard for the achievement of others should not therefore be measured by the quotations made from individual authors. In a debate it is not possible to address all one's partners equally. What had to be done was rahter to expound in a positive way my own view formed from the New Testament sources.

Rudolf Schnackenburg

The Church in the New Testament

The Church is everywhere present in the New Testament even where it is not manifest in concepts and imagery. The Church gave birth to the New Testament writings and they all bear witness to its existence and life. Not a single New Testament author wrote as a mere private individual, but all took up their pens only as members and for the benefit of the society to which they professedly belonged and impelled by motives which concern all who believe in Christ. The New Testament documents, so different in literary category and the style of their authors, were not simply linked together artificially in the canon authorized by the later Church, but are held together by the intrinsic bond of the witness they bear to Jesus Christ. Prior to all deliberate reflection on this society from which they sprang and which they serve, prior to any theology of the Church, therefore, there stands the reality, the existence and the vitality of the community confessing Jesus Christ. Consequently, an exposition of the teaching of the New Testament regarding the Church will not only have to take into account the explicit statements and express pronouncements regarding the *ecclesia*[1], but must also ponder and judge the New Testament documents themselves as expressions of the

9

Church's life and as speaking testimony to the way the Church viewed itself[2].

Since all the New Testament writings have this character, it is legitimate to take the testimony of the New Testament to the Church together as a unit, even though shades of distinction concepts, imagery and ecclesiological views remind us not to overlook differences and lines of development in the idea of the Church. It will, therefore, be necessary to combine a critically analytical point of view taking into account the historical and theological development, with a more systematic, synthetic vision. It would seem appropriate to take as starting point that reality of the Church of Jesus Christ which lies behind all New Testament writings and in doing so to envisage the varied nature of the Church's life as well as the profounder harmony of the essential manifestations of that life (Part One). Then the development of the early Church's own understanding of its nature and the growth of a theology of the Church must be followed as far as the sources permit (Part Two). And when in this way a firm foundation has been laid by an historical and theological mode of investigation based on the sources, we can attempt to trace the nature and mystery of the Church by striving to penetrate through the multiplicity of theological concepts and pronouncements and at least approach the central nature of the Church in the New Testament (Parts Three and Four).

PART ONE

The Reality of the Church
Fundamental Characteristics of its Origin and Life

The existence of the redeemed community of Jesus Christ is expressly attested in the Acts of the Apostles and its origin and growth is presented in what is certainly a definitely Lucan perspective, but not one that is unhistorical on that account[3]. We have reason to be grateful for this account which describes with many details the life of the original community in Jerusalem and the mission which was initiated by God's dispensation and under his guidance, until the gospel reached the capital of the Roman Empire. For the Acts of the Apostles permit us to survey coherently, at least in its main features, what we only know in a fragmentary way, or infer, from the other New Testament writings. The particular picture of the Church and of history proper to Luke, where this author places his emphasis, and the theological views which characterize him, will be evaluated later (see Part Two, § 2 below). At this point it is a question of observing in the events and circumstances described by him the emerging reality and activity of the early Church, and of doing this despite the fact that we are obliged to trust to the guidance of a man who himself was a believer and personally committed. Will he not have observed the phenomenon of the original community better and more deeply than would have been possible for a merely critical historian?

11

We do not need to abandon historical criticism on that account, and may not do so, precisely when we seek to penetrate the mystery of the early Church triumphant despite all human inadequacies. But on the other hand we can never approach that mystery if we close our minds on principle to the view of faith. But the other documents of the New Testament are also indispensable in this perspective and wherever possible must be taken into account as well.

1. The post-paschal assembly

For a long time, liberal critical scholarship has repeatedly affirmed that the primitive Church originated in the Easter faith. Without going into the problem of the founding of the Church by Jesus[4], we propound the opposing thesis, one which corresponds to the early Church's own conviction, that the band of Jesus' disciples assembled (again) after Easter and, on the basis of the divinely effected events of Jesus' resurrection and the outpouring of the Spirit, formed itself into Christ's community. Luke himself creates the impression of a band of disciples which persisted without interruption from the days of Jesus' early life into the time after Easter, not dispersed by the passion of Christ nor completely cast down by his death, and which re-formed after Easter and became firmer, consolidated and expanded (cf. Acts 1 : 14, 15). He omits all indications relating to a return or flight of the disciples to Galilee, for the sake of theological concentration on Jerusalem[5] (cf. Mk 14 : 27 f. par. Mt; Mk 14 : 50 par. Mt; Mk 16 : 7 par. Mt), and links his two books by the command of the risen Lord to the disciples to remain in Jerusalem to await the descent of the Holy Spirit and then as his witnesses to carry the gospel from Jerusalem into the whole world (Lk 24 : 47–49; Acts 1 : 8). But even if we give the return or "flight" of the disciples to Galilee due weight from the historical point of view, the assembly of the scattered band (which receives its theological interpretation in Mark 14 : 27 f.[6]), remains a fact which is not adequately explained without real appearances of the risen Christ[7]. In the same way there can be no doubt about the remarkable fact that the disciples, whose origins were in Galilee, settled in Jerusalem and that the original community was formed in the holy city of Israel[8].

The community contained in the bosom of Judaism and then emerging from it cannot be understood without the coming and work of Jesus of Nazareth. It continues on a new plane that movement of assembly which he had begun with his message of the approaching kingdom of God[9]. Consequently the interest of the primitive Church in the Jesus of history was a living and indispensable one, as is shown not only by the missionary discourses in the first part of the Acts of the Apostles[10], but also by the fact of the composition of the gospels, even if the predominant interest that led to this was not a biographical or merely historical one. The early Church knew itself to be the community of Jesus the Messias whom God raised to his right hand (Acts 2 : 32–36; 3 : 13–15, 20 f.; 5 : 30 f.; 7 : 55 f.; 9 : 4 f.; 10 : 37–43; 13 : 27–31). A strong indication that the primordial Jerusalem community traced itself back to the intentions and fundamental actions of Jesus is its maintenance of the circle of the Twelve, listed once again by name (less the traitor) in Acts 1 : 13, and completed at the apostolic election (1 : 15–26) by casting lots (behind which the hand of God was seen)[11]. The original community represented and made authoritative by the Twelve is, however, also recognizable apart from the Acts of the Apostles in the oldest parts of the tradition, above all, for example, in the fragment of that tradition recorded by Paul in 1 Corinthians 15 : 3–5, where Cephas and the Twelve, to whom the risen Christ appeared, figure as guarantors of the fundamental kerygma of salvation[12], and in the other important fragment of tradition, 1 Corinthians 11 : 23–25, according to which the

13

central liturgical celebration of Christ's community, the Lord's Supper, is shown to be an inalienable, integral part of their life, inviolable in content. Already at this point the fact cannot be sufficiently emphasized that Paul himself, who did not belong to the circle of the Twelve, and who in his work decisively advanced beyond the initial situation in Jerusalem, attributed the greatest importance to the fact that his churches were rooted in the soil of the original community. Preaching and divine worship were not separable for him from the original cell of the "Church of God" of the New Testament (1 Cor 11 : 22). All ecclesiastical growth, expansion into the Hellenistic world, the creation of new forms and groupings, adaptation to the Hellenistic mind, does not sever the living connection with the motherland of the Church of Jesus Christ assembled and constituted in Jerusalem.

From this, two provisional conclusions may be drawn. In the first place, an individual Christianity which was to or would wish to form apart from and outside the community is unthinkable for the primitive Church; belief in Christ, communion with Christ, life deriving from Christ, are only found within the society of believers joined to their Lord. The Church is constitutive of authentic Christian life. Consequently all the writers of the New Testament are churchmen who, for all their individuality, write as members of the one Church of Jesus Christ. Secondly, there is no "separated" Christianity either, that is to say, no division into disparate groups only linked externally by a common profession of faith in Jesus Christ and common religious rites and practices, or which were later to be conceptually linked by an emerging theology of the Church. The formation of groups in early Christianity, often postulated to excess by scholars[13], must in accordance with the early Church's own conception of itself, never be imagined as if a unitary entity, the "Church", were merely a later fiction; the multiplicity of historical phenomena, all the differences of local organization, all the shades of difference in

14

the formulation of theological teaching, cannot conceal the hidden ground of unity. In reality God's Church of the new Covenant by its very basic constitution and fundamental understanding of itself from its very beginnings was built solely on the "foundation of the apostles and prophets" and assembles all its members into the building whose corner-stone is Christ (Eph 2 : 20).

2. *The outpouring of the Spirit*

The descent of the Holy Spirit at Whitsun (Acts 2) is for Luke a fundamental event for the whole epoch and efficacy of the Church. It is not indeed the hour of the Church's birth, at least not in the sense that from then onwards Jesus Christ's community existed (it was already there in Acts 1 : 15); but it is the moment of its endowment with the "power from on high" (Lk 24 : 49; Acts 1 : 8), which alone qualifies it for its earthly task, its work of salvation in the world, and confers on it the mystery of its supernatural mode of existence. Whatever judgment may be passed on the Lucan account of Pentecost, which in the eyes of the critics involves difficulties of various kinds[14], for the early Church the outpouring of the Spirit and the importance of this for the Church's life was an established fact, even according to non-Lucan testimony in the New Testament. The charismatic manifestations of the Spirit in the Pauline communities are not in doubt, in view of the apostle's concrete instructions for Corinth (1 Cor 12–14). The Corinthians were not wanting in any charisma (1 Cor 1 : 7); but even in Thessalonica the gift of the Spirit must have been perceptible (cf. 1 Thess 5 : 19), as well as in the Galatian churches (Gal 3 : 2–5) and in Rome (Rom 12 : 6–8). However various the operations of the Spirit, the Spirit is the gift of God to all who believe and are baptized (cf. Acts 2 : 38; Gal 4 : 6; Rom 5 : 5), and according to Paul, he is the Spirit of

15

holiness who impels and engages to a holy life (cf. Gal 5 : 16 to 25; Rom 8 : 13). Already in 1 Thessalonians 4 : 8 the apostle had understood this Spirit to be God's eschatological gift to Christ's faithful (cf. Ezek 36 : 27). But this conviction is also expressed in 1 Peter 1 : 2 (cf. vv. 11f.); Hebrews 6 : 4; Jude 19f.; and in 1 John 3 : 24; 4 : 13, the phrase "God has given us the Spirit" already has the appearance of a fixed formula of the early Christian catechism. The imparting of the Spirit as a mark of the eschatological occurrence of salvation (cf. Acts 2 : 17–21, quoting Joel 3 : 1–5) is bestowed on all the baptized, but also makes of Christ's community as such, the temple of God (1 Cor 3 : 16; 2 Cor 6 : 16; Eph 2 : 22), a spiritual building in which the true "spiritual sacrifices" are offered (cf. 1 Pet 2 : 5), and the true worship "in spirit and truth" takes place (Jn 4 : 23 f.) [15]. It is precisely through this Spirit which fills the whole Church, that all its members obtain common access to the Father and become fellow citizens of the saints (in heaven) and members of God's household (cf. Eph 2 : 18 f.). Scarcely any thought intensified the Church's eschatological awareness and feeling of solidarity so much as this conviction of having received from God the gift of the Holy Spirit through the medium of Christ. It is the Spirit who, according to the Acts of the Apostles, guides the early Church and its missionaries (cf. 5 : 3, 9; 8 : 29, 39; 9 : 31; 10 : 19; 13 : 2; 15 : 28; 16 : 6f.; 20 : 23; 21 : 11), and according to the Apocalypse speaks to the churches (2 : 7, 11, 17, 29; 3 : 6, 13, 22; cf. 19 : 10).

Once again consequences are implied by this for the reality and self-awareness of the primitive Church which stands behind the whole New Testament. It cannot be understood without its foundation and endowment which took place "from on high" by God's eschatological action. Every attempt to understand it purely from the point of view of religious sociology for example, as the formation of a group within Judaism, as a sect with an apocalyptic bent which then developed in the Hellenistic world into an independent yet syncretist religious society, breaks down because of the witness it bears to itself. Though it is legitimate to draw analogies from the history of religions, such as are suggested by certain features in Judaism (apocalypses, Qumran) and in Hellenism (mystery cults, Gnosticism), these remain superficial and ignore the "showing of Spirit and of power" to which the early Church appealed for its formation and consolidation (cf. 1 Thess 1 : 5; 1 Cor 2 : 3; Acts 4 : 33; 19 : 11; 1 Tim 1 : 7 f.; Ignatius of Antioch *Ad Rom.* 3, 3). The consciousness of having received the Holy Spirit from the exalted Lord and Messias, as the first fruits and pledge of redemption (cf. Rom. 8 : 23; 2 Cor 1 : 22; Eph 1 : 13 f.; Tit. 3 : 6 f.), distinguishes its character from the whole of Judaism, including the Qumran community, to say nothing of paganism and its cults. Consequently, it was not merely a question of historical development and of adaptation to life on earth, when primitive Christianity, at the beginning still very close to Judaism, became an independent religious society; on the contrary it was much rather an intrinsically inevitable achievement of independence despite the ties which at first bound it to Judaism, and later it was an astonishing but intrinsically intelligible resistance to the temptation of losing its identity in syncretism. Paul was not the man of genius who saved the early Church from the danger of remaining or becoming a Jewish sect, but the enlightened mind who, perhaps like the "Hellenes" of Acts 6–7, recognized the special position of "the Church of God" side by side with the Jews and pagans (cf. 1 Cor 10 : 32) and who more than any other, threw open to it the gate into the world.

3. *Living communities*

The Acts of the Apostles gives an affectionate but not altogether clear and unified picture of the religious and social life of the original Jerusalem community. In the "summaries" (2 : 43–47;

4 : 32–35; 5 : 12–16), in which the outlines of the Lucan ideal can already be distinctly discerned[16], three things in particular are emphasized: the activity of the apostles[17], supported by healing and miracles which led more and more new members to the Church; the harmony and community of goods of its members; the liturgical life and worship which developed partly in a special meeting-place in the Temple (Solomon's Porch, 5 : 12; cf. 3 : 11), partly in the houses of members of the congregation (2 : 46; cf. 5 : 42). In these private meetings "they broke bread" and "took their meat with gladness and simplicity of heart" (2 : 46), a custom that was not limited to Jerusalem, for a gathering of the church in Troas in which Paul took part when travelling through is described in exactly the same way. All had assembled on Sunday "to break bread"; Paul spoke during the service, himself broke bread and "tasted" (food) (Acts 20 : 7, 11)[18]. The essential agreement of this common meal and eucharist with the Pauline "Lord's Supper" (1 Cor 11 : 20) can scarcely be disputed[19]. The celebration of the eucharist was from the beginning the central and common worship of the Christian churches; it was peculiar to them in commemoration of their Lord and in fulfilment of his sacred command, and intrinsically bound them together (cf. also below, Part One, § 6). Other characteristics, on the other hand, belonged particularly to the original Jerusalem church: the strong attachment to the Temple (which, however, was clearly opposed by the "Hellenists", cf. Stephen, Acts 6 : 13 f. and the speech in c. 7[20]), the continuance of outward life within the body of the Jewish people (and that means also in the practice of religion and the Law), and finally the voluntary and in some respects problematic community of goods[21]. The certainly idealized picture given by Luke may very well soften many weaknesses, tensions and developments, for instance the dispute between the "Hebrews" and "Hellenists" (Acts 6 : 1 to 6)[22]; the emergence of a radical legal tendency which wanted to hold fast to the Torah as an obligatory norm for all

18

Christian believers (Acts 15 : 1; cf. 21 : 20); the ruling of the "Council of Jerusalem" which did not itself suffice to settle all questions of corporate life (cf. Acts 15 : 23–29; 21 : 25 with Gal 2 : 1–10, 11–14)[23]. But it is not an artificially constructed picture, for it is partly confirmed by indications in Paul's letters; for instance the material distress of the Jerusalem church is shown by the great collection organized by Paul (cf. 1 Cor 16 : 1–4; 2 Cor 8 : 9; Rom 15 : 25–28), and the fundamental agreement with Jerusalem is shown by the description he gives in Galatians 2 : 1–10.

Another important community is vividly described in the Acts of the Apostles, that of Antioch in Syria. In this city, which was at that time the third largest in the Roman Empire (Fl. Josephus, *Bell. Jud.* III, 29), the first Christian community gathered, and was composed of former Jews and pagans, for some "men of Cyprus and Cyrene" preached with success the message of salvation of Jesus the Lord also to "Greeks" (cf. Acts 11 : 14–26). The common life of Christians of Jewish and gentile origin must have assumed harmonious form in this vast metropolis and this is once more indirectly confirmed by Paul in Galatians 2 : 1–14. The Christian community which subsequently was to become the centre and capital of the mission to the pagans, developed independently, as is seen by the fact that the disciples, Luke tells us, were here first called Christians[24]. There were regular meetings of this community, at which the considerable congregation was "instructed" (11 : 26), that is, as well as the missionary preaching there was doctrinal teaching within the church, probably within the framework of divine service. From the brief account in Acts 13 : 1–3, which is based on reliable information, however, as is shown by the list of names, we learn that in that church, "prophets and teachers" were active. So there were charismatic gifts here as well as in Jerusalem (cf. the "prophets" of 11 : 37 and 15 : 32), and in the Pauline churches (1 Cor 12–14 and *passim*). Probably they were at the same time the leading men

19

in the church at Antioch[25]. During a solemn service of prayer
(λειτουργούντων.) intensified by a fast "for the Lord", which
probably these men (αὐτῶν) were holding, perhaps with the
thought of the mission already in mind, the Holy Spirit
through prophetic voice designated Barnabas and Paul as
those whom he wanted to see set apart for the work he
had determined (v. 2), and after more fasting and prayer the
two chosen were sent out after imposition of hands (v. 3).
The ritual referred to certainly sprang from Jewish customs,
but they now subserved guidance by the Holy Spirit and took
place with the Lord in mind.

With the original, purely Jewish-Christian Church of Jerusalem and the mixed community of Antioch, that of Corinth
might be given as an example from Paul's missionary terri-
tories of a church of predominantly pagan origin and whose
life is well known to us from the two epistles to the Corinthians. What is striking about this church in the busy port of
Corinth is its rich charismatic endowment (1 Cor 1 : 5 ff.;
12 : 8 ff.) and, on the other hand, its human inadequacy and
frailty. We hear of assemblies in which many charismatics
wanted to come forward but only caused confusion (1 Cor 14).
At the most sacred assemblies, namely for the celebration of
the Lord's Supper, serious disorders arose, because on account
of the behaviour of the rich, no fraternal social spirit developed (1 Cor 11 : 20–34). There were also divisions into groups
which lauded some particular missionary, to whom they gave
preference over others (1 Cor 1 : 11; cf. 3 : 4 f., 22). Not a few
paid heed to opponents of Paul who made their way into the
congregation (cf. 2 Cor). Some misunderstood the gift of the
Spirit, became conceited and, perhaps infected with gnostic
ideas, became fanatics. In addition there were the still un-
mastered pagan vices, particularly of a sexual kind (1 Cor
5; 6 : 12–20). In short, the picture of the church was anything
but gratifying and Paul had to employ his whole personality
to prevent the community from slipping from him. Never-

theless, the epistles to the Corinthians, for all this human inadequacy, bear witness to the existence of a flourishing church life which was evident in morality too. They themselves, read in the assemblies as they were, give a most vivid and beautiful idea of the apostolic preaching and instruction (2 Cor 3 : 4 – 4 : 6), admonition and encouragement. The common worship of God, on which Paul has much to say and many instructions to give (cf. 1 Cor 11 : 14), occupies a central position. Baptism and eucharist (cf. 1 Cor 1 : 13–16; 6 : 11; 10 : 1–11, 16–22), become deep religious experiences, sources of strength and motives for improvement (cf. also below, Part One, §§ 5 and 6). The awareness is present of forming a new religious society side by side with the Jews and pagans (cf. 1 Cor 10 : 16–22), "the Church of God" (1 Cor 1 : 2; 10 : 32; 11 : 22; 2 Cor 1 : 1), which in Jesus Christ honours its own and the only true Kyrios (cf. 1 Cor 1 : 2, 9; 8 : 6; 10 : 21; 12 : 3; 2 Cor 3 : 17 f.; 4 : 5). Furthermore Paul understood how to tighten the link between Corinth and Jerusalem (the great collection), and the other churches (cf. 1 Cor 1 : 2; 7 : 17; 11 : 16; 16 : 1, 19; 2 Cor 1 : 1; 8 : 24; 12 : 13; 13 : 12).

There prevailed, therefore, everywhere in the Christian communities a new life, full of promise. Despite all local differences, what is common to them stands out clearly: faith in Jesus the Messias and Lord, baptism and eucharist, apostolic preaching and instruction, high regard for brotherly love, and eschatological expectation. In the differences of practice from place to place, in discussion about the actual conduct of life, in the judgment passed in deciding special questions regarding church life (charismata, veiling of women, etc.), in settling difficult individual cases (the incestuous man, 1 Corinthians 5, litigation in pagan courts, 1 Corinthians 6 : 1–11 etc.), the freedom of the early Church is evident, and in failure and guilt too, the human limitations which, despite the guidance of the Holy Spirit, were still left in it.

4. Order and constitution

It is difficult to make out the order that prevailed in the first Christian communities, because it varied according to place and time. Even the picture drawn by the Acts of the Apostles of the Jerusalem mother-church gives ample occasion for questions. What was the position of the Twelve whom the author identifies in 1 : 26 with the "apostles"? Why do they strikingly recede into the background after 6 : 2 (cf. 6 and Acts 8 : 1, 14, 18), and why are the "elders" or "the ancients" mentioned with them at the "Council of Jerusalem"? Especially, however, what rank and position had "the Seven" who were chosen by the full assembly and according to Acts 6 : 6 were appointed by the "apostles" with prayer and imposition of hands? They were chosen to serve tables (6 : 2 f.), but according to the description that follows, undertook much more far-reaching activities such as, for example, preaching inspired by the Spirit and supported by miracles (Stephen, 6 : 8–10), and the mission (Philip in Samaria, 8 : 4–13, and in the coastal towns, 8 : 26–40)[26]. There is no doubt about Peter's special position, because the account in Acts is supported by various remarks of Paul in his letters[27]; but the question arises what the nature of his pre-eminence was, and above all, what is to be thought of the growing importance of James the "brother of the Lord" in Jerusalem, by his side (Acts 12 : 17; 15 : 13–21; Gal 1 : 19; 2 : 9), and after him (Gal 2 : 12; Acts 21 : 18). These problems have been much discussed and have received divergent answers[28], but cannot be dealt with here. We are not concerned with the concrete "constitution" of the original community but with the fundamental question whether and how an order appeared for the community life of the first Christians in Jerusalem and in the later churches.

As the Acts of the Apostles does not give adequate information about constitutional questions, there is a preference for using the authentic material that is available in Paul's epistles regarding conditions in the Pauline churches. But here, too, a warning must be given against wanting to obtain an adequate picture of the actual situation, though it is easier, nevertheless, to perceive the apostle's fundamental conception in this matter from his living speech with his churches. In that we encounter the problem which we are dealing with: whether, at least as regards Paul's way of thinking, we can speak of an "earthly constitution" of the churches (or of the Church as a whole) at all, or whether the whole life of the Church was based on guidance by the Holy Spirit, that is, on a purely pneumatic or charismatic order. The thesis of the democratic and charismatic constitution without special ministers, finds advocates even today though mostly no longer in the radical form represented by R. Sohm, who set the "Church of the Spirit and of love" in contrast to the "legalist Church", the model being considered to be the church of Corinth in particular[29]. Characteristic of the judgment of Protestant scholars of the present day is perhaps the remark of H. F. von Campenhausen: "The Church with Paul is therefore not regarded as an organization constituted in some way with ranks and grades, but as a single living cosmos of free spiritual gifts which serve and complete one another, but whose bearers can never rise above one another or shut themselves off against one another. To the extent that all compulsion and all lasting authority to command is expressly excluded, the picture of the Church that emerges, understood in the sense of a human social order, is utopian."[30] Further, "For a directing ministry such as the order of presbyters or the later monarchical office of bishop, there is no place in Corinth either in practice or in principle."[31] Now it would certainly be erroneous to try to affirm and defend in opposition to this an ecclesiastical juridical organization for the Pauline churches based on a starting-point of later conditions and views. The apostolic period has its own special criteria because the apostle in the Pauline sense,

23

the "envoy of Jesus Christ" (cf. the addresses of the epistles), personally called by God to his service, is just as much an exceptional phenomenon as the charismatic who is directly endowed by the Spirit for his service in the Church. But it is questionable whether this "apostolic" and "pneumatic" order (the two are to be carefully distinguished, though at that time they coincided in fact) was different in kind from the "juridical" or "hierarchical" one with which the attempt is made to contrast it. E. Schweizer correctly observes that "freedom of the Spirit and juridical order" cannot be opposed as they used to be, namely as contradictory and mutually exclusive. But he would like to define the order as the Christian community understood it, as follows: "It is God's Spirit which in freedom marks out what is then subsequently recognized by Church order; this order is, therefore, functional, regulative, instrumental, not constitutive, and this is precisely the decisive point."[32] This is where Evangelical (Lutheran) and Catholic thought is still divided even at the present day.

Before we actually attempt to deal with the question which is in fact decisive, that is, whether a definite order and constitution was essential to the early Church, it will be as well to bring out a few points which it is only possible here to affirm and emphasize.

1. The inner structure of the Church is fundamentally different from any purely humanly constituted community or society. The Church is conscious of being subject to its heavenly glorified Lord who guides and builds it up by his Spirit. Even external growth is attributed to him: "The Lord, however, each day added those who were to be saved" (Acts 2:47; notice the use of the passive voice in 2:41; 5:14; 11:24); the success of the preaching is an increase of the "word of God" (Acts 6:7; 12:24; cf. 19:20); the "hand of the Lord" is with the missionaries in Antioch so that a great number turned to the Lord in belief (11:21). And that is not only Luke's view, for Paul, too, is convinced that "the door" is

opened "to him" by God (1 Cor 16 : 9; 2 Cor 2 : 12; Col 4 : 3), that God gave power to Peter for the apostolate among the circumcised and to him the mission to the gentiles (Gal 2 : 8; cf. 2 Cor 2 : 5 f.), that Christ works through him and his words in order to call the gentiles to the obedience of faith "by the power of signs and wonders and by the power of the (divine) Spirit" (Rom 15 : 17–19; cf. 1 Thess 1 : 5; 1 Cor 2 : 3–5). Yet even the inner building up of the churches is not so much the result of the successful efforts of the men concerned, as the work of God or the Holy Spirit. Luke expresses his own, but not only his own, conviction in the fundamental statement: "The Church (ἡ ἐκκλησία in a supra-local sense) now had peace in all Judaea, Galilee and Samaria, (was) built up and walking in the fear of the Lord and grew by the consolation (τῇ παρα-κλήσει) of the Holy Spirit" (Acts 9 : 31). Paul develops a whole theology of "growth" (1 Cor 3 : 6 f.; Col 1 : 6, 10) and of "building up" (1 Cor 3 : 9–11; 14 : 5, 12, 26; 2 Cor 12 : 19; Eph 2 : 21; 4 : 12–16)[33], in which God and his powers take the first place. Consequently all the men who are entrusted with tasks and services in the Church are simply God's instruments, servants of Christ, organs of the Holy Spirit (1 Cor 4 : 1; 12 : 4–6), and so possess an essentially different character from all bearers of office appointed by merely human statute and constitution.

2. The law valid for all members of the Church, whatever functions they exercise in the whole and for the whole, is that of service and love which Jesus himself laid down for his disciples and inculcated (cf. Mk 10 : 42–45 par.), in the paradoxical sense that precisely the man who humbles himself will be exalted (by God) (Lk 14 : 11; Mt 23 : 12). That the early Church applied this "new order" to itself and indeed in its historical reality, is shown for example by the framework in which such sayings of Jesus are set by the tradition of the gospels (cf. Mt 23 : 8–10; Lk 22 : 24–27)[34]. Particularly strik-ing are the words that Paul uses from this point of view for

his apostolic office (1 Cor 4:1f., 9–13; 2 Cor 4:5, 12, 15; 6:4–10; Phil 2:17). The original Christian idea of service went much deeper than any comparable ideas and demands in the domain of human social life, for the early Church was not only concerned with the prior claims of the common good (although this point of view, *mutatis mutandis*, is not lacking, cf. 1 Cor 12:7), but also with the eschatological order.

3. Consequently the offices and ministries which appear from time to time, their number, the way they are named, and their nature, are not the decisive factor as long as the order willed and determined by God is maintained (cf. 1 Cor 14 : 33). Measured by this the "constitutional history" of early Christianity appears in fact lacking in uniformity and full of changes, for they seem to have drawn partly on Jewish models (cf. the elders or ancients in Jerusalem), and in Christian communities of pagan origin perhaps also on Hellenistic forms (cf. the ἐπίσκοποι and διάκονοι in Philippi, Phil 1 : 1). Even the much discussed question whether side by side with the charismatic offices, those that is which were occupied by reason of manifest gifts of the Spirit, there were also institutional or administrative ones whose bearers were appointed by simple conferring of office and were tied to a definite locality[35], also becomes less important if every office in the early Church was considered to be conferred by God and endowed with the Spirit[36]. Similarly the division into permanent and temporary ministries or offices is of less importance. The only thing that matters is that there is an order which derives from and is willed by God and in which Christ is the head of his earthly community and rules it by his Spirit. The decisive question (and the one which separates Catholic from Protestant scholars) is whether the Church of the new Covenant according to the will of God and the disposition of its founder Jesus Christ is in its earthly form to possess an articulated, graduated (hierarchical) order with certain organs empowered

to rule, or whether the "holy people of God", as such, possesses all authority and the necessary order is produced by
disposition of the Holy Spirit at any particular time, in
whatever way this may find expression. To put the matter
more briefly, is a definite fundamental order constitutive of
the Church of Jesus Christ?

There is no question of sharply opposing, as K. Holl does[37],
the concept of the Church held by the original Jerusalem
community to that of Paul. As regards the former, Holl concedes that "we find in the Christian community from the very
beginning a regular hierarchy, an order established by God,
divine ecclesiastical law, a Church which is an institution into
which individuals are received" (page 54). In Paul, however,
he thinks he discerns a new and entirely different concept of
the Church. The "apostles" (for Holl that means James and
the Twelve) who possessed in Jerusalem "a lasting, divine pre-
eminence unattainable by any others" and who "therefore
were empowered to guide", were now regarded by Paul merely
as instruments, servants, preachers, and messengers of Christ.
It was not a question of individual persons as such, but of their
testimony to Christ. The independence of the community and
of the individual Christian, he thinks, has greater weight
(page 63). Although this sharp contrast was rejected by
Lutheran scholars too[38], its influence is still felt. Paul's link
with Jerusalem and the original apostles is acknowledged and
also his awareness of himself as an apostle, but neither is
envisaged in the perspective of an hierarchical order. We do
not wish to go further here[39] into the rather difficult question
of the relation of the great apostle of the gentiles to the
authorities in Jerusalem; after all, he knew he was an apostle
directly called by God and authorized by the Lord just as they
were, and sought contact and agreement with them (cf. Gal
1; 2 : 2–10; 1 Cor 15 : 3, 9–11). But what are we to say of
his relationship as an apostle of Jesus Christ to his churches?
Is he not conscious of being endowed with an authority over

27

them that includes rule and jurisdiction? On this, von Campenhausen affirms that "Paul, though called as an apostle by Christ and though as teacher of his churches their highest authority, nevertheless does not deploy this authority directly and does not build it up into a sacred relationship of spiritual leadership and subordination but rather the opposite."[40] "However imperiously Paul the apostle demands a hearing for Christ, however unaffectedly he presents himself as a model to be imitated, he nevertheless cannot simply give commands; he himself does not create the norm which would then have to be obeyed without further ado, but the community of those who possess the Spirit must rather follow him in freedom and it is to this freedom of theirs that he addresses himself" (ibid., page 51). That surely cannot be an accurate picture. Von Campenhausen indicates that Paul's concept of the apostolate is related "wholly and entirely to preaching the word and not to organization" (page 57); it must be added, however, that he also wrote his letters to the churches from very definitely pastoral points of view. He did not want to give orders but to exhort with kindness, not repel by strictness but win over by gentleness. It is a question, however, whether he does not all the same, claim a special authority granted him by the Lord. There are sufficient signs of this. Paul is conscious of the "full power" (ἐξουσία) which the Lord had given him (2 Cor 10 : 8; 13 : 10), but he does not want to use it "for the destruction" but for "the building up" of the community[41]. His apostolic power in no way makes him dependent on the "freedom of the community" to follow him. But unmistakably he asks the Corinthians, "What will you? Shall I come to you with a rod, or in love and the spirit of gentleness?" (1 Cor 4 : 21). Despite his absence from Corinth he himself decided the case of the incestuous man, though it is true he expected the assembled congregation with which he felt himself present in spirit to carry out the excommunication; the passage is not clear syntactically (1 Cor

5 : 3–5), but permits scarcely any doubt that the apostle "allows no freedom of decision of any kind to the community"[42]. The apostle's directions for divine service, too, have an authoritative tone (1 Cor 11 : 17, 33 f.); he not only admonishes, but gives concrete prescriptions (διατάσσω cf. 1 Cor 7 : 17; 16 : 1; Tit 1 : 5), using the same word as in 1 Corinthians 9 : 14 for an ordinance of the Lord. It is true he distinguishes a plain command of our Lord (1 Cor 7 : 10) from a merely personal decision (1 Cor 7 : 12); but he expresses the latter also with a definiteness that brooks no contradiction. His instructions for the moral conduct of life, too, expressed by παραγγέλλω or similar word, which he gives "by the Lord Jesus" (1 Thess 4 : 2)[43], are definite and concrete (cf. 1 Thess 4 : 11; 2 Thess 3 : 4, 6, 10, 12). The church of Corinth must have recognized this apostolic leadership; otherwise it would not be intelligible why they submitted certain questions to him for decision (cf. 1 Cor 7 : 1; the subsequent chapters concern those inquiries). Paul remarks in so many words "And that is what I prescribe in all the churches" (1 Cor 7 : 17).

On this basis and quite apart from the question of authorship, we must also dispute the justification for dissociating the Paul of the pastoral epistles from the Paul of the epistles to the churches and for seeing in them not merely more highly developed conditions (which no one denies) but also a fundamentally different conception of official ministry. Do the epistles to the churches really give a complete picture of the apostle's behaviour and actions, dispositions and prescriptions in his new foundations? In them too, though more incidentally, men are mentioned who have undertaken tasks in church life, and it is difficult to contest that among these functions of presiding and governing are also meant such as we find in 1 Thessalonians 5 : 12[44], and also in 1 Corinthians 12 : 28 (κυβερνήσεις); 16 : 15 f. ("be subject to such"); and Romans 12 : 6–8. Even if the activity and competence of such local

29

ecclesiastical assistants of Paul (in contradistinction to his envoys) was limited to care for the poor, and administration but included pastoral tasks also, the principle is nevertheless apparent here that Paul appointed or acknowledged such men, upheld their position in the church and endorsed it with his authority. Yet he himself remained the father and leader of the churches. This is the way the appointment of "presbyters", or "elders" must be understood, which is reported in Acts 14 : 23. Consequently the picture presented by the pastoral epistles is not improbable for the period of consolidation of the Pauline churches; we cannot go further into the question here[45]. It must only be clearly realized that Paul must not be viewed one-sidedly as preacher of the word and servant of his churches, but also as the authorized apostle, conscious of his authority and power to govern and who, when it seems necessary, makes use of it.

The question whether the primitive Church regarded a definite order as constitutive of its structure cannot be decided by peremptory treatment of the sources, but the whole testimony of the New Testament must be taken into account. And in doing so, it is not possible to pass over the gospels which, however important the rôle of the evangelists in their redaction, a matter much studied at the present time, nevertheless primarily transmit the primitive Church's own conception of itself based on Jesus' words and deeds. And in them special dignity and authority is attributed to Jesus' envoys. The saying handed down in different forms "He who listens to you, listens to me and he who rejects you, rejects me, but he who rejects me, rejects him who sent me" (Lk 10 : 16; cf. Mt 10 : 40; Jn 13 : 20)[46], indicates the general principle by which Jesus' messengers are to be judged. They continue his mission and consequently share in his mandate and authority which comes from God. That even during his earthly activity Jesus gave his disciples a limited share in his own powers and authority is shown by Mark 3 : 15; 6 : 7, 11, 17 f. par.; Luke

10 : 19. The opinion sometimes met with, however, that the Twelve had originally nothing to do with the later office of apostle (their actual designation "apostles" in Luke 6 : 13 is secondary [47]), but were rather only the circle of those who already knew about the coming kingdom and lived in its light and for that very reason regarded themselves as messengers who had to call all Israel to conversion, and who one day were to judge Israel in the "future kingdom", [48] does not take the text Mark 3 : 14 f. seriously enough. The purpose indicated for Jesus' choice here, that they "should be with him and that he might send them to announce (κηρύσσειν) and have power (ἔχειν ἐξουσίαν) to cast out devils" repeats precisely what Jesus regards as the content of his own mission, namely, to announce the approaching kingdom of God and to make it visible in its already present power (cf. Mk 1 : 39). The task and activity of the Twelve (Mk 6 : 7, 13) are, therefore, entirely in line with Jesus' own work. Providing Jesus is regarded as more than an eschatological prophet, a direct commission to form the eschatological redeemed community must also be attributed to these men who were chosen by him, who gathered around him and shared his work [49]. They have not only a symbolic significance (that of the full Israel of the time of final salvation intended by Jesus), a prophetic task in the present (the call to the people of the twelve tribes), and an eschatological function (judges over Israel cf. Luke 22 : 30b; Matthew 19 : 28), but also are empowered to gather together in the present, in Jesus' name, the redeemed community.

That, however, is not itself sufficient. There is no question of ignoring in this connection the saying regarding binding and loosing (Mt 18 : 18); for even if it has been handed down without direct indication to whom it was addressed, it would be difficult to postulate any other circle of recipients of this conference of authority except the Twelve, especially as the cognate saying in John 20 : 23 can only have been addressed to them [50]. If the power of binding and loosing designates "the

31

authoritative proclamation and mediation of the salvation which is God's rule" and comprises "an action of proclaiming and teaching, imposing obligation and order, effecting grace and judgment, in principle, therefore, full sacred teaching and juridical authority",[51] then it can hardly be "the Church as a whole" which is the "bearer of the great authority".[52] This interpretation receives a certain confirmation from some things that are reported in the Acts of the Apostles (cf. 5 : 1–11; 6 : 2–6; 15 : 6–29), but also from Paul's own conception of himself as an apostle. Though "the multitude" or congregation may be involved in important decisions (Acts 15; 1 Cor 5), nevertheless the authoritative leadership of the apostles can be recognized. The assembly in Jerusalem which discussed the necessity of circumcision for gentile Christians had as members "the apostles and presbyters with the whole church congregation" (Acts 15 : 22; cf. 6, 12, 23). The local churches are directed by presbyters (colleges of presbyters) and it is to such community leaders in Ephesus that the words are addressed which are so significant for the whole picture of the Church: "Take heed to yourselves and to the whole flock in which the Holy Spirit has appointed you overseers (ἐπισκόπους) to tend as shepherds the Church of God" (Acts 20 : 28)[53]. It is not only Lucan theology that we find here. At the basis of the Pauline conception in 1 Corinthians 12 : 28, too, is the picture of an articulated community with graded functions: "And God has appointed some in the Church, first apostles, secondly prophets, thirdly teachers, then miraculous powers, then gifts of healing, of giving assistance, of governing, and various kinds of languages." For all his endeavour to overcome a false estimation in judging the charismata and to emphasize the necessity of the collaboration of all members, Paul does not blur the differences and the articulated structure, and he too derives appointment to the various offices from God (cf. also Eph 4 : 11). Mention of the apostles in the first place and after them prophets and teachers (in Ephesians 4 : 11: apostles,

ORDER AND CONSTITUTION

prophets, evangelists, pastors and teachers), cannot be chance[54].
The picture does not yet correspond to the later hierarchy,
but exhibits the principle of a sacred order which God has
given to the Church. The holy people of God is also led by
earthly, human pastors who are responsible to their heavenly
chief shepherd (cf. 1 Pet 5 : 2–4)[55].

If the apostolic constitution of the primitive Church is
perceptible in this way, the further question must now be
raised of the primacy of Peter, which peremptorily calls for
examination in view of Matthew 16 : 18 f. and also Luke
22 : 31 f. and John 21 : 15–17. These various items within the
tradition of the gospels, themselves demonstrate that the question is neither peripheral nor to be restricted to a particular
community or group in the early Church. That Simon Peter
occupied a special position in the college of the Twelve is not
only shown by the account in the gospels, by his being named
first in all the lists of apostles, by the name Cepha(s) given
him by Jesus (cf. also John 1 : 42)[56], but is also supported by
the old tradition transmitted by Paul according to which the
risen Lord "appeared to Cephas and then to the Twelve"
(1 Cor 15 : 5). This appearance which is also mentioned incidentally in Luke 24 : 34 must have had decisive importance
for the authority of Simon Peter which was recognized in the
original Jerusalem community (cf. Peter's discourses and
his prominence in Acts 1–15); it is revealed in John
21 : 15–17, a piece of tradition the juridical and constitutional significance of which must not be overlooked[57]. But even
with Paul himself the outstanding and undisputed position of
Cephas is clear, not, it is true, from the point of view of
ecclesiastical law but, if we may use the expression, from that
of ecclesiastical politics. Why else did Paul attribute importance to going to Jerusalem "in order to make Cephas'
acquaintance" (Gal 1 : 18), and why is he concerned in
Antioch precisely about Peter's conduct in the dispute about
the mode of life of gentile Christians which was free of the

Law, and their association at table with their brethren in the faith who were of Jewish origin (Gal 2:11–14)? The days when people following the lead of F. C. Baur set up an irreconcilable opposition between Petrine and Pauline early Christianity are presumably over[58]. The controversy nowadays has focused on the manner in which Peter's primacy is to be understood, above all whether it was only a personal privilege of limited duration and validity, or whether it possessed fundamental and more far-reaching significance. O. Cullmann has put forward the theses that Simon Peter occupied only a representative position in the circle of Jesus' disciples and played no directing rôle, that in the original Jerusalem community he withdrew after a certain time from the leadership in favour of the "brother of the Lord", James, and went on the mission to the Jews; and in particular that the significance given him by Jesus as "rock" of the Church (Mt 16:18), concerned only his personal historically restricted position, not a strictly fundamental and enduring position in the building of the Church, so that no legitimate successors took over his primacy but rather Christ himself continues to build his Church on Peter the rock[59]. We cannot here enter into the lively discussion of this problem that has ensued[60]. For our purpose of recognizing the essential constitutive order of the Church willed by God, announced by Christ and followed by the early Church, it is already significant to observe not only the leading rôle of the Twelve but also the outstanding position of Simon Peter in the circle of the Twelve; to confirm his primacy of jurisdiction and the requirement of the apostolic succession, would only be possible within the framework of a more far-reaching inquiry which would have to include other fundamental topics such as tradition, the operation of the Holy Spirit and the continuance of Christ's work.

It is at least possible, however, to affirm at the end of this section overshadowed by controverted questions, that the primitive Church, whether as a whole or in its individual communities, did not lack order and that this order was not one which had to be created each time by the Holy Spirit, and which had to be recognized and acknowledged by the community, but was based on a fundamental constitution of the Church determined by God and obligatory from the start, and followed from the "mission from on high". That just as little excludes the continual guidance and immediate direction of the Holy Spirit as it does the collaboration of the community. In addition, enough scope was left the Church for giving concrete form to the constitution and sufficient freedom in establishing necessary offices and services as occasion arose. But the primitive Church nevertheless did not simply view itself as "the people of God" which must wait and listen to the direct instructions of its heavenly Lord, but rather as the "flock of Christ" for which its Lord has also appointed human pastors on earth who rule and guide it in his name.

5. *Proclamation of the Word*

Proof is scarcely needed that the proclamation of the word (of God) occupied the foreground in the early Church. Just as Jesus as God's eschatological messenger of good news (cf. Is 52 : 7) announced the approach of the kingdom of God (Mk 1 : 14 f.) and charged his envoys to transmit this message (cf. Lk 10 : 9), so after Easter it was the requirement of the hour in sacred history to link with the gospel of Jesus the gospel about Jesus the Messias and "leader (author) of salvation (life)" (Acts 3 : 15; 5 : 31)[61]. It is not our purpose here to unfold the contents of this kerygma (1 Cor 2 : 7; cf. Rom 16 : 25); but it is probably advisable, in order to picture the primitive Church as it really was, to emphasize the importance of the preaching of the word and the function of this proclamation in early Christian life and activity.

Even on a superficial view the multiplicity of terms which

are used to designate this activity is striking. "To announce salvation" (εὐαγγελίζεσθαι) is a favourite word of Luke, (10 and 25 times in gospel and Acts), but no less of the apostle Paul (21 times), who uses it in evident connection with his rich, profound idea of "the gospel" (60 times). It is a characteristic and comprehensive expression for the function of the messengers of the Christian faith (cf. Acts 5 : 42; 8 : 4 and *passim;* 1 Cor 1 : 17; 9 : 16), and refers to missionary preaching as well as to sermons to church congregations (cf. Rom 1 : 15). The depth of this concept which it is scarcely possible to render adequately in English can be perceived when we find it said in Acts 10 : 36 that "God announces peace through Jesus Christ" or in Ephesians 2 : 17 that Christ by his coming "announced peace to you who were afar off and peace to those nearby". The "evangelist" is similarly only the mouthpiece of God who is making known his salvation; he does not deliver the word of men but truly the word of God (1 Thess 2 : 13). His action is not only "speaking and preaching but announcing with authority and power"[62]. Closely related to this is the "proclaiming" (κηρύσσειν), like the cry of a herald. The gospel, of course, in order to develop its saving power, must be heard and accepted in obedience and faith (cf. Rom 10 : 14–18). Just as Jesus as God's herald declared the saving message of the approaching kingdom of God and so in fact proclaimed "the year of grace of the Lord", brought to the poor the news of salvation and to prisoners the notification of their liberation (cf. Mk 1 : 14; Lk 4 : 18; 8 : 1), so also this gospel must be proclaimed throughout the world for all nations (Mk 13 : 10 par. Mt); after Easter, however, it becomes the message of salvation about Jesus crucified and risen (cf. Acts 8 : 5; 9 : 20; 1 Cor 1 : 23; 15 : 12). This preaching is itself an eschatological event (2 Cor 4 : 3–6) of cosmic scope (cf. Col 1 : 23) and is of the nature of a public proclamation (cf. Gal 3 : 2 with 2 : 2). At the same time this kerygma which concentrates entirely on Christ "the power of God and the wisdom of God" (1 Cor 1 : 24) must also continue to ring out before the Church (cf. 2 Cor 4 : 5), so that God with his constant encouraging exhortation to reconciliation may reach the heart of the hearers through the mouth of the preacher (cf. 2 Cor 5 : 20). Of course, it is not a question of transferring the redemptive event so exclusively to the kerygma that the unique historical saving event of cross and resurrection only have power and efficacy in it[63]; but the "service of reconciliation" in the proclamation of the word is nevertheless much more profoundly envisaged by Paul than it is in our current conception of preaching[64].

The various functions that belong to the preaching of the word are also mirrored in an abundance of further verbs, from the simple "saying, speaking" (λέγειν, λαλεῖν), "testify" (μαρτυρεῖν), "persuade" (πείθειν), via compound words with the stem — ἀγγέλλειν or — ἡγεῖσθαι, to special expressions like "exhort" (παρακαλεῖν), "prove, convince" (ἐλέγχειν) and "reprimand" (νουθετεῖν), The "theology of the word"[65] is not limited to Paul, but also appears in the language of the first Christian missions and community and made its way even into the gospels, as for example into the explanation of the parable of the sower (Mk 4 : 13–20 par.), and in particular expressions such as "to speak the word (that is, of the message of salvation)" (Mk 2 : 2; 4 : 33; cf. 16 : 20), "the word of the kingdom" (Mt 13 : 19), "eyewitnesses and ministers of the word" (Lk 1 : 2). In this respect the language of the Acts of the Apostles is particularly rich and varied.

One expression deserves special notice: "the teaching of the apostles", in which the first Christians "persevered" (Acts 2 : 42). The "teaching" (Acts 4 : 2, 18; 5 : 21, 25, 28; 5 : 42; 11 : 26; 15 : 35; 18 : 11; 20 : 20; 28 : 31), expresses essentially more than our "instruction"; following Jewish tradition in its external form (cf. Acts 5 : 25), with the Christian preachers it was nevertheless entirely in the service of their message of salvation and powerfully penetrated the hearts of the hearers just as Jesus' "teaching" and "doctrine" were authoritative, new and startling (Mk 1 : 22, 27; 4 : 1 f.; 6 : 6, 30; 11 : 17 f.; 12 : 38). It occurs publicly (in the Temple) and in houses (Acts 5 : 42; cf. 20 : 20), and by Christian interpretation of Scripture, of which we have illustrations in the missionary discourses of Acts, it serves to provide the foundation of faith in Christ and to consolidate this[66]. Here, then, we have evidence of the early Christian "preaching", just as Acts 20 : 7, 11 provides an account of a sermon of Paul during divine service. The apostles themselves undertook this important function which took place before the celebration of the meal (cf. "the breaking of bread"). Unfortunately we are given no details about the nature of such sermons to a congregation; but just as all "teaching" according to Jewish habit[67] was based on the word of Scripture, the apostles too will have argued from Scripture, not in the rabbinical way inferring legal instructions, but throwing light on the message of Christ, strengthening and heartening. We hear nothing of Scriptural readings; it is possible that in the first period in contrast to practice in the second century, this was dispensed with and all attention was directed to the testimony and message of Christ crucified and risen[68]; but the whole New Testament bears eloquent witness to Christian study of the Scriptures[69]. But there was never lacking either, in the instruction of the congregation, an encouraging and hortatory application of the Scriptures to the faithful (cf. Acts 11 : 23; 14 : 22; 15 : 32; 20 : 2; and also 1 Thess 2 : 2; 1 Cor 14 : 3, 31; 2 Cor 5 : 20; 6 : 2; Phil 2 : 1). The early Christian sermon was an address preached in faith, based on Scripture, praising God's deeds in sacred history and culminating in the most recent saving events, but it also made plain the consequent obligation to a life of holiness, love, and brotherly spirit, and it gave courage and consolation for endurance in this world. Not infrequently it may have been followed by a warm prayer of thanks and petition to God (cf. Acts 4 : 23 to 31).

One particular form of the proclamation of the word came from the Christian "prophets". That such charismatic gifts were not rare in the early Church is testified not only by the Acts of the Apostles (cf. 11 : 27; 13 : 1; 15 : 32; 19 : 6; 21 : 9–10), but also by Paul's epistles (1 Thess 5 : 20; 1 Cor 12 : 10, 28; 13 : 2, 8 f.; 14; Eph 2 : 20; 3 : 5; 4 : 11; 1 Tim 1 : 18; 4 : 14) and the Apocalypse of John, that chief testimony to Christian prophecy, clearly presupposes the existence of a more closely associated group of prophets (cf. 11 : 18; 16 : 6; 18 : 24; 21 : 9). The prophetic gift could find expression in different ways; as well as prediction regarding the future, prophetic speech played a large part in divine worship. A fairly clear picture of this is given by Paul's description in 1 Corinthians 14. In preference to glossolalia, which manifested itself in an unintelligible manner, the apostle recommends that prophets should be allowed to speak, but not more than two or three, and that in succession, vv. 29 ff. "He that prophesies speaks to men for edification, exhortation and comfort" (v. 3). Such discourse inspired by the Spirit, has much to say to the faithful (v. 22); but an unbeliever, too, who perhaps may have come to the assembly is affected by it. By all those who are speaking prophetically he is "convinced, judged by all; the hidden things of his heart are made manifest and so he falls on his face, adores God and confesses: truly God is among you!" (vv. 24 f.)[70] In this way the primitive Church admitted discourse that came directly from the Holy Spirit, and esteemed the prophets. They are listed even before the "teachers" (1 Cor 12 : 28; 4 : 11); the faithful are "built up on the foundation of the apostles and prophets" (Eph 2 : 20; cf. 3 : 5). Their importance must not, however, be exaggerated; there is no proof at all that the early Church recognized their utterances as words of the Lord and even incorporated them in the gospels[71], and there is no mention in the New Testament of their being in any way rivals to the official ministry[72]. It was only against pseudo-prophets that the early Church had to take timely measures and inculcate discrimination (cf. 1 Thess 5 : 21; 1 Cor 12 : 3; 1 Jn 4 : 1–3).

In all this it is clear how rich the early Church was in its proclamation of the word. It was conscious of this, and Paul exhorts, "Let the word of Christ dwell among you in all its abundance" (Col 3 : 16).

·6. Worship and sacraments

Even though the Christians of Jerusalem who originated in Judaism and had been brought up in the Law, continued to assemble in the Temple (Acts 2 : 42; 5 : 12), prayed there (3 : 1), and were "zealous for the Law" (21 : 20, 23 f., 26, 23), that does not make it clear to what extent they took part in sacrificial worship. The information that a "great multitude of priests" accepted the Christian faith (6 : 7) also scarcely permits any conclusions to be drawn[73]. The Jewish Passover, the highest and most vivid expression of the religion of the Old Testament, would hardly still be celebrated by the first Christians in the old way; there are several indications which point rather to their celebrating from the beginning a new Christian "Passover", with Jesus' Last Supper (Lk 22 : 15–18)[74] in mind[75]. Though the Acts of the Apostles reports nothing about such an Easter celebration (cf. 20 : 6), there is reference to another frequently occurring liturgical celebration. The striking term "breaking of bread" (2 : 42, 46; 20 : 7, 11; cf. above, Part One, § 3), can scarcely mean anything but the eucharist[76]. Probably the "breaking of bread" took place within the framework of a service which also comprised preaching of the word, a common meal and prayers (cf. 2 : 42; see above Part One, § 5); and the atmosphere was an intensely eschatological one ("gladness", 2 : 46). The communal meals of the Essenes, including those of the Qumran community, do not bear comparison with this early Christian celebration, which already bore a character of eschatological fulfilment[77]. Nor, however, can the Jerusalem type be opposed and contrasted to other early Christian types of meals. Both Lietzmann's thesis, that the Jerusalem communal meal with its eschatological emphasis was far removed from the Pauline memorial celebration, as well as Lohmeyer's modified thesis of a Galilean and a Jerusalem type, have proved untenable[78]. Paul, who in Corinth had to reject a false, enthusiastic conception of the Lord's Supper, only places the emphasis differently when he insists on the remembrance of the death of the Lord (1 Cor 11 : 26). He not only retained the eschatological outlook ("until he comes," ibid.), but he too knows the eschatological gladness. On another occasion he speaks of "psalms, hymns, and spiritual canticles" which the faithful are to sing in thankfulness (Col 3 : 16), and in the parallel passage, Ephesians 5 : 18–20, this "being filled with (holy) spirit" and "thanksgiving" stands out even more strongly; both passages markedly point to assemblies for divine worship with celebration of the eucharist[79]. In reality both elements, the memory of the death and the eschatological anticipatory joy already have their basis in Jesus' institution of the Last Supper, and are linked in the gospel accounts[80]. The eucharist established by Christ has its place in redemptive history in the intermediate period between cross and Parousia and derives its profound significance from this position as well as from the will of its founder.

From the ecclesiological point of view it may be sufficient to bring out the following features.

1. The central act of worship of the early Church testifies to its characteristic eschatological awareness of already having experienced the happiness of the time of salvation, and yet of still looking forward to the "restoration of all things" at the Parousia of its exalted Messias (cf. Acts 3 : 20 f.). It must have been in the liturgical celebration of the eucharist that the old cry rang out which has been handed down in its original Aramaic,

41

Marana-tha ("Our Lord, come")[81]. However close the congregation at the "breaking of bread" knew itself to be to its Lord and however much it rejoiced at the common meal "giving thanks" (εὐχαριστοῦντες Eph 5 : 20) to God the Father for everything in the name of Jesus Christ, it did not forget, nevertheless, that ultimate society with the Lord had not yet been granted to it, and ardently implored his coming. Probably the peculiar concluding verses of the First Epistle to the Corinthians have a liturgical background. The apostle imagines the celebration of the meal beginning in the church assembly after the reading of his letter and his gaze moves from the greetings in the letter to the holy fraternal kiss with which those who had assembled greeted one another (16 : 20); he includes himself in spirit with a greeting written in his own hand, and then uses formulas from the liturgy: the anathema on the man "who does not love the Lord" and the *Marana-tha* (v. 22, cf. *Didache* 10, 6)[82]. The congregation's "Amen" when someone had pronounced in the Holy Spirit words of praise and thanksgiving (cf. 1 Cor 14 : 16) was a liturgical custom and confirmed in the Christian community (as opposed to the Jewish) that in Christ the "yes" had become an event, because in him God's promises were fulfilled (cf. 2 Cor 1 : 19 f.)[83]. Only where people thought they already possessed the whole wealth of gnosis and all the fullness of redemption (as with the Corinthian enthusiasts, cf. 1 Cor 2 : 8) and wanted to celebrate an exuberant and drunken liturgical meal, was it necessary to emphasize the gravity of the religion of the cross (cf. 3 : 9–13), the commemoration of the death of the Lord (11 : 26), the fact that they still stood under judgment (11 : 27 to 29). The unity in tension of the Christian eschatological attitude must not disintegrate.

2. In the celebration of the eucharist, the primitive Church experienced in a unique way the proximity, presence and society of its Lord. Precisely by this it became conscious of its essential difference from the Jewish worshipping community

and even more emphatically, of its contrast to all pagan religious associations and sacrificial fraternities (cf. 1 Cor 10: 16–22). Its meeting and bond with the exalted Lord in this celebration was based on a sharing in his blood and his body (v. 16), and is therefore thought of and explained much more realistically than all "analogies" in Judaism ("partakers of the altar", v. 18), or in paganism ("partakers with devils", v. 20). It is a "sacramental realism"[84] which, however, does not admit any magical conceptions because the gifts simply form a bond with the Lord and impose the obligation of holy service for his sake (cf. also 10: 1–13). It is not, of course, the eucharist which first joins together the faithful into Christ's community (that has already been done by faith and baptism), but it represents that community of Christ precisely as such in an incomparable way, perpetually effects, renews and strengthens its bond with Christ and repeatedly subjects itself anew to its heavenly Lord.

3. The assemblies for divine service which culminated in the celebration of the eucharist also, however, required inner cohesion among the faithful. The early Church's conception of itself as "the Church of God" scarcely, of course, had its basis in the celebration of the eucharist, but was nourished and confirmed by it. In this celebration the nature of the "Church of God" as the holy "assembly" of the Lord or of the people of God (cf. Deut 4 : 10; 9 : 10; 18 : 16; 23 : 2f.; Jgs 20 : 2) found particularly clear expression (cf. 1 Cor 11: 22 with 11 : 18). Perhaps the term originally was peculiar to the first community in Jerusalem (Paul uses it when he is recalling the time when he was a persecutor, Gal 1 : 13; 1 Cor 15 : 9) and was then extended to the Christian communities both of Jewish and of gentile origin[85]. Certainly the Jerusalem Christians at an early date called themselves "the saints" (cf. Acts 9 : 13, 32, 41; 26; 10; Rom 15 : 25ff.; 1 Cor 16 : 1; 2 Cor 8 : 4; 9 : 1, 12). However this manner of designating themselves may be viewed[86], it must also have a connection with an independent

43

liturgical life of their own. Paul perceived the relation of the eucharist to the unity of the Church in the profoundest way. The thought was so familiar to him that he even wanted to supplement the rather different argument in 1 Corinthians 10:16 (see above) with it. Verse 17 is like a small ecclesiological interpolation: because there is one bread, namely the eucharistic bread which is a partaking of the body of Christ, and because all share in this one bread, the many are therefore also one body. The concise mode of speech itself throws profound light on the Pauline conception of the "body of Christ"[87].

4. Finally the primitive Church receives from its liturgical life and especially from the eucharist, powerful impulses for its moral endeavour. That is particularly plain in the disorders in Corinth which Paul censures (1 Cor 11:20–34). Lack of consideration for poor people who came late destroyed fraternal harmony and made impossible the celebration of the Lord's Supper, for which friendly association at the meal and in the eucharist which followed was essential (v. 20). Such behaviour, however, signified unworthy reception of the eucharist and involved being guilty of the body and blood of the Lord (v. 27). Paul demands serious self-examination so that the Lord will not have to intervene further in judgment or discipline; for the many cases of illness and death in the congregation were, according to the apostle, a sign of salutary correction by the Lord, intended to preserve the guilty community from the last judgment (vv. 30–32). It is plain that the eucharist educated and formed both the individual, especially through the realistic conception of the sacraments (v. 29), and the whole congregation, namely by the intrinsically communal aspect of the sacrament. The sacrament of unity is also the sacrament of love. No believer can place himself outside the church community; even to the "strong" in Corinth Paul, still thinking of the obligations imposed by sharing in the body and blood of the Lord and also of the congregation

celebrating the eucharist, as being "one body" (10:16 f.), cries: "Be without offence to the Jews and Greeks and the Church of God" (10:32). As regards Jerusalem there is the word of the author of the Acts of the Apostles that even the serious difficulties between "Hebrews" and "Hellenists" in the daily ministrations to widows were not able to destroy concord (cf. 6:1–6)[88]. For Antioch the incident described in Galatians 2:11–14 testifies to the endeavour not to end fellowship at table between groups of Christians who followed Jewish or gentile customs. Behind these tensions after all there was always tacitly the question of the eucharistic association which imperatively demanded union.

All this shows the great ecclesiological significance of the early Christian worship with its culmination in the eucharist. This legacy of Jesus contributed to the early Church's keeping itself separate and apart from all other cults, to its awareness of the profound bond between the faithful, and to the development of a rich liturgical life. As however in this perspective the eucharist also already figured as "sacrament", as a gift of God (or more precisely here, of Christ), conferring salvation, it is imperative to raise the further question whether the primitive Church was at all open to a "sacramental" mode of thought. The question is important for a picture of the Church, because a religious society's conception of itself must be more clearly recognizable if it makes the claim to possess definite and perhaps indispensable means of salvation. Attention must therefore immediately be given to baptism.

There can be no doubt that the primitive Church from the beginning practised and required baptism "in the name of Jesus Christ" (Acts 2:38; 10:48; 19:5; cf. 1 Cor 1:13, 15; James 2:7)[89]. It is a question, however, of what meaning was attributed to it. It was not a mere rite of reception to incorporate the believer visibly and legally into the community, although this significance too cannot be overlooked (cf. Acts 2:41). An answer is given in the additional phrase in Acts

45

2 : 38, "for the remission of your sins". Baptism has a redemptive function; it confers salvation in a fundamental way that provides a foundation so that the recipient can thereby receive all the further gifts and benefits of redemption. In the Acts of the Apostles the eschatological redemptive gift, absolutely speaking, is the Holy Spirit; but the Spirit is as a general rule (10 : 44 is an exception determined by the situation), only conferred by God on those who are baptized in the name of Jesus Christ (cf. 19 : 2–6), even if the conferring of the Spirit sometimes seems to be connected with the imposition of hands by the apostles after baptism (cf. 8 : 15–17; 19 : 6). It is not necessary here to inquire further into the relation between baptism, the imposition of hands, and the reception of the Spirit[90]; it is sufficient for the present purpose to observe that baptism is not only an external institution but also a means of salvation of eminently religious significance. It frees the contrite and believing recipient from sin and guilt by subjecting him to the Kyrios Jesus (baptism "in the name of Jesus Christ"), in whom alone there is deliverance (Acts 4 : 12). Jesus' atoning death "for our sins" (1 Cor 15 : 3), becomes effective in baptism for those who attain belief. Even if the Acts of the Apostles nowhere formally and expressly state this, it is implied by their whole teaching. The conversion which is required of the Jews that their sins may be blotted out (3 : 19), only leads to its goal in actual fact via baptism (cf. 2 : 38). This, however, is not a magical device but establishes a bond with Jesus Christ whom "God has raised to his right hand to be leader and saviour and to give repentance to Israel and remission of sins" (5 : 31). Jesus' death, however, is viewed in the light of Isaias 53, as the scene between Philip and the Ethiopian treasurer shows (8: 31–35). The fundamental "preaching of Jesus" by Philip is immediately followed by baptism (vv. 36–38), perhaps the most vivid description of early Christian baptismal instruction. If the external and inner effect of baptism is viewed simultaneously,

it is impossible to avoid describing it as a sacrament[91] and indeed as the basic sacrament which gives a share in the salvation won by Jesus Christ and at the same time incorporates into his redeemed community. There is an indissoluble connection: all deliverance comes from Jesus Christ; there is no (true and full cf. Acts 18 : 24–28) fellowship with him except in his community; in order to win salvation and be added to his Church, one must be baptized in Jesus' name.

Without going into the question of the origin of early Christian baptism[92], it is to be observed that this conception of baptism is shared completely by Paul[93]. He too speaks of "washing" and the "sanctification" and "justification" which ensue "in the name of our Lord Jesus Christ and in the Spirit of our God" (1 Cor 6 : 11). The baptism "into the name of Jesus Christ" which can be more easily inferred from 1 Corinthians 1 : 13, 15 and the effects of the cleansing bath of baptism which are if anything more insisted upon by the apostle, are unmistakable views which he had already adopted, even if his conception of the Spirit as the divine agent and again as the gift of God conferred by baptism itself (cf.. Rom 5 : 5), appears, as compared with Acts, to be theologically more developed. Paul grasped more deeply also the relation of baptism to Jesus' death on the cross and resurrection, namely as the old man being crucified with Christ in order to rise to a new life which will find its ultimate fulfilment in the future eschatological life "with Christ" (cf. Rom 6 : 2–8). This close connection of the baptismal event with Jesus' cross and resurrection (cf. also Col 2 : 11–13; 3 : 1–4; Eph 2 : 5 f.), and the inner basis this provides for the sanctification which takes place in baptism, forms the great strength of Paul's christocentric theology. The early Christian ideas of baptism were developed in another way in the notions of regeneration (Tit 3 : 5), being engendered anew (1 Pet 1 : 23) "birth from the Spirit from above" (Jn 3 : 3, 5), and this brings out even more strongly the necessity of baptism for salvation. But it is not only at this stage that baptism becomes a "sacrament", perhaps on the basis of analogous ideas in the mystery cults[94]. It was one from the beginning. The thought of the Holy Spirit in particular which is still dominant even in the late texts (Tit 3 : 6), points to the basis in the thought of the Old Testament and Judaism, which hoped for an eschatological outpouring of the Spirit and a resultant change of heart (Ezek 36 : 25–27; on this cf. also now *1 QS* IV, 20 f.).

In this way the primitive Church in fact developed a sacramental mode of thought and was aware of being in possession of the saving means of grace (cf. also 1 Pet 3 : 21; Eph 5 : 25 f.; Jn 3 : 5; 6 : 53; 19 : 34; 1 Jn 5 : 6)[95], which, however, do not abolish moral endeavour but rather actually demand earnest striving for holiness (cf. 1 Cor 10 : 1–13; 1 Pet in its entirety; Heb 6 : 4–8). The early Christian paraenesis is to a great extent baptismal paraenesis in the sense that the God-given holiness is to result in a holy manner of life, that a "new man" and indeed a new humanity is to come into being in Christ (cf. Col 3 : 11), and one which is also mindful of its task of sanctification of the world around which is still far from Christ (cf. Eph 5 : 7–14).

7. Mission

To the picture of the early Church there finally belongs the mission. There was never a time in which the original congregation in Jerusalem was satisfied with an esoteric life of joy in salvation, fraternal association and waiting for the Parousia of its Lord as quietly as possible and without opposition, in the bosom of Judaism. Luke may have put the powerful stamp of his missionary interest on the Acts of the Apostles, but the preaching of the apostles and especially of Peter before the "whole people" is transmitted with convincing details (cf. Acts 3 : 11 f.; 4 : 1 f.; 5 : 25, 40, 42), is confirmed by the reaction of the Jewish authorities (4 : 1 f., 5 ff., 18, 21; 5 : 17 f., 40), and can be measured by the growth of the community which is not only represented in schematic fashion (cf. 1 : 15 with 2 : 41, 47; 4 : 4; 5 : 14; 6 : 7; 9 : 31; but also 15 : 5, 22). There is no room for doubt about a relatively early mission to the Jews by the apostle Peter, extending beyond Jerusalem (9 : 32–43; cf. Gal 2 :8; 1 Cor 9 : 5)[96]. The concern and zeal of the primitive Church for the mission are to be inferred above all from the tradition of the gospels, too. Although the gospels of Mark and Matthew are not missionary writings in the narrower sense, that is to say, writings intending to canvass those outside the Church, but are primarily addressed to the Christian communities, the missionary interest is unmistakable in both. In Mark, as well as individual sayings such as 13 : 10; 14 : 9 (cf. also 11 : 17 "a house of prayer for all nations"), the sections 6 : 6b–13 and 7 : 24 to 8 : 26 have to be taken into account in accordance with the way form criticism regards them, for they perhaps express "the outlook of the missionary Galilean community"[97]. In Matthew there are in addition to the parallels with Mark, even clearer passages, especially for example the missionary commission of the risen Lord (28 : 18–20) as well as parables with missionary reference (cf. 21 : 43; 22 : 9 f.), and sayings of universal scope such as 5 : 13 f.; 13 : 38[98]. All the early Church's preaching (cf. above, Part One, §5), even when aimed at those within the Church, bore the stamp of its missionary activity.

From the gospel texts quoted from Mark and Matthew, to say nothing of Luke, the universal orientation of the mission of the early Church can be recognized, in other words, a drive beyond Israel to the gentile peoples. Precisely the mission to the gentiles, however, raises special problems, in the first place whether it lay within Jesus' intention and could appeal to the special mandate of the risen Lord (whether, therefore, Matthew 28 : 18–20 is not a later community formation), and secondly the other question when and how the transition from the Jewish mission to the gentile mission took place. That Jesus did not wish to exclude the gentiles on principle from redemption is amply evidenced merely by the logion at Matthew 8 : 11 f., and parallel, Luke 13 : 28 f.; consequently the words at Matthew 10 : 5 f.; 15 : 24 must be understood as referring to the limits set to Jesus' mission (or that of his disciples) by the circumstances of redemptive history [99]. But that does not itself prove that Jesus' intention was that the gospel was to be preachead to the pagans later by missions; the texts on the matter are controverted [100]. In the perspective of our subject we do not need to enter into this discussion, but it is necessary to deal with the actual practice of the early Church.

The hesitation and initial resistance of the Jewish Christians of Jerusalem, including the apostles, in regard to the mission to the gentiles is not passed over in silence by Luke, either; in the Acts he wishes in fact to point out the way of the gospel to the gentiles and give a theological foundation to it (cf. merely 28 : 25–28). He traces the decisive turning-point in their attitude to the intervention of God and the authority of Peter (10 : 1 – 11 : 8). The opposition of the first Christians may have had various grounds especially their still very close ties with the Jewish people and its way of thought (cf. the apostles at Acts 1 : 6; Peter at 10 : 14), but cannot be connected with a fundamentally different conception of the mission imposed by the Lord and an essentially different idea of "God's Church" (cf. below, Part Two §1). For it is a fact that at the "council of Jerusalem", James the "brother of the Lord" who was clearly at that time already leader of the Jerusalem church, declared himself in agreement with the Pauline gospel (free of circumcision as it was), and with Paul's mission among the gentiles (cf. Acts 15 with Gal 6–10). That cannot have been a concession to faits accomplis; for previously Barnabas, the envoy of the Jerusalem church [101], had already approved the conversion of "Greeks" in Antioch, had brought Saul of Tarsus to the flourishing metropolis of the gentile Christians and himself collaborated for a whole year in the church there (Acts 11 : 22 to 26), and then actually accompanied Paul on his first missionary journey (Acts 13–14).

It is true, of course, that the opposition of the first apostles to the mission seems to create exceptional difficulties regarding the authenticity of the Matthean "missionary mandate" (Matt 28 : 18–20). Yet it must not be overlooked that in Luke 24 : 47 what is clearly the same command of the risen Lord is referred to (". . . to preach in his name repentance for forgiveness of sins to all peoples"), but there is also the supplementary phrase "beginning from Jerusalem". This command is then developed in Acts 1 : 8: "You shall be my witnesses in Jerusalem, and in all Judaea and Samaria and to the ends of the earth". The mission to the gentiles therefore was not to be the first step after Easter or Pentecost (the event which "prophetically announced" the opening out of the gospel to all nations[102]); Israel's privilege as the ancient people of God is preserved even in the "era of the Church"; Paul the apostle of the gentiles is also convinced of this as can be seen from his practice (according to the account in Acts), and his theological reflections (Rom 9–11). First of all Israel was to be given its last opportunity of repentance by the apostolic preaching (cf. Acts 2 : 38; 3 : 19; 5 : 31; cf. also the πρῶτον in Mark 7 : 27 and also in Romans 1 : 16; 2 : 9f.); this thought seems to have taken complete possession of the original apostles and blinded them to the more far-reaching command of the Lord. Luke at all events plainly sees in their conduct no contradiction to the missionary command, which he reports, to announce the gospel to all nations. Now Matthew dates Israel's obduracy as early as Jesus' time[103] and at the end wishes to throw open the perspective of the "true Israel" comprising Jesus' disciples universally, from all nations[104]. Consequently he leaves out of account the prospect of the mission going to the gentiles by way of the Jews first. His gospel itself, however, which after all probably was addressed to Christians of Jewish origin, shows that he, too, did not wish to deny or omit the mission to the Jews. For that reason the emphatically universal missionary mandate in Matthew should not be set against the narrowly Jewish conduct of the apostles described in Acts. The Lucan missionary command which is differently formulated even as regards its wording generally, shows clearly enough the conviction that the risen Lord desired in the mission a certain economy or plan of redemptive history which the Acts of the Apostles aim at indicating in broad lines. Historically speaking, the "Hellenists" who from the start had a freer and more open attitude to paganism, may have been the first to proclaim the gospel to the gentiles even if the story of Cornelius apparently attributes the initiative to Peter.

If Luke describes the beginnings and divinely directed course of the mission as seen by the believer in the perspective of redemptive history, Paul, the greatest missionary to the gentiles, also became the theologian of the missionary idea. The necessity of the mission, here understood in its original sense as a "sending", is given its basis by him in Romans 10 : 14f. by a sorites: "How then shall they call on him (the Lord) (in order to be saved) in whom they did not believe? But how are they to believe in him of whom they did not hear? But how were they to hear without anyone preaching? But how are there to be preachers unless they are sent?" Then he adds the scriptural text "How opportune[105] are the feet of those that preach salvation" (Is 52 : 7 in a divergent text). He describes the service of the missionary to the gentiles which Paul despite his privileged vocation (Gal 1 : 16; cf. Acts 9 : 15: "chosen instrument"), does not claim for himself alone[106], perhaps most beautifully in Romans 15 : 16 as, "administering as a priest the gospel of God so that the oblation of the gentiles may be acceptable and sanctified in the Holy Spirit". By this liturgical image he shows that God himself wishes the gentiles as a gift of mankind that belongs to him but which, of course, must first become obedient to him through belief in Jesus Christ, and pure and holy through the Holy Spirit. This gift of humanity, however, will not merely in the end fall to God's share like a ripe fruit, but already in the eschatological time of harvest is to be presented to God by means of the service of the missionaries. Paul was profoundly convinced of the eschatological urgency of this event. He was as it were filled with a holy anxiety to carry the gospel of Christ, after he had "unfolded it from Jerusalem round about as far as Illyricum", via Rome to Spain (Rom 15 : 19, 28). He sees it as a mystery of the history of redemption that "the fullness of the gentiles" is to "go in", so that then "all Israel will be saved" (Rom 11 : 25). However this apocalyptic saying is interpreted[107], it brings out very well the dynamic aspect of the mission in sacred history. But the deeper connection between Church and apostolic proclamation is revealed in Ephesians 3: 1–13 (cf. Col 1: 25–29). The mystery that the gentiles are "co-heirs in Christ, of the same body, and co-partners of the promise by the gospel" has only just been revealed to the holy apostles and prophets in the Spirit (vv. 5 f.). The service of the gospel, that is to say the proclaiming of the unsearchable riches of Christ (v. 8), is a service of mediation by the "apostles and prophets" chosen for this, in order to lead the gentiles into full and closest fellowship with Christ, to an equal sharing in the "body of Christ" and so at the same time to realize God's saving plan which culminates in the mystery of Christ (v. 9). The gentiles are comprised in God's dispositions in view of salvation (οἰκονομία); only by their incorporation into the "body of Christ" does the Church receive its actual full concrete form and so reveal the "manifold wisdom of God" (cf. v. 10)[108]. The organs by which the Church realizes itself in this way are the preachers of the gospel called and endowed with grace by God.

These deep Pauline thoughts simply bring into prominence what ultimately lay as a conviction behind the whole missionary activity of the early Church. The mission is a task set the Church by the very nature of its vocation as Christ's redeemed

53

community, and in accordance with its position in redemptive history, namely in the era between the exaltation and the second coming of Christ, a function that is essential to it and which the Church has to fulfil within the framework of the divine plan of salvation. It does not simply take place "in accordance with orders received", through men acting to the best of their ability, but always proceeds under the secret guidance of God, who chooses his instruments, and of the fullness and power of the Spirit of God bestowed on the Church.

PART TWO

The Theology of the Church. Theological Guiding Ideas of the Church and their Basic Unity

Already in our glance at the reality of early Christian life, we have frequently come across the primitive Church's own view of itself which that life reveals. A society which has formed itself on the basis of a common religious belief must of course necessarily manifest in the expressions of its life the thoughts and strivings which occupy its members. Until now, however, we have not uncovered this fundamental basis in its entirety, nor have we examined whether the conception the young Christian community had of itself did not perhaps gradually develop and change. This question must now be gone into from the historical and theological points of view as far as the sources permit. It is imperative for several reasons to do this. In the first place it will only be possible to work out clear theological conceptions of the Church if we do not prematurely mingle ideas which occur in the various individual writings but instead take into account the particular outlook of each author. Secondly, in view of the characteristics of the sources and especially of the synoptic gospels, the fact must be reckoned with that tradition and the author's views are so interwoven that in certain cases the traditional material embodies a different conception from that found in the work as we have it now in the definitive form given it by the sacred writer.

Thirdly, and this is of great importance, there could have been in the course of development changes and perhaps even "radical changes" in the early Church's conception of itself, whether as a whole or in particular groups or trends within it. For historical criticism it is tempting to oppose the original Jerusalem community with its close connections with Judaism, to the later gentile Christian communities which were conscious of their independence from Judaism and were not infrequently in opposition to it, and to seek the reason for this difference of attitude not only in human and historical factors but in differences of fundamental views and ideas. Consequently attention must be paid to the chronological occasion and historical point of origin of the ideas noted and also to their development, even though it seems impossible from the sources to trace anything of the nature of a history of ideas in regard to the concept of the Church at that early period[1]. Only certain questions will be dealt with here: was there a radical change from the conception of the Church held by the original congregation of Jewish Christians to the universal conception of Hellenistic Christianity? And was there a further break between for example the Pauline theology of the Church and what has been called "early Catholicism?" It is not intended to deal with these matters in a mainly polemic or apologetic way, but positively and theologically, in order to survey, compare and as far as possible put in order the rich and developing ideas about the Church. Clearly nothing more than an attempt can be made.

1. *The primitive Church's view of itself*

As the Acts of the Apostles unmistakably owes its form to Luke, and as scholars are increasingly inclined to question whether it is possible to reconstruct the sources used by Luke[2], there is no direct access to be had through Acts to the way the original community envisaged itself. We do not even know with certainty what words its members used to describe it, but have to fall back on inference. It can be assumed that the first Christians called themselves the "saints" (cf. Acts 9:13, 32, 41; 26:10; Rom 15:25f., 31; 1 Cor 16:1; 2 Cor 8:4; 9:1, 12), and further that they claimed to be "the Church of God", if it is correct that Paul originally applied this predicate to the Jerusalem community (cf. Gal 1:13; 1 Cor 15:9; also Phil 3:6 Vulgate) and only secondarily (as with "the saints") to Jewish Christian communities (cf. 1 Thess 2:14 and probably also 1 Cor 11:16: notice in both cases the use of the plural), and finally extended it to his own community in Corinth (1 Cor 1:2; 10:32; 11:22; 2 Cor 1:1), certainly in the sense of its being representative of the Church as a whole[3]. With him the expression indubitably possesses high theological significance which cannot without further ado be transferred to the Jerusalem community's own view of itself. The striking expression "the way" (Acts 9:2; 19:9, 23; 22:4; 24:14, 22) cannot have meant the community itself but the doctrine and way of life it represented[4]. Whether from certain pieces of tradition in the Gospel according to Matthew (not the redactional treatment), inferences may be drawn regarding what the original Jewish Christian and still Aramaic speaking community considered itself to be, is questionable, but must be kept in view. In particular with regard to the famous passage Matthew 16:18f., a problem now arises more seriously than before as a consequence of the discovery of the Qumran texts, and this must be gone into rather more closely.

Through certain Qumran parallels to the metaphor employed in Matthew 16:18 of the building of the Church on a rock[5], the formerly prevalent view that the term ἡ ἐκκλησία goes back to the Old Testament *qehal Yahwe* has been called in question. In the Greek Bible (LXX), ἡ ἐκκλησία usually renders the Hebrew word *qahal;* it often simply means "assembly",

57

but in important passages it bears the theologically important sense of "the community of Yahwe" (Deut 23 : 2 f.; 1 Chr 28 : 8; Neh 13 : 1; Mic 2 : 5), because it is a question of "the assembly of the people of God" (Jgs 20 : 2). This meaning must probably be implied in other passages as well, particularly in the Psalms and Chronicles, where simply ἡ ἐκκλησία is used[6]. The idea of "God's community" now transferred to the New Testament people of God is certainly present in Acts 20 : 28; 1 Corinthians 1 : 2; 10 : 32; 11 : 22; 2 Corinthians 1: 1 (and cf. also 1 Tim 3 : 5, 15), and is probably also behind many passages where merely "the Church" is mentioned without further qualification (for example Acts 9 : 31; 1 Cor 12 : 28). In other passages, it is true, ἐκκλησία continues as in the Old Testament simply to signify an assembly, and quite often of course the local congregation without any theological overtones (notice also the plurals used). Although the linguistic usage was still hesitant and not uniform, it cannot be doubted that in the early Church it largely expressed the idea of the "community of God" of the New Testament, the new people of God not restricted to the old Israel[7]. But the question is whether the oldest, Jewish Christian congregation already shared this view. Its consciousness of its mission in regard to Israel and its continuing close ties with the body of the Jewish nation make caution advisable. Even earlier, as a matter of fact, another Aramaic equivalent for μου τὴν ἐκκλησίαν in Matthew 16 : 18 has been conjectured by some scholars, in particular *kenishta*'[8]. On account of the Qumran texts there is now also a possibility of *sōd* (*1 QH* VI, 26: "Thou placest a *sōd* on a rock"; cf. *1 QS* VIII, 5; XI, 8; CD VIII, 21 b etc.[9]), and especially *'edhah* (*1 QpPs* 37, Kol. II, 16: "in order to build the *'edhah* of his elect" [probably plural] and elsewhere very frequently[10]). It seems that these expressions were deliberately chosen by the Qumran community and served to signify their own particular view of themselves. For them their community was the chosen holy Remnant of Israel which represented the true Israel, faithful to God and his Law, making atonement in the present age "for the land" and in the end will receive all Israel into itself (cf. CD I, 9 f.; II, 11 f.; *1 QS* VIII, 5 f.; *1 QSa* I, 1–3; *1 QH* VI, 8, 15; VII, 19; VIII, 6–11). Must not the original Aramaic speaking community when it used the same terminology (cf. also "the saints", "the brethren", "the way"), have linked the same thoughts to it, especially as it, too, of course, according to Acts, was seeking to call Israel to penance or atonement (cf. 3 : 19 f.; 5 : 13)? Did it perhaps assimilate such ideas under the influence of Qumran?[11] In that case, of course, the oldest Christian community would certainly have had a different conception of itself from the later primitive Church even from the "Hellenists" and certainly from Paul. It would only have seen one task before it, and that in regard to Israel, and would have aimed at being nothing else than the true Jewish Israel or the kernel of the eschatological Israel[12].

Nevertheless this conclusion would be premature and mistaken. A general caution must be given against inferring from an identity of terms an identity of conceptual content. The primitive Church when it spoke of ἡ ἐκκλησία τοῦ θεοῦ, "the Church of God", gave the Old Testament *qehal Yahwe* a new content. The Church of God of the New Testament is by reason of Jesus' atoning death (cf. Acts 20 : 28) a reality of quite a different kind. There is no sign at all that the primitive Church ever ascribed to this atoning suffering of its Messias any but a universal saving efficacy (cf. Mark 14 : 24 ὑπὲρ πολλῶν). Even if ἡ ἐκκλησία were originally derived from the expression *'edhah* preferred in Qumran[13], that does not of itself imply that the original Christian community meant the same thing by it as the Essenes of Qumran. As regards Matthew 16 : 18, the Qumran parallels are striking and show that this saying, which Matthew alone transmits, has by its mental outlook and linguistic expression an origin in the Palestinian past. Even if τὴν ἐκκλησίαν does presuppose *'edhah*,

59

the μου is also to be noted. Jesus is speaking about *his* Church. Quite apart from the question whether the word was actually used by Jesus himself, or, as not a few present-day critics maintain, first arose in the oldest congregation, it indicates a definite characteristic view[14]. And for this the other parts of the triple saying are not to be overlooked namely, the "keys of the kingdom of heaven", and the "binding and loosing". The relation of the ἐκκλησία to the βασιλεία τῶν οὐρανῶν (an expression that has no particular significance in Qumran), is very important for an understanding of the conception of the ἐκκλησία that is implied here[15]. If we now raise the decisive question regarding the content of the ἐκκλησία idea for Jesus and in the primitive Church, it is possible to observe various factors which plainly exclude the Essene view. The idea of the holy Remnant, so essential to Qumran, is completely lacking. The primitive Church did not separate itself from the people, laid down no special conditions for admission and did not itself seek at all to "atone for the land". Its call to repentance aimed at union with Jesus; special works of penance were not required[16]. If the first Christians called themselves "the saints", their holiness had quite a different air from that of the "saints" of Qumran. If the latter did choose the word 'edhah to refer to themselves, with the linguistic usage of the Book of Numbers in mind because "the desert life of the sect" found its "perfect model" in that book[17], the Christian community had a considerably different conception of its own life. Such possible linguistic parallels, therefore, do not permit any conclusions regarding essential agreement in ideas. E. Schweizer rightly observes, "Two things were impossible for the primitive Church, to distinguish itself from the 'people of the land' as a superior nucleus on a higher plane, or to view the Israel which rejected Jesus and would not hear the call to repentance, as the authentic Israel, at least for the time of salvation."[18] For the rest, the comparison with Qumran will have to be pursued in the third part of this essay.

Only a few cautious remarks of a positive kind are possible regarding the original community's view of itself, if this view is not thought to coincide with that of those who spoke about it. A more marked inclination towards the old Israel is unmistakable; the mission to the gentiles at first still lay outside the field of vision (cf. above, Part One, § 7). Since the eleven whose origins were in Galilee soon after Easter moved to Jerusalem and made the holy city the centre of their activities, this must be regarded as implying the intention of winning the whole of Israel to belief in Christ, or at least of confronting the members of the old chosen people with a decision whether they would accept the Messias Jesus for their salvation or reject him to their judgment (cf. Acts 2 : 36 πᾶς οἶκος Ἰσραήλ and also 3 : 22–26). In this the primitive Church remained quite in line with Jesus who was conscious that he was sent to the "lost sheep of the house of Israel" (Matt 15 : 24), and during his life on earth only sent his disciples to them (Matt 10 : 5 f.). But just as little as Jesus thereby intended to exclude the gentiles from salvation did the apostles who were acting in his name. It is possible that the latter according to old Jewish views were thinking that the gentiles after the conversion of Israel would be "added by God"; but if James' speech at the "Council of Jerusalem" is historically reliable (and the decision taken speaks in its favour), the leading men maintained an open attitude regarding a settlement of the question of the gentiles by God, whatever concrete form this would take. James declares that God himself was making his will known even at that moment "to take of the gentiles a people for his name" (Acts 15 : 14) and in this James seems to have seen the signs of the fulfilment of the prophetic promise for the age of salvation (cf. Zech 2 : 15)[19]. That required a fundamental assent to the mission to the gentiles which was a sign and indeed a confirmation of the belief of the primitive Church that it stood in the eschatological age, even if the apostles themselves, and in particular Simon Peter, felt themselves

61

called to the mission to the Jews (cf. Gal 2:8f.). It is legitimate to say, therefore, that the original community precisely on account of the memories of the Twelve of their instruction by Jesus, still felt itself more strongly bound in the perspective of redemptive history to the people of Israel, yet was convinced in principle that a new people of redemption had been constituted by the blood of Jesus.

This invalidates those theories which claim to observe a radical break in thought between the original Jewish Christian congregation and the Hellenistic Church. The different manner of thought recognizable in Acts 6–7 of the Jewish "Hellenists" who had been converted to the Christian faith relates not to a quite different conception of the redeemed community of Jesus Christ, but to the attitude to the Temple and the Law (cf. 6:13), a question in which the "Hebrew" Jewish Christians with the Twelve at their head were clearly more conservative in their thinking, without, however, denying their own liturgical life, their new bond to their Lord which alone ultimately was decisive (cf. above, Part One, § 6). The attitude towards unbelieving Judaism which rejected the apostolic preaching of salvation and consequently God's last proffer of salvation to Israel, raised a new and difficult problem for the early Church which, especially after A.D. 70, could not but contribute to further clarity its own conception of itself. And so the Jewish Christians, too, even heretical splinter-groups, found their way into the universal "Catholic" Church and endured without inner breach the loss of the greater part of their former compatriots and brethren in faith (cf. below, Part Two, § 3 on the Gospel according to Matthew).

2. The Lucan conception

The considerable contribution which Luke made to a theology of the Church in his double work (Gospel and Acts), will probably be thought chiefly to consist in his having brought

Church and history into relation to each other and of having assigned the Church its era and its tasks between the taking up of Jesus into heaven (Lk 9 : 15; Acts 1 : 2, 11, 22) and his return (Acts 1 : 11; cf. Lk 21 : 27 f.). The beginning of Acts is particularly significant. In the first sentence he surveys once again Jesus' deeds and teaching as he described these in his "first book" and so contrasts Jesus' time with that of the Church. This epoch which began with the Lord's departure is marked by the charge given by the risen Lord to his disciples who have remained behind and is clearly delimited in v. 11 by the words of the angels: "This Jesus who was taken up from you into heaven will so come as you saw him going into heaven." Then full "redemption" will take place (Lk 21 : 28). The period of history that belongs to the Church, however, is determined in content by the task of the mission: "You will be my witnesses in Jerusalem in all Judaea and Samaria and even to the uttermost part of the earth" (Acts 1 : 8). That an ecclesiological conception is implied by this is shown by the context of this saying of the risen Christ. The disciples had previously asked him whether he intended "at this time to restore the kingdom for Israel" (v. 6). The Lord first rejected the question about fixing a date: "It is not for you to know times and moments which the Father has put in his own power" (v. 7). In this way the time that lies before them is left indeterminate in extent and any further questions about it excluded by the reference to the power of the Father to dispose. That can hardly be regarded as unintentional when the similar question raised in the Gospel according to Luke is taken into consideration (cf. 17 : 20; 19 : 11; 21 : 7; 24 : 21), but is meant to forbid calculating the end in advance (cf. 17 : 20 f.), and to discourage too eager an early expectation (cf. 21 : 24 "till the times of the gentiles be fulfilled"), and give the Church calm and confidence for its mission[20]. But the narrowly Jewish manner of thought of the disciples (cf. 19 : 11; 24 : 21) is tacitly corrected; their task is not restricted to Israel, but reaches "to the uttermost part of the earth" (Acts 1 : 8).

This reveals what the theologian Luke has most at heart. He is concerned about the Church's place in the context of redemptive history and the tasks which, according to the will of God, it has to fulfil in its time. Perhaps he did not possess any clearly defined concept of the Church at all[21]; but "the standpoint from which Luke develops his view of history is the Church which believes in Jesus Christ".[22] His own life is bound up with the Church and he writes according to the living picture of the Church that he bears within him. He expresses this by depicting the Church's beginnings, origin, and growth, and what is the basis and ground of its history. Here only the attempt can be made to develop a little further his conception which is rooted in redemptive history and his view of the Church as a factor in that history, and in doing so to note a few questions raised by Luke.

H. Conzelmann has correctly observed that for Luke the age of the Church is already the third great period of sacred history[23]. The first age is that of Israel, characterized by "the Law and the prophets" and reaching down to John the Baptist; "from that time the reign of God is preached" (Lk 16 : 16). Baptizing by the Jordan, John forms the bridge to the age of redemption (cf. Acts 13 : 24) in which Jesus the Messias, anointed by the Spirit (Lk 4 : 18 f.) works, and it is only to this "mid-point of time" (Conzelmann) that the age of the Church is fitted as the third period of redemptive history. This observation is important for the theology of the Church for several reasons. (1) The Church stands in continuity with God's saving plans and dispositions. The old Israel had *in its own place* just as much a legitimate rôle as Jesus' redeemed community has in its time, and in fact the Church stands as it were on the shoulders of Israel. The promises to Israel which are so significantly brought out in the infancy narrative (Lk 1 : 32 f., 54 f., 68–75) and the expectation of its pious members living at that time (cf. also 1 : 76–79; 2 : 25, 38) are fulfilled in Jesus and the Church. Luke takes up a positive attitude to the ancient people of God as such (cf. Lk 1 : 68, 77; 2 : 10, 32; 7 : 16; 24 : 14; Acts 4 : 10; 13 : 17) and does not place the terrible passage about hardening until the end, after the greater part of Israel had refused faith in Jesus (Acts 28 : 26 f.) [24]. (2) The geographical framework of the activity of Jesus and his apostles also serves to emphasize the privileged position of Israel in sacred history (cf. the use of πρῶτον in Acts 3 : 26; 13 : 46). The holy city of Jerusalem stands at the centre of the salvation occurrence. In it the divinely appointed lot of the Messias is fulfilled as that of the prophets had already been — that incomprehensible turn of events whereby God's city kills the prophets and stones those sent to it (Lk 13 : 34); yet "it cannot be that a prophet perish outside Jerusalem" (Lk 13 : 33). Consequently Jesus' journey to Jerusalem forms a central part of the gospel (9 : 51–19 : 27), and Jesus undertook it deliberately, fully conscious of what awaited him there (cf. 9 : 51). After the violent drama, however, Jerusalem is also the place where the risen Christ appeared to his disciples (Lk 24 : 33–43), and from it the gospel goes forth into the whole world. The "beginning with Jerusalem" is just as important for Luke as the "to all nations" (24 : 47). Just as it is the divine plan of salvation that the Messias must suffer death and so enter into his glory (Lk 24 : 26, 46), so also that the message of salvation and salvation itself should, because of Jewish unbelief, pass over to the gentiles. That already finds expression at the beginning of Jesus' public life, in the tradition only found in Luke of the rejection of Jesus in Nazareth (Lk 4 : 24–27), and that is what by his two works Luke sought to prove theologically, in the light of the facts: the universality of the Church has its basis in God's decree, in the charge that was laid on Jesus and in the actual course taken by the history of redemption. (3) Just as the Messianic prophecies made to Israel in the first period of sacred history are fulfilled in Jesus (cf.

65

Lk 4 : 18–21; 7 : 21–23) so too the age of the Church represents the age of fulfilment: the outpouring of the Spirit at Pentecost is, on the one hand, the eschatological event announced by the prophet Joel (Acts 2 : 16–21), but on the other, it is also the accomplishment of the promise made by the departing Lord to his disciples to send them "power from on high" (cf. Lk 24 : 49; Acts 1 : 8). This conferring of the Spirit on the whole community in the time after Pentecost is indubitably for Luke a counterpart to the personal anointing of the Messias by the Spirit for the time of his earthly activity (Lk 4 : 14, 18; Acts 10 : 38). Jesus' period continues in the age of the Church and, furthermore, the latter is a development of what the former promised and it is so precisely by reason of the intervening elevation and establishment of Jesus in power (cf. Acts 2 : 34–36), as well as by the gift of the Spirit. Between the time of Jesus and the period of the Church there is no hiatus. The gospel is preached here as it was there, though after Easter, of course, it is enriched by the message regarding Jesus the crucified Messias raised from the dead, the exalted Lord. The powers of God's reign, in concrete terms, of the Holy Spirit, which made their presence felt with Jesus, are more and more widely operative. The Church is, we may state in Luke's case too, the domain ruled by the exalted Christ and is his instrument in the world until his coming in glory. And the latter must occur all the more certainly by the fact that Jesus' first promises have already been fulfilled. For the Lucan conception of the Church the last words of Jesus with his disciples in the room of the Last Supper are also important (Lk 22 : 31–38); for they were certainly assembled by Luke with the future community in mind and this for him is the direct continuation of the group of disciples round Jesus[25]. Without going into all details the following is to be noticed.

(1) The celebration of the eucharist (cf. Part One, §§ 3 and 6) is Jesus' farewell gift before his passion (v. 15) and is established for the whole era of the Church.

Through it he remains linked with his community of disciples until the "fulfilment" of the company at supper in the kingdom of God (vv. 16, 18, 30a) and applies continually to it the saving effect of his violent death (ὑπὲρ ὑμῶν, vv. 19, 20). It is a command he expressly imposes in "commemoration" of himself (v. 19). And so for Luke the "breaking of bread" (perhaps as a continuation of sharing the earthly Jesus' company at table but on a new plane, cf. Luke 24 : 30 f.), is the kernel of the religious life of the primitive Church, the source of its eschatological joy (Acts 2 : 46), but it also imposes an obligation of fidelity to the Lord (cf. the words about the traitor, Luke 22 : 21 f.), of steadfastness in temptation (v. 28) and of fraternal fellowship which finds expression in the love banquet (cf. vv. 24–27; Acts 2 : 42).

(2) Despite this joy animating from within and despite the "consolation" deriving from the Holy Spirit (Acts 9 : 31; cf. Lk 11 : 13; 12 : 12), the age of the Church is characterized by temptations, sufferings and persecutions; Christ's community is an *ecclesia militans et pressa*. According to Luke 22 : 31, (the) Satan had asked (of God) to sift the disciples as wheat is sifted. With the passion, Satan, whom the Lord had repelled at the beginning of his public mission (Lk 4 : 1–13) and had repressed during his work done under the impulsion of the Spirit (10 : 18), appears on the scene again (cf. 22 : 3, 53). Now he is also permitted to shake Jesus' disciples, too, in order to "sift out their guilt"[26]; he even has access to the "saints" of Jerusalem and contrives to fill the heart of Ananias (Acts 5 : 3). Jesus' grave words at Luke 22 : 32 f. also hold good for the age that is coming; they express in metaphorical form distress and conflict. But that is only in harmony with earlier sayings of Jesus about persecution and the lot of the disciples, which Luke will similarly hear and understand, with the situation of the later Church in his mind (cf. Lk 6 : 22 f.; 11 : 49 ff. [ἀποστόλους] 12 : 4–12; 14 : 25 ff.; 21 : 12 to 19), as applying to the age of the Church: the law holds

67

good that Jesus is to be followed by the cross to glory: "Through many tribulations we must enter the kingdom of God" (Acts 14 : 22; cf. with this Lk 24 : 26). The Church is still the time of tribulation and martyrdom (Acts 7 : 54–60), until the kingdom of God comes and also the time of temptation, which must be withstood through persevering prayer (cf. Lk 21 : 36; 22 : 40, 46 and also Acts 4 : 29 f.; 12 : 12; 20 : 36; 21 : 5).

(3) The "apostolic" constitution of the Church is also to be recognized from the discourses of the Last Supper; for the saying at Luke 22 : 28 ff., is specially addressed to the Twelve but the words in verses 31 f., are addressed to Simon Peter. Even if no direct light is thrown on the position of the Twelve in the original community, their pre-eminence is nevertheless evident; it was they "who had persevered with him in his temptations" [27] and to whom Jesus on that account promised eschatological "rule"; they will "sit on thrones and judge the twelve tribes of Israel". Simon, however, receives the special task of strengthening in the faith his "brethren", not by his own strength, but by virtue of Jesus' prayer. The expression "brethren" indicates at least in Luke's view, that the whole community is meant (cf. Acts 1 : 15; 6 : 3; 9 : 17, 30; 10 : 23 etc.), and in fact the picture drawn by Luke in Acts 1–12 of Peter as the leader and spokesman of the original community corresponds to what was said in the room of the Last Supper. It is true that that does not itself explain his official position in the Church, but it does reveal his intrinsic importance for the primitive Church. (The question of the value of these words to Peter as a piece of tradition cannot be discussed here.)

(4) Finally, something of Luke's conception of offices in the communities is probably to be recognized from his description of Jesus' farewell celebration. It has always been remarked that the third evangelist, and only he, has transferred the dispute among the disciples about precedence into the room of the Last Supper (22 : 24–27); if the rather peculiarly

formed saying of Jesus regarding serving (v. 27) is compared with the "serving of tables" spoken of in Acts 6 : 2, it will not be difficult to recognize the contemporary context in the life of the Church which explains the order in which Luke has arranged the material of tradition. Luke is writing with the circumstances of the early Church in mind and in verse 26 (cf. ὁ ἡγούμενος, cf. Acts 15 : 22) he is aiming at the overseers who had to attend to the serving of tables and look after the poor. He is concerned with the "task of those who have position and responsibility in the community".[28] In the Acts of the Apostles he not only reports the appointment of the Seven for the serving of tables (6 : 1–6), but also of presbyters whom Paul appointed in his missionary churches (14 : 23; cf. 20 : 17), no doubt for similar presiding functions. There are other passages in the gospel, too, which also very likely refer to the later pastors of the Church (cf. Lk 6 : 39 f.; 12 : 39 f., 42 to 46, 47 f.). Luke demands from them, in accordance with Jesus' words, readiness to serve and fidelity in small things (cf. Lk 16 : 10; 19 : 17) in responsibility before the Lord. As regards external organization and classification of offices, on the other hand, he shows no particular interest.

Rudiments of a theology of the Church appear in Acts 20 : 28 (cf. also Luke 12 : 32, the metaphor of the flock); but there Luke is no doubt echoing universal early Christian ideas. His special contribution was to have ensured for the Church its era and its space, its mission and road into the future.

3. *The idea of the Church in Matthew*

The problem of Israel which was essentially settled for Luke both historically (by the destruction of Jerusalem) and as regards the economy of salvation (Acts 28 : 25–28) is still, or once again, for Matthew a matter of debate. That is doubtless connected with the readers he had in mind who probably for

the most part consisted of Jewish Christians[29], though, of
course, ones who had long since overcome any narrowly
nationalistic modes of thought and had found their way into
the breadth and openness of the universal redeemed community
of Jesus Christ[30]. It is only when due account is taken of the
two points of view, Jewish Christian origin and universal
outlook that the themes and "dogmatic theology" of the
Church in the Gospel according to Matthew can be understood.
It is precisely the argument with unbelieving Judaism, its particularism, its boast of the Torah and its legalist accomplishment,
its pride in achievement and striving after merit, which created
that consciousness of the Church which is perceptible in
Matthew's gospel and also contributed to its favour in the
Church and its position as the "ecclesiastical gospel".

The best starting-point is Matthew 21:43, a verse only
found in Matthew in connection with the parable of the wicked
husbandman (cf. v. 41): "Therefore I say to you that God's
reign will be taken away from you and given to a people
yielding the fruits thereof". By "you" only the old Israel can
be meant, even if in the parable it is in particular the leaders
of the nation (who had charge of the vineyard = Israel, cf.
Isaias 5:7) who were attacked; for Matthew the whole Jewish
people shares responsibility for the rejection and crucifixion
of the Messias Jesus (27:25 πᾶς ὁ λαός). It is from this
unbelieving nation, which by its decision against Jesus gave
judgment against itself, that "God's reign will be taken away";
that is to say that the privileges and blessings will be withdrawn which belonged to and were promised to it as God's
chosen possession (cf. Exod 19:5f.; Deut 7:6; 14:2; 26:18).
Matthew must have seen this withdrawal of divine guidance
by grace in quite a concrete form in the judgment of condem-
nation that had already taken place over Jerusalem and in
the loss of national independence (cf. 22:7). The "people",
however, which now takes the place of the old Israel is no longer
an ethnic, national reality but a spiritual unity, an association

of men who "yield fruits of divine rule". But precisely this image of the fruits shows that Matthew was thinking of the Church, for he applies various sayings and parables of Jesus which employ this metaphor paraenetically to his Christian readers (cf. 7 : 15–20 against false Christian prophets; 13 : 8, 23 regarding tried and tested hearers of the "word of the kingdom"; 13 : 26, cf. 38, about the "sons of the kingdom") whilst the unbelieving Israel is burdened with the curse of barrenness (cf. 21 : 19). The "people" is, therefore, the true people of God which is being formed on a new foundation. It comprises members who were Christian believers from Israel as well as converted and tested adherents from the gentiles (cf. 12 : 21; 24 : 14; 25 : 32; 28 : 19); it is a purely religious society made possible by the atoning blood of Jesus (cf. 26 : 28), called together by his messengers, constituted by baptism and obedient discipleship (28 : 19) but this society is also under an obligation to bear moral fruit especially in love for the brethren and neighbours and even for enemies (cf. the passages peculiar to Matthew, 5 : 43–48, with characteristic differences from the Lucan parallel; 18 : 23–35; 25 : 31–46). This new people of God, this special community of Jesus (16 : 19), is throughout strongly contrasted with the unbelieving Israel which persisted in the old legalism and "hypocrisy" (cf. also 5 : 20–28; 8 : 10, 11 f.; 15 : 7 ff.; 21 : 31 f.; 22 : 1–10; 23). In the great discourse of woes (c. 23) the evangelist clearly also has in his mind the circumstances of his own time (vv. 7–11, 34–36), so that Jesus' sharp attacks on the Scribes and Pharisees must probably in the evangelist's perspective also be directed against the unbelieving Judaism of his time[31]. His positive ideas about the Church are only fully intelligible against the background of this polemic; consequently the fundamental concept of his gospel can scarcely be better summarized than by the ideogram "the true Israel"[32], even though the new people of God is never actually designated by the term Israel (even in 19 : 28).

For this reason the question of the Law occupies considerable space in Matthew. The interpretation of the relevant texts, especially 5 : 17–20 is of course difficult and controverted[33]; we do not need, however, to go into this more closely because one thing in any case is certain: the "Law" which is binding on Christ's community is a *lex Christi* surpassing the old Torah which Jesus, the eschatological envoy of God (5 : 17; cf. 12 : 41 f.) has authoritatively promulgated (cf. the Sermon on the Mount cc. 5–7), a "fulfilment" of sacred history (5 : 17, 18), a transcending of the Law in content (5 : 20 and the antitheses which follow), a perfect exposition of the old Torah, taking the will of God seriously (cf. 5 :19; 7 : 21) and yet not tied to the letter (purification and Sabbath prescriptions). This law of Christ which is summarized in the chief commandment of love (cf. the Matthean formulation, 22 : 40), applies to all aspirants to the kingdom of God in exactly the same way wherever they come from and whoever they may be, and is valid for the whole Church of Jews and gentiles. Although Matthew is familiar with Jewish thought and perhaps takes account of special problems and answers given among Jewish Christians (cf. 5 : 19, 32; 19 : 3–9; 23 : 3, 23), and although he adapts himself to that thought in the concepts he uses (cf. "justice", "perfection", the title "Son of David"), he represents no narrow and re-Judaized Christianity. The common foundation is belief in Jesus the Messias and Son of God, as only through him can the will of God be known and in obedience to him fulfilled (cf. 21 : 32; 28 : 20a).

That in itself shows the universality of the Matthean idea of the Church. But there are passages which bring out this characteristic even more clearly. The important saying of Jesus regarding the gentiles streaming into the eschatological kingdom of God is linked by Matthew to the story of the centurion of Capharnaum and in fact to the saying which in Matthew is found in even more emphatic form: "*in no one* in Israel have I found such great faith" (8 : 10, 11 f.). In Luke it is a threat to Jesus' contemporaries with a subsequent announcement of the conversion of the gentiles (Lk 13 : 28 f.), in Matthew a general promise starting with the pagan centurion in mind and with the announcement attached that "the sons of the kingdom" will be cast out into the darkness. And so the centurion appears as a hopeful sign, and for Matthew that will be even truer of the gentiles won in his time (cf. also 21 : 9 f.). The quotation from Isaias 42 : 1–4 inserted by Matthew at 12 : 17–21 by way of comment is instructive. Although primarily intended to provide a reason for the order to be silent given in v. 16 (cf. v. 19), it nevertheless opens out a perspective towards the gentiles who according to the last verse also quoted (in the clearer, Septuagint version), "hope in his name", that is, of the Servant of God. Even though the conjecture remains hypothetical that Matthew was guided in his universal outlook (cf. also 13 : 38; 24 : 14; 25 : 13) by Deutero-Isaias with its missionary sympathies (cf. 42 : 6; 49 : 6)[34], it is possible to say that here and there even in his description of Jesus' activities he allows a hope to shine through, which is then fulfilled in the missionary mandate given by the risen Lord. It is precisely Matthew who is not silent about the restriction of the mission of Jesus and his disciples to Israel for the time of his earthly life (10 : 5 f.; 15 : 24). The discourse on the sending out of the disciples (c. 10), does not contradict the universal missionary mandate of the risen Lord for it is not a missionary catechism but rather from v. 17 onwards a discourse about the lot of a disciple[35] and indirectly in v. 18 even presupposes work in gentile territory. The solemn commission by the Kyrios established in rulership of the world (28 : 18, 20) does not come as a surprise, therefore, but is the intended culmination of the book. This carefully contrived final scene[36] corresponds to the picture of Christ in this gospel (cf. 11 : 27; 14 : 33; 16 : 16; 27 : 54) as well as the significance ascribed to the disciples (cf. 5 : 13–16) and reveals a consciousness of the Church as possessing a universalism which sets to it "no limits either in principle or on account of conditions of situation or time" (W. Trilling).

73

For the inner structure of the Church, according to Matthew's conception, nothing is as significant as the so-called "community rule" in 18 : 1–20. Here many important terms (ἡ ἐκκλησία v. 17; the "little ones who believe in Jesus", vv. 6, 10; "brethren" v. 15 ff.) and also ideas are brought together (exercise of divine authority v. 18; presence of Jesus v. 20; position and function of those presiding, cf. vv. 1–4, 12 f.; dignity of the Church, v. 17; association in prayer v. 19). We can only bring out a few characteristic features. (1) The fundamental idea of the ἐκκλησία which Matthew has already taken over from the saying reported by him at 16 : 19 (cf. Part Two, §1 above), is built on the thought of the people of God. It is true that instead of God's assembly of the old Covenant we now have Christ's community (16 : 19), but the old dignity of the people chosen by God also attaches to the latter. That is shown in the second saying regarding the ἐκκλησία (18 : 17): anyone who does not listen to the community is regarded as expelled and thereby separated from the redeemed society. If this is compared with 22 : 11–14 (wedding garment) where Matthew apparently wishes to warn people streaming into the Church in response to the call of missionaries not to neglect moral consequences and to show themselves "chosen"[37], it may be said that for him the ἐκκλησία is the place of assembly and preparation of the ἐκλεκτοί, the society confessing salvation but not guaranteeing it without moral results, and, if one prefers and does not shun the term, an establishment or institute for salvation. That is confirmed by the power given to Peter or, as the case may be, to the Twelve "to bind and loose" (16 : 19; 18 : 18; cf. below Part Two, § 4). (2) This itself implies that in the Church there is an authority conferred by God and concerning salvation which, according to the evangelist's conception, can hardly repose in the community as such, but is rather made over to certain persons. The connection of v. 18 with v. 17 in no way demands that in v. 18 it is the ἐκκλησία as a whole that is addressed; for the

"community rule" is composed of numerous individual sayings
which to some extent are only joined together on the link-word
principle (cf. the transition from v. 4 to v. 5, from v. 5 to
v. 6 f., and from v. 7 to 8 f.), and partly fit together from the
point of view of content (cf. v. 10 with 12 f., and v. 14 which
rounds it off). Verses 15–17 form a self-contained unity; v. 18
starts again with ἀμὴν λέγω ὑμῖν, has a change of object (from
thee to you), and is also of a different literary kind; the saying
in verses 15–17 contains a rule of conduct, v. 18 a conferring
of authority. Consequently those addressed must be ascer-
tained from the content and as in the parallel passage, 16 : 19,
it is a question of a single person, here too a definite circle
of persons suggests itself, and this for the evangelist by the
very setting in 18 : 1 can be no other than the (twelve) disciples
(cf. also Jn 20 : 23)[38]. Conversely even for v. 17 it would be
necessary to consider that the authority of the ἐκκλησία
mentioned there rests not only on its dignity as representative
of the people of God, but also on its guidance by those
empowered by God. (3) But it is not only the disciples authorized by Jesus who have ruling functions, but there must also be
"community shepherds". The parable of the lost sheep which
in Luke 15 : 3–7 symbolizes God's love for sinners and his joy
at the rescue of the one that was lost is applied by Matthew
at 18 : 12–14 to the diligent care of a shepherd for "one of
these little ones"; this is clearly intended for church leaders who
must care for even the least in the community, in this case, in
contrast to v. 6, the weak and erring (cf. vv. 15–17). It is also
possible to suppose, however, that the exhortation to "humble
oneself" (v. 4) which closes the dispute about precedence among
disciples is intended to be the basis of all order in the Church
and so concerns not only the Twelve but also anyone distinguished by a "rank" in the Church. The paradoxical requirement of service holds good throughout for all who "desire
to be great" in the Church (cf. 20 : 26 ff., parallels)[39]. Perhaps
even the question: "Who is the greatest in the kingdom of

heaven?" (v. 1) in which "in the kingdom of heaven" is a Matthean addition in contrast to the scenes of argument about precedence in the other synoptics (Mk 9 : 34; Lk 9 : 46; 22 : 24) is understood as a question about order of precedence in the Church; "The question and its summary answer (v. 4) nevertheless sound as if the relative positions that hold good here and now 'among us' are meant"[40]. But such an identification of "God's reign" and Church cannot be exemplified elsewhere in Matthew and it will be better to interpret it so that the Church is a preliminary stage and school which prepares for and perhaps in some way represents the future *basileia* (cf. also 5 : 19). At all events Matthew knows and acknowledges presiding functions and offices in the Church but also subjects them all to the law of service and responsibility before the Lord (cf. 24 : 45–51; 25 : 14–30).

(4) Matthew is convinced of human deficiency and sinfulness even in the Church of Christ. No one warns as much as he does against scandals which can occur even in the Church. In the context of the "community rule", the terrible saying in v. 6 f. should perhaps be referred to scandals in the Church (cf. 13 : 41) or else perhaps as an admonition to its pastors to protect simple believers from perils whatever their source. In Luke 17 : 1 ff., that logion is taken as a warning to the disciples themselves ("take heed for yourselves"); and is immediately followed by the saying regarding the sinful brother who must be forgiven (v. 3). In Matthew 18 : 15–17 this has become the three stages of treatment shown to a brother who offends against the spirit of the congregation, clearly on the Jewish pattern (cf. *1 QS* V, 26–VI, 1). Similarly, the ecclesiastical application of the logia 7 : 15–19 (false prophets, who are certainly to be thought of as Christian teachers of error), 7 : 22 f. (workers of miracles, workers of iniquity) and the two parables of the cockle (13 : 24–30; 36–43) and of the fishing-net (13 : 47–50) may also be recalled.

(5) At the same time the Church is certain of the presence

of its Lord and (leaving the holy eucharist out of account) in two ways. There is a "mystical" presence of the Lord attainable in prayer in common (v. 19), namely when two or three are gathered together in his name the Lord is "in the midst of them" (v. 20), just as the *shekinah* according to Jewish belief rests amind two or more men who busy themselves with the Torah[41]. Then also the risen Lord also promised his apostles that he would be "with them" (μεϑ' ὑμῶν) all days until the consummation of the aeon (Mt 28 : 20). By that he assures them of the assistance of his grace, just as Yahweh was close to his people, guiding, protecting and powerfully helping. The mystical, liturgical and the dynamic, active presence of the Lord are the sources of strength, the consolation and mystery of the Matthean Church which is certain of its indestructibility (cf. 16 : 19) until "the Son of man shall come in the glory of his Father with his angels" (16 : 27).

4. *The Pauline theology of the Church*

To expound the Pauline theology of the Church would require a separate book[42]. Here we can do no more than raise the question what special importance Paul had for the development of the idea of the Church in the primitive Church, that is, what his personal theological contribution consisted of, what particular ideas he sketched and what fruitful impulses he bequeathed to the period that followed. In view of our imperfect knowledge of Hellenistic Christianity before and contemporary with Paul, it will not be possible to say with certainty to what extent he had assimilated the ideas of other missionaries and theologians; nevertheless his originality (cf. "Body of Christ") is incontestable and his deeper penetration into the idea of the Church is evident. For that reason his ecclesiology has not been dealt with until this point, although chronologically it takes precedence over Luke and Matthew.

Very probably Paul, trained in Jewish theology as he was, had reflected on the "people of God" very soon after his vocation and particularly in view of his mission to the gentiles. The relation between Israel and the gentiles in God's saving plan deeply preoccupied him, most of all in Romans 9–11 where he presents a unique survey of sacred history [43]. This great conception cannot, however, be taken as a starting point, for it was drawn up when he was already at the height of his missionary activity, after the conclusion of his work in the eastern half of the Roman Empire (cf. Rom 15 : 9), and, in view of the readiness of the gentiles to believe, it is written from a special standpoint: "Has God cast away his people?" (11 : 1). In order to harmonize with the divine promises to Israel the fact, so hard for him as a Jew, that the greater part of his nation was obdurate in unbelief regarding Christ, he puts very penetrating questions: Whether the word of God had become ineffectual (9 : 6); whether there is injustice with God (9 : 14); whether perhaps God was responsible for Israel's failure (cf. c. 10), and whether God's promises for Israel will still be fulfilled after all in an unsuspected way (cf. c. 11). And with this he even warns the converted gentiles against arrogance towards Israel, which indeed in large part was faithless then, but remains nevertheless the root of the olive tree onto which the gentiles have been grafted and in regard to which God still remains faithful to his promises (cf. 11 : 17–24). All that is envisaged from a definite angle which is partly explained by missionary experience; it must first be asked therefore what positive judgment Paul passes on the vocation of the gentiles and what picture of the Church he draws from it.

On this, the Epistle to the Galatians is significant, the document in which Paul emphatically defends both his apostolic office, namely his legitimate right as apostle to the gentiles and his equality of rights with the original apostles, as well as his gospel without circumcision and legal observances, the foun-

dation of his unrestricted world-wide preaching. In an allegorical exposition of Scripture he views in one passage (4 : 21
to 31) Abraham's two wives as types of freedom and bondage.
The bond woman Agar who only bore "according to the flesh"
is linked by him with the Covenant of Mount Sinai which
bears children into bondage; she corresponds to the "Jerusalem which now is" and which lies in bondage as its children
do. The free Sara, however, who bore her son "by reason of
the promise", becomes for him the representative of the "Jerusalem above" which is "our mother"; "you, however, brethren,
are like Isaac, children of the promise". It must be remembered
that Paul is writing to combat the old obsolete order of
bondage to the Law to which, for him, the "Jerusalem which
now is" is clinging, and furthermore, that Paul saw that that
empirical Israel as it in fact existed, closed against Christ, was
persecuting believers in Christ (v. 29). This is a different
viewpoint from that of Romans 9–11 in which, as it were, the
obverse of the phenomenon "Israel" is shown. Paul is torn
between the two extremes: on the one hand, Israel as the
people of God of whom the promises hold good, on the other,
Judaism unbelieving in regard to the heir to the promises in
the absolute sense, Christ (Gal 3 : 16), persisting in bondage
to the Law in opposition to the will of God and even
persecuting the Christian believers submissive to the new order
of salvation. But from this dialectic, however, there emerges,
when Paul is judging calmly without regard to the empirical
Israel, his positive conception of the true people of God, which
equally comprises believers from Israel and the gentiles and
has become "in Christ" a totally new unity: "There is neither
Jew nor Greek, neither bond nor free, neither male nor
female; for you are all one in Christ Jesus" (Gal 3 : 28). So
it is clear that for Paul a new people of God has taken the
place of the old, and one which, it is true, is formed on the
basis of the old and more precisely on the promises of blessings
made to it but for the rest stands on an entirely new foundation

79

that of belief in the one heir to the blessings and sole mediator of salvation, Jesus Christ.

Paul, as we have just seen, regards this new people of God as the "Jerusalem on high" (Gal 4 : 26), or as its earthly manifestation (it is the "mother" of the Christians), and he also terms it "the Israel of God" (Gal 6 : 16). The attempt has been made of course to interpret this expression in another way[44]; but the benediction should probably best be understood as follows: "The Galatian Christians whom Paul primarily in mind when he speaks of those who are following his rule, and in addition, the Israel of God as a whole, the ἐκκλησία, wherever it may be, are to be blessed with peace and mercy from God. The apostle probably had the nineteenth blessing of the Qaddish in mind . . .[45]" For here something very characteristic is occurring. The apostle is transferring the old title of honour to the new society of those who believe in Christ (something that was not to be observed even in Matthew, see above, Part Two, § 3). In fact this must be regarded as a very deliberate theological proceeding; for something similar occurs more than once in Paul: the blessing that was promised to Abraham for his physical offspring is transferred to Christ and through him to all who are bound to him by faith and baptism (Gal 3 : 14, 16, 29), and in the Epistle to the Romans the spiritual descent from Abraham is directly ascribed to all who, like Abraham, allow themselves to be justified by faith, the uncircumcised equally with the circumcised (Rom 4 : 11–17). Where it seems appropriate, Paul can also reinterpret the terms "circumcision" and "Jew" (Rom 2 : 25–29) or deny to some "from Israel" membership of "Israel" and of some of Abraham's offspring, that they are his children, and of his children in the flesh, that they are God's children (Rom 9 : 6–8). For him the unbelieving Israel is the "Israel according to the flesh" (1 Cor 10–18) and to the unbelieving Jews and Greeks he opposes "the Church of God", that is to say, the Christian community (1 Cor 10 : 32). He is not alone in the primitive Church in this view (cf. above, Part Two, § 1–3); but as well as the titles of honour of Israel, he also laid full claim to its actual privileges, and presents the Church as the legitimate heir of the old people of God. Furthermore, he attempted to provide a theological basis for this inheritance by seeking to recognize the lineaments of the new people of God of believers in Jesus Christ, in the text of the Old Testament itself newly interpreted. By that he certainly heightened and developed the primitive Church's consciousness of being an independent society and even more prepared the way for the conception of the Christian believers as the "third race"[46].

The bond between Jews and gentiles in the Church is most profoundly indicated in the Epistle to the Ephesians. It is "the mystery of Christ, which in other generations was not made known to the sons of men as it has now been revealed to his holy apostles and prophets in the Spirit" (3 : 4 f.). Through Christ who proclaimed peace to "those afar off" (gentiles) and to "those that were near" (the Jews), both groups who formerly were separated have equal access to the Father in the one Spirit (cf. 2 : 16 ff.). It is only with the incorporation of the gentiles that the essential eschatological picture of the Church emerges and God's economy of salvation reaches its culmination and "the manifold wisdom of God" is "made known to the principalities and powers in heavenly places through the Church", that is, through her actual reality and her preaching, and so the destruction of their power is announced (cf. 1 : 21–23; 4 : 8–10). In this perspective the Church cannot be envisaged in any other way than as comprised in God's eternal salvific plan as the Church of Jews and gentiles which Christ represented in his body on the cross and made into "a new man" (3 : 15), and which he has redeemed (5 : 23) and sanctified (5 : 26 f.); the one Body of Christ directed and built up by him, its heavenly head, whose growth is promoted and brought to the "full measure of the plenitude of Christ" (cf. 4 : 11–16).

That Paul also ensured the freedom of the gentiles in the Church is already sufficiently plain from what has been said. It was chiefly due to him that the settlement at the "Council of Jerusalem" which accorded the gentiles entry to the Church without circumcision or adoption of the Jewish Law was not only maintained in the ensuing period despite the intrigues of Judaizers, but was also understood. His thesis of the one way of salvation for all in faith in Jesus Christ, presented with polemic intensity in the Epistle to the Galatians and with doctrinal serenity in the Epistle to the Romans, dissipated any doubts that might have been possible: "There is no distinction; for all have sinned and have need of the glory of God, but are (all) justified by way of gift by his grace on the ground of the redemption in Christ Jesus" (Rom 3 : 22 f.). Consequently the gentiles have equal rights as brethren in Christ and there may not be any tutelage or neglect of the gentile Christians by the former Jews (cf. Gal 2 : 15–18). On the other hand, of course, this must again be stressed, the gentile Christians must not despise the old Israel on account of its failure (cf. Rom 9–11 *passim*) and must show loving consideration for their Jewish Christian brethren who perhaps may have a more rigid conscience in matters of food and drink (cf. Rom 14). And so Paul admonished and educated all his churches to Christian concord and also promoted harmony between the mother-church in Jerusalem and his new foundations (cf. the great collection). In that way he made an essential contribution, both theological and practical, to the formation of a common consciousness of the Church as a whole. One of the chief reasons, humanly speaking, why the Church which was quickly growing in extent, did not split up, is to be found in Paul's theology, which made all the faithful vividly conscious of the unity conferred on them by God and which imperatively called for concord: the one faith in Jesus Christ the Lord (cf. 1 Cor 8 : 5 f.), the one baptism knitting into unity in Christ (Gal 3 : 26 ff.; 1 Cor 12 : 13;

Col 3 : 11; Eph 4 : 3–6), the common sharing in the one eucharistic bread and thereby in the Body of Christ whereby the many are themselves a single body (1 Cor 10 : 16 f.).

From this it is clear that Paul had reflected profoundly on the nature of the Church. For him it is not merely the association of those who believe in Christ, the people of God of the new Covenant, the earthly community of the exalted Lord. The metaphor of the temple of God (1 Cor 3 : 16; 2 Cor 6 : 16) which the apostle probably took over from later Judaism and early Christian views (cf. Ezek 40 : 44; Is 28 : 16 f.; *1 (Ethiopic) Enoch* 90 : 28 f.; 91 : 13; *Jubilees* 1 : 17; *1 QS* VIII, 5 f.; Mk 14 : 58 and parallel), gave him the opportunity of bringing out the holy nature of the Church. In this sanctuary God's Spirit dwells and anyone who destroys it, God will destroy (1 Cor 3 : 16). His clear and realistic conception of the Holy Spirit who fills every individual believer (1 Cor 6 : 19) as well as the whole edifice of the Church (cf. Eph 2 : 22) gave the old idea new richness and depth. His sacramental theology penetrating to the inner process of sanctification was also an enduring vital influence for the idea of the Church. "The saints", probably originally a term used by the Jerusalem Christians to designate themselves (cf. above, Part Two, § 1), now become "those who are sanctified in Christ Jesus" (1 Cor 1 : 2) in a sense understood quite realistically on the ground of baptism (cf. 1 Cor 6 : 11), but not only as individuals but also precisely taken as a whole (cf. Gal 3 : 27 f.). The congregation renders actual again and again this unity in Christ (1 Cor 10 : 16 f.) which at the same time imposes the obligation of holiness and brotherly love (cf. 1 Cor 10 : 1–13; 11 : 20–29). The whole assembly stands responsible before the Lord and is chastised by him (1 Cor 11 : 30–32). Even the idea, familiar from the people of God of the old Testament, that the community must watch over its purity and remove offenders from its ranks, is placed on a new plane in view of the sanctification that has taken place in Christ (cf. 1 Cor 5 : 7 f.).

The decisive advance over previous ideas, however, was taken by Paul with his view of the Church as the Body of Christ. This conception which appears in the First Epistle to the Corinthians and is immediately richly developed (6 : 15–17; 10 : 17; 12 : 12–27) is also met with in the Epistle to the Romans and then under a new aspect reaches its full splendour in the Epistles to the Colossians and the Ephesians, must probably be considered a creative achievement of, and theological concept proper to St Paul, for in this form it is not found anywhere else in the New Testament. On account of its importance for an understanding of the nature and mystery of the Church, it is to be dealt with separately later (cf. below, Part Four, § 4). Here it may be sufficient to indicate that it is only in this perspective and especially when it is fully unfolded in the Epistles to the Ephesians and Colossians that Paul fully and completely envisaged the heavenly dimension of the Church, its reality under which earthly categories break down. Nevertheless, the Church also appears with him under other aspects, too, as a society centred in heaven and striving towards eschatological fulfilment and the real nature of which is not grasped in its earthly, historical shape and form. It has already been seen as the "Jerusalem on high" which in accordance with the old Jewish personification of the holy city is also regarded as the mother of many children (Gal 4 : 26 f.). In another metaphor the Church (or the church of Corinth which is directly addressed here) is the chaste virgin who is espoused to Christ (2 Cor 11 : 2) and who is led to him (for the Messianic marriage at the Parousia). In Philippians 3 : 20 the apostle says that "our citizenship is in heaven", so that is where we have our true home[47]. Certainly in these passages the Church is not expressly named; it is rather the life of the Christians that is characterized as being eschatological and only externally linked to this aeon; but that occurs in symbolic language which adopts metaphors, some of which had already been created in the Old Testament and

Judaism to express the eschatological fulfilment of the old people of God or of the city of God (temple, Jerusalem, marriage) and which therefore have ecclesiological significance. Like all the early Church, Paul knows no "individual" Christianity but always has the church community in mind in which the individual accomplishes his Christian life. Consequently the eschatological conception of the Christian life which is so powerfully worked out by him also benefits the concept of the Church: the Church itself becomes an ultimately non-cosmic reality, one already removed from this aeon in Christ. Even without the idea of the Body of Christ it is the sphere of rule of the heavenly exalted Christ enthroned with God (cf. Col 1 : 13) and looks towards its fulfilment in the future kingdom of glory (cf. below, Part Four, § 6). This idea, perceptible in the primitive Church from the beginning but not yet clearly formulated, regarding the essentially spiritual, eschatological character of the Church, was considerably assisted by Paul to establish itself and find characteristic expression. The Epistle to the Hebrews then shows it perfectly worked out (cf. below, Part Two, § 5).

The attempt has already been made to show that Paul nevertheless also recognized an earthly structure and constitution of the Church (cf. above, Part One, § 4). The pastoral epistles, which present precisely this aspect of the Church, will, in accordance with their unmistakably late position in the development of the idea of the Church (despite their Pauline or Paul-inspired authorship), be dealt with later (cf. below, Part Two, § 6).

5. The ecclesiology of the First Epistle of Peter and of the Epistle to the Hebrews

Theological conceptions regarding the Church also underlie the First Epistle of Peter and the Epistle to the Hebrews. Furthermore, Pauline influence is operative in the first of these

85

and the second is distinguished by particular originality. But the First Epistle of Peter also has its characteristic features; it takes up certain ideas of the original community and links them with Pauline ones[48]. This is seen most clearly in 2 : 4 to 10, a passage which expresses the author's conception of the Church concisely by means of various images and terms taken from Scripture[49]. The "spiritual house" to which the Christians as "living stones" are built up (v. 5 a) is similar to the picture in Ephesians 2 : 20–22. The kinship with the Pauline idea of the Body of Christ is unmistakable even though this concept never appears in the work. The growth of the newly-baptized (v. 2) is accomplished in this building (cf. also Eph 4 : 12–16) and at the same time they are living stones. Two features, however, ensure the author's originality; first the striking change from the figure of the Temple to that of the "holy priesthood" which is "to offer up spiritual sacrifices acceptable to God through Jesus Christ" (v. 5b)[50], and secondly the rôle which he assigns to Jesus Christ. The latter is the "living stone" rejected indeed by men but chosen and made honourable by God (v. 4) and this stone, in an explicit quotation from Scripture (from Isaias 28 : 16), is then designated as the corner-stone which allows no one to be confounded who trusts in it (v. 6). In Ephesians 2 : 20 "the apostles and prophets" form the foundation and Jesus Christ is to be regarded as the corner-stone which holds the edifice together; only in this way does the idea correspond with that of Christ as head of the body. According to the First Epistle of Peter 2 : 4, however, the baptized have "come" towards him and the quotation brings to mind the powerful foundation stone which gives the building support and security from below[51]. Here the greater proximity to the tradition of the community is evident; this had preserved the saying of Jesus which probably used the same image (Mk 12 : 10 parallels) with reference to Ps 118 (117) : 22 f.; the community's interest in this passage of Scripture is also perceptible in Acts 4 : 11

where Peter applies it to Jesus in a discourse to the people. Used by Jesus as a weapon in argument (cf. also Lk 20 : 18), the image is at first given a positive interpretation in the First Epistle of Peter 2 : 6 (in accordance with the more appropriate passage 28 : 16), but after that, again with reference to Psalm 118 (117) : 22 and Isaias 8 : 14 f., is turned as a weapon against unbelievers (vv. 7–8). In contrast to this the author describes those addressed as "a chosen generation, a kingly priesthood, a holy nation, a purchased people" (v. 9); with this he takes up the old idea of the people of God which with Paul is only preserved in the concept of "the Church of God" or "the Israel of God". Whilst, however, Paul always has the community of Jews and gentiles in mind, this author applies all those titles of honour emphatically to the gentile Christians. It is precisely to them whom God "has called out of darkness into his marvellous light" (v. 9) that his mercy is revealed. Once they were "not a people" now they are "the people of God"; once they had "not obtained mercy"; now they "have obtained mercy" (v. 10); once again the transference of a prophecy that once applied to Israel (Hos 1 : 6, 9; 2 : 25) to the converted gentiles. Even the Epistle to the Ephesians had not gone as far as this; in it the gentiles once "afar off", have become by the blood of Jesus "nearby" (2 : 13). However, the Jews who believe in Christ are also included, according to the First Epistle of Peter, in this new people of God, for it is only against the unbelieving Israel that polemic is perceptible (cf. 2 : 7) and perhaps chiefly against its' responsible leaders (the "builders"). "The idea is that God has turned the very rejection of the stone into the laying of the foundation stone of his house."[52] The metaphor of the "house of God" also recurs in 4 : 17, probably more in the sense of the members of the household. This easily leads to the other old image of "God's flock" (5 : 2) which is also a totality even when dispersed but it manifests itself in a special way in the local church ("the flock of God which is among you"). The passage which turns in exhortation to the presbyters (those presiding over the local church or churches) is also important for the concept of official ministry[53]. Ultimately these are only various images to express the idea of the people of God (cf. on this also below, Part Four, § 2).

Such a fusion of numerous passages of Scripture and employment of a variety of thoughts for the benefit of the recipient of the epistle indicates an advanced ecclesiology open to many-sided influences. If a particular guiding idea is looked for in the First Epistle of Peter, it is that of "strangers and pilgrims" that is most indicated. These terms are already found in the Epistle to the Ephesians (2 : 19) but in significant contrast to the "community of Israel" (2 : 12); in Christ the former gentiles are no longer "far away" and "strangers", as they were in the time of the old theocracy, but "fellow-citizens of God" (2 : 19). In the First Epistle of Peter this reference to Israel is lacking; the new people of God is immediately envisaged and seen as foreign to this world. In the salutation itself the addressees are described as "elect ... strangers dispersed through Pontus, Galatia, Cappadocia, Asia and Bithynia" (1 : 1). The dispersion here can scarcely mean the Jewish diaspora in the literal sense; the spiritual meaning must be understood, which was already signified by "strangers"[54]. The new people of God too is still dispersed "among the gentiles" (cf. 2 : 12) and that corresponds to a new "diaspora situation" in this world generally. So we find a similar transposition of the concept as we observed in 2 : 9f. The Christians during the time of their "pilgrimage" (παροι-κία)[55] must lead their lives in fear of God (1 : 17), and, as "strangers and pilgrims", refrain from carnal desires (2 : 11). The same fundamental idea is present therefore, as in Philippians 3 : 20: the State to which the Christians interiorly belong, is in heaven. They are not only juridically citizens of the heavenly city of God, but thanks to their new engendering by God (1 : 3, 23), they await in "lively hope" the "incorruptible, undefiled and unfading inheritance which is reserved in heaven" for them (1 : 3 f.). As this condition of being strangers on earth extends right through the period in which the Christians are held fast in this world (cf. 1 : 17; 4 : 2; but "the end of all is at hand", 4 : 7), it constitutes them at the same time as pilgrims, even if the idea of the "pilgrim people of God" does not yet formally emerge (as it does in Hebrews 3 : 7–4 : 11). The author has felt strongly the distance and alien character of this world under the impression of many temptations and sufferings (cf. 1 : 6; 2 : 20; 3 : 14–17; 4 : 12 to 19); yet the joy of election and deliverance keeps breaking through and the society of the brethren gives support (cf. 2 : 17; 5 : 9). In a similar way to Paul, the author sees the life of Christians in this world and the character of the Church as eschatological. "The Church as diaspora, which is not so merely in what was called the diaspora but essentially, has according to biblical witness a particular distress, promise and task, which determines its eschatological character and attitude."[56]

The idea of the journeying of the people of God is developed in a new way of his own by the author of the Epistle to the Hebrews. Once it is recognized that this theological thinker is not aiming at showing polemically the superiority of the worship of the new Covenant over that of the Old Testament and of Judaism, but is rather seeking to say something positive to the people of God of the new Covenant by means of Old Testament typology and through a special ("Alexandrian") kind of scriptural exegesis, in order to stimulate it on its way to the heavenly future world[57], the various typological notions employed have to be brought together for the theological guiding principle to emerge. The Son (c. 1), who as "leader", "author" of salvation, leads "many sons", his "brethren", into glory (2 : 5–18); the Son set over God's "house", who is higher than Moses, the true administrator in the house of God (that is, in God's community of the Old Testament), and

89

possesses God's community of the new Covenant as the eschatological "house" of God (3 : 1–6) [38]; the guide to salvation leading
the new people of God into "rest" as Moses once led the old to
the promised land (3 : 7–4 : 11); above all the true high priest
who entered once and for all through his blood sacrifice into
the heavenly sanctuary and so opened up access to it to those
who are united to him (cc. 7–10): all these are changing and
partly overlapping typological expressions for the redemption,
sanctification and perfecting by Jesus Christ of the people of
God of the new Covenant. The Christological interest is at
first in the foreground: the Son as image and as equal in nature
with God, his superiority to the angels, his position as cosmic
ruler (1 : 3–14); but the soteriological and ecclesiological point
of view is linked to this. The Son for whose sake and through
whom all things were created, is to lead many sons into glory
to share in his inheritance (cf. 1 : 2, 14; 2 : 10; 9 : 15). The
"Son" and the "sons", sanctifier and sanctified (2 : 11), the
mediator of the Covenant and the people of the Covenant,
he who offers sacrifice (of himself) and the worshipping community, the high priest and the people whom he represents,
belong inseparably together. Those united with Christ are the
eschatological people of God (4 : 9; cf. 13 : 12), with whom
God concludes through that true "mediator", the new and
definitive Covenant of salvation (cf. 8 : 8–12).

The author, however, directs particular attention to the
eschatological situation of the people of God of the new
Covenant. On the one hand it already shares in the redemption
accomplished by the blood of Christ (cf. 9 : 11–28). Through
the oblation of the body of Jesus Christ, we are sanctified
once and for all (10 : 10); through his blood we possess well-
founded confidence of entry into the heavenly sanctuary, we
have a new and more living way which he has inaugurated
for us through the veil, that is, through his flesh (10 : 19 f.).
We have come "to Mount Sion and to the city of the living
God, the heavenly Jerusalem and to thousands of angels, to

the festive gathering and Church of the first-born who are written in heaven, and to God the judge of all and to the spirits of the just made perfect, and to Jesus the mediator of the new Covenant..." (12 : 22ff.). This reality of the redemption experienced particularly in Christian worship[59], no longer any "shadow" of the future blessings but the real and authentic "image" (cf. 10 : 1); this union with the heavenly Church of God, this entry into the divine domain, is taken so seriously that there is no longer any turning back; those who "were once enlightened, tasted the heavenly gift and became partakers of the Holy Spirit and tasted the good word of God and the powers of the future aeon", and then have fallen away, cannot be renewed again to repentance (6 : 4ff.). And so, on the other hand, it becomes clear that this redeemed and sanctified community which already belongs to heaven must still prove itself on its earthly journey and in the combat of afflictions (cf. 10 : 32—36). "For we have here no lasting city, but strive for one that is to come" (13 : 14). Like the ancient people of God in its wanderings through the desert, the new one also hears perpetually the voice of its God: "Today if you hear his voice do not harden your hearts as (happened) in the 'provocation'" (3 : 15). That is the eschatological "today" which compels a decision, which summons each individual and the whole people of God not to remain behind as long as the promise of entry into "rest" is still open (4 : 1). Great exertions are still needed in order to reach this goal of Sabbath rest (4 : 9ff.). And so fulfilment and expectation, deliverance and promise of perfect accomplishment compenetrate and that tension still persists which must be mastered in earthly trial. The fundamental eschatological promises are already fulfilled in the order of the new Covenant (cf. 8 : 6), but the culminating promise of entry into "rest" is still unrealized (4 : 1). "So every promise fulfilled is once again a promise of what is definitive; it is as it were an adumbration in which what is heavenly and invisible already

91

in some manner assumes shape and form." [60] In the meantime, however, the condition holds that the people of God must "hold fast" to what has already been given (3 : 6, 14; 10 : 23). Filled with the powers of God, it must employ its own endeavour and is urgently exhorted "to lift up the hands which hang down and the feeble knees" (12 : 12), following its saving leader and model it must "in perseverance" run to the goal and overcome indolence of soul (cf. 12 : 1 ff.). Indeed the community must be vigilant for the holiness of all its members "so that no bitter root may spring up and be troublesome and so that many may not be contaminated by it" (12 : 15). Under different forms of presentation this is precisely the same eschatological attitude that we also find in the great epistles of Paul and which finds expression there in the juxtaposition of eschatological proclamation of salvation (with the use of the indicative mood) and of ethical admonition (in the imperative mood). In the Epistle to the Hebrews, this very definite "word of exhortation" (13 : 22), the consequence that follows after doctrinal exposition is always immediately, clearly and urgently drawn in warmly encouraging admonition (cf. 2 : 1–4; 3 : 12 ff.; 4 : 1, 11; 6 : 9–12; 10 : 19–39 etc.).

It is unmistakably a complete ecclesiological conception that is expressed here, which itself implies a theological and ecclesiastical development of some duration and which adopts many ideas and metaphors (people of God, pilgrimage, the house of God, the future city, the heavenly Jerusalem), but also adds new elements and is shaped into an original whole by the author's synthetic power. The question is not without importance, how the author arrived at this impressive idea of the Church. A one-sided derivation from gnostic themes (Käsemann) is just as unconvincing as the more recent attempt to discover all the concepts and imagery and even its function and the context of its composition in the Qumran community (H. Kosmala), although light is thrown from both of these sides on the mentality of the Epistle to the Hebrews. The author's generally recognized Alexandrian mode of scriptural argument as well as his genuinely Christian conception should no longer be contested. Then it can only be a question of what proportion is to be ascribed to gnostic or Qumran themes and elements. Even if some knowledge of, or contact with, gnostic ideas (yet of what kind?) were thought to be possibly implied by the conception of the close connection of the "Son" with the "sons", nevertheless the images centring on the high priest (according to the order of Melchisedek, c. 7), which are so important to this work, seem after all to be very remote from gnostic imagery[61]. The liturgical terminology, the sacerdotal attitude of mind concerned with "purification" (cf. 9 : 13 f.; 10 : 2, 22), the doctrine of the Messias which takes greatest interest in his character as high priest, the prominence given to the angels, on the one hand creatures placed "far beneath the Son" (cc. 1 and 2), on the other a heavenly festive gathering linked with the Church (12 : 22), the paraenesis, and also many individual turns of phrase[62] suggest close contact with the spirituality of Qumran[63]. Of course, just as in the case of the Gospel of John, various relations and degrees of kinship are possible in this. The least convincing hypothesis is that the work is a "proclamation of the Son of God-Messias Jesus, the first of its kind, to a group of men who were not yet believers in Jesus", namely Essenes of Qumran[64], for the work clearly enough presupposes Christian recipients who have already belonged to the Church for some time and have already endured trials and sufferings (cf. 10 : 32–39; 12 : 1–6; 13 : 7 f.), and threatened to slacken in their previously strong faith (cf. 4 : 1; 5 : 11 f.; 10 : 23 ff.; 12 : 12 f.). Even the famous glance back to the foundation of faith in 6 : 1 f., the "illumination" (10 : 32, cf. 6 : 4), can only refer to the adoption of Christian belief (τὸν τῆς ἀρχῆς τοῦ Χριστοῦ λόγον)[65]. Greater inclination might well be felt to agree with the thesis of C. Spicq, that the author (according to Spicq, Apollos), was probably addressing "Essene Christians,

93

Jewish priests, among whom there may have been a certain number of former members of Qumran"[66]; but again, it must have been a whole relatively closed community which in a Christian area it is difficult to imagine consisting only of former Essenes or even Jewish priests. The recipients of the epistle among other things had suffered loss of their possessions in a former persecution (10 : 34), and that does not exactly suggest the Essene "poor". There also remains the possibility that the author himself had imbibed, as well as other influences, something of the Qumran spirit, perhaps had come into contact with Essenes and learnt something from them. That could have served to promote his ecclesiological thought, for in that regard it is certain that valuable treasures were guarded and sought out in Qumran, such as the idea of "the (new) Covenant", the "(holy) people of God", "the (eschatological) community", "the exodus and the sojourn in the desert", and the link with the "saints" (that is, the angels), in heaven. But that scarcely meant more than an enriching for our author, for the whole conception, the scriptural foundation, the characteristic mode of thought on the two planes of what is earthly and a shadow and of what is heavenly and real, remain his own and form a theological synthesis of unique originality. Nor did any other theologian follow him in this comprehensive and unifying mode of vision.

6. *The Church in the pastoral epistles*

Inquiry into the concept of the Church in the pastoral epistles leads into quite a different atmosphere. It must be remembered that this group of letters is concerned with questions of organization, with the regulation and stabilization of ecclesiastical conditions, with pastoral instructions for bearers of office and others in already quite complex situations. By the very purpose of these writings, addressed to deputies of the apostle Paul, we can scarcely expect great theological expositions from them; on the other hand, however, such instructions from a superior for the carrying out of the ministry must probably presuppose as a basis an idea of the Church which supports and permeates all admonitions. Here the question immediately arises whether we have the same Paul before us as in his indisputably genuine letters; but this problem is complicated and difficult precisely from the point of view which concerns us here. If the authenticity of the pastoral epistles is maintained, an aspect of the great apostle of the gentiles is revealed which is less apparent in his epistles to the churches but, according to the account in the Acts of the Apostles, cannot be excluded from his missionary undertakings: the ecclesiastical organizer and missionary making preparations in advance for the period after his death. If their genuineness is disputed, perhaps precisely by reason of the surprisingly new and different picture of the Church, it must be explained who could write in this authoritative way and when, to two outstanding disciples of Paul, or could instigate the fiction of such writings. There are certainly also possibilities of holding firm to the Pauline substance and of assuming perhaps a later revision, completion or adaptation. Consequently it will be preferable to leave aside the difficult set of questions regarding the origin and literary character of the pastoral epistles[67] and be content to extract in a positive way the concept of the Church from these writings, which in any case merit attention by their antiquity and incorporation in the canon.

The Church or community is mentioned in only three passages in the First Epistle to Timothy (3 : 5, 15; 5 : 16); of these the first two are theologically important. If the pregnant statement in 1 Timothy 3 : 15 is taken as a starting-point, where mention is made of the "house of God" which is "the Church of the living God, the pillar and ground of truth", a significant picture is immediately presented and one which points in a certain direction. The old term "Church of God" is adopted, but is scarcely being understood as "the people of God" but (in conjunction with the likewise old image of the "house of God"), is rather being understood as a holy institution. The view of the Church as a building or temple was, of course, already powerfully developed in Judaism (cf. Qumran: *1 QS* V, 5f.; VIII, 5–9), as well as in Paul (1 Cor 3 : 16; 2 Cor 6 : 16; Eph 2 : 20f.) and in 1 Peter 2 : 5 ff.; but there are perceptible differences in the application of the metaphor. Especially with Paul, the proximity of the image of planting (1 Cor 3 : 6–9), the insistence on the holy temple filled with the Holy Spirit (1 Cor 3 : 16), the interchange of the idea of the people of God (2 Cor 6 : 16ff.), and the emphasis on growth (Eph 2 : 21), all give the idea dynamic character [68]. The edifice is no finished, well-constructed fortress equipped against attacks, but a structure that is still being built, striving towards heaven, led by inner forces towards completion. In 1 Timothy 3 : 15, however, the "Church of the living God" is a firmly based and well-furnished house, in which it is possible to move and which possesses its own order (cf. the list of qualifications for bearers of office, 3 : 2 ff., 8 f.). That is made even clearer through the comparison drawn in 1 Timothy 3 : 5 with the earthly house of a family (οἶκος in Greek has this meaning too); "for if a man does not know how to rule his own house, how shall he take care of the house of God?" "Church of God" has already become a definite concept, probably in catechetical and liturgical use, which in fact brought the picture of a furnished building before the mind, just as the English word "church" does, and which to a Greek could also suggest the closed circle of a household. This last idea is prominent in the passage, for the thought moves from the good administrator of his own house (the bishop, 3 : 4; the deacons, 3 : 12), to correct behaviour "in the house of God" (3 : 15); but then there is mingled with this the image of the edifice which is strong (στῦλος = support) and firmly founded (ἑδραίωμα = foundation) [69].

96

The expression "ground of truth" has a parallel in *1 QS* V, 5 f., where the Qumran community describes itself as "foundation of truth *(mosad 'emeth)* for Israel" and "house of truth *(beth ha'emeth)* in Israel"; the metaphor and the idea recur frequently[70]. The closer connection with these Qumran passages consists in the following points: (a) The community itself serves as foundation whilst in the earlier Pauline texts Christ or as the case may be, the "apostles and prophets" (Eph 2 : 20) are described as such; (b) the house appears fortified ("bulwark") just as in the Qumran texts the metaphor is in fact exchanged for that of a fortified city in which the "wall" is formed by members of the community (cf. *1 QS* VIII, 7; *1 QH* VI, 25, probably following Is 26 : 1–6); (c) the idea of "truth" is bound up with it. Nevertheless the differences must not be overlooked. The holy foundation in Qumran, the spiritual temple, what is holy and most holy (laymen and priests?), God's house and God's city, is intended for Israel and what constitutes the strength of the building is different from what it is in the Christian Church. For life in "the house of truth" of Qumran is entirely regulated by the Torah which "the men of truth" strive to realize according to the measure of their knowledge (cf. *1 QpHab* VII, 10f.); and so the community is "as it were a spiritual house of instruction"[71]. In the pastoral epistles truth signifies belief in Jesus Christ and indeed true and right belief as opposed to false doctrines (cf. 1 Tim 1 : 19; 2 : 7; 4 : 1, 3, 6; 6 : 5, 10; Tit 1 : 13f.; 2 Tim 2 : 15 etc.), which alone guarantees salvation (cf. 1 Tim 2 : 4; 4 : 16; 2 Tim 2 : 10, 25). Despite the different way of salvation a certain similarity is nevertheless recognizable in "awareness of the Church", and it is not by chance that this shows itself in the same imagery. Established in a different way, the Church is nevertheless a strictly constituted society, a bulwark on a solid foundation. With its right belief and baptism which brings deliverance (cf. Tit 3 : 5 f.), its instruction and formation (Tit 2 :12; 2 Tim 2 : 25), its offices and discipline (cf. 1 Tim 1 : 20), it is a refuge, guarantor of salvation, a strong and fortified city of God.

The metaphor of the house appears again in 2 Timothy 2 : 19 ff., this time employed independently and carried further. With reference to two heretical teachers named Hymeneus and Philetus infected with Gnosticism, "who say the resurrection has already taken place" (2 : 18), it is said: "God's sure foundation stands firm and bears this seal: 'the Lord knows those who are his' ..." That is once again primarily the idea of the divine foundation, the holy edifice formed of those who are called. Then, however, a comparison is drawn with an earthly house and its furnishing: "In a great house are not only vessels of gold and silver but also of wood and clay, some for honourable, the others for ignoble use" (v. 20). To this is added, moving forward paraenetically to the relevant point, "If any one cleanses himself from these things, he will be a vessel unto honour, sanctified and profitable to the Lord, prepared for every good work" (v. 21). Here the Church appears even more clearly as a well-furnished house of God formed of human beings among whom there are also unworthy ones, but nevertheless as a house not threatened in its internal stability; for the Church remains God's foundation and has in it the power of repelling what is bad and dangerous. But it is scarcely envisaged as a reality that belongs more to heaven than to earth, as a society mysteriously united with Christ its heavenly head, as in Ephesians.

The order and proper furnishing of this earthly house of God is ensured above all by the official ministries. In this picture of the Church they have the essential task of continuing to build on the "foundation of God", protecting his house from dangers but also developing the inner life. Full authority still continues to rest with the apostle; but Paul allows a share in it to his intimate friends Timothy and Titus whom he appoints as a kind of pastoral superiors over a wider area and these again are to appoint presbyters for the local communities

(Tit 1 : 5; 2 Tim 2 : 2). The principal service of the apostle remains the proclamation of salvation as herald of Jesus Christ "who destroys death but has brought life and immortality to light by the gospel" (2 Tim 1 :10 f.; cf. 1 Tim 2 :7). In this time of stabilization of ecclesiastical conditions and of emergent heresies, however, that also becomes a teaching obligation which the apostle imposes on his pupils and representatives, and which is administered in the local churches by the bishops or presbyters. Consequently, teaching and, as opposed to pernicious false teaching, the "sound doctrine" (Tit 1 : 9; 2 : 1; 2 Tim 4 : 3), combined with urgent exhortation (παρακαλεῖν), receive special emphasis (cf. 1 Tim 4 : 11; 6 : 2; Tit 1 : 9; 2 Tim 1 : 11; 2 : 2; 4 : 2). And so the apostolic doctrine also becomes a "deposit" (παραθήκη), which Paul commits to Timothy and which the latter must preserve (1 Tim 6 : 20) "by the Holy Spirit who dwells in us" (2 Tim 1 : 14). In this way the Church's principle of tradition and succession begins to become apparent. In these writings, as well as teaching the authoritative guidance by the apostle, or, as the case may be, by his representative, is everywhere prominent and the offices are conferred by official consecration (ordination). Timothy was authorized and consecrated to his position as pastoral superior *(ad nutum apostoli)* in a solemn act by the imposition of hands by Paul (and of the college of presbyters?) (cf. 1 Tim 1 : 18; 4 : 14; 2 Tim 1 : 6); he in turn is to appoint "trustworthy men capable of teaching others also" (2 Tim 2 : 2). If 1 Timothy 5 : 22 does not refer to the reconciliation of sinners[72], and that can hardly be the case, the passage formally testifies that the transmission of authority to the presbyters of the church is likewise to take place by the imposition of hands; but this is in any case likely. Consequently the local holders of office also share in the authority to teach and direct which was originally concentrated in the apostle, and it is understandable why careful lists of qualifications were laid down for such men. It is not necessary here to investigate more closely the various offices and terms used to designate them[73]; it is sufficient to recognize their essential function, their hierarchical structure and their indispensability for the "domestic order" of the Church of God.

There can be no doubt then that the Church in the pastoral epistles assumes a more institutional appearance which seems to contrast with the "pneumatic" and indeed heavenly nature of the Church in Paul's earlier letters. If closer attention is given, however, to the message that is contained in these epistles to the churches, many familiar echoes can be heard of the Pauline gospel. What the Church has to announce is here also the grace and goodness of God (in more Hellenistic terminology, it is true, cf. φιλανθρωπία, χρηστότης, σωτήρ), which has appeared in Jesus Christ (Tit 2 : 11; 3 : 4 f.; 2 Tim 1 : 9 f.), in order to save all men (cf. 1 Tim 1 : 15; 2 : 3 f.). The idea of the people of God is also touched upon in Titus 2 : 14, quite in line with Pauline and early Christian theology generally. The Church sees itself situated in the time between the first and the second, glorious manifestation of its Lord and saviour (1 Tim 6 : 14; Tit 2 : 13; 2 Tim 4 : 8), filled with blessed hope (1 Tim 4 : 10; Tit 1 : 2; 2 : 13; 3 : 7). The Church is not spared earthly combat and tribulation (with the emphasis on combat); for its members the rule is: "If we die with (Christ) we shall also live with him; if we persevere we shall also reign with him" (2 Tim 2 : 11 f.). It is vividly aware of the sacrificial death of Jesus Christ, the only "mediator between God and man" (1 Tim 2 : 5 f.; Tit 2 : 14). It is true that the dominant mood tends more to victory and glory. The Church sings a hymn to Christ describing the way of the redeemer from the flesh into the divine spiritual sphere, his heavenly triumph and cosmic success (1 Tim 3 : 16); it may be assumed that it recognized its own way in this and hoped for faith throughout the whole world. The Church sees more clearly its tasks in the world but must not on that account install itself in the world or fall a victim to convention and routine. It would be one-sided to regard the Church in the pastoral epistles only as an institution established on earth and settling down for a long time, a "spiritual welfare institute"; but it is true that the eschatological tension is fading, the "civic" virtues are insisted on, the conflict with heresies causes difficulties, and a more rigorous order and discipline are becoming apparent.

In this way a change certainly took place, but whether this really was a "change in the Church's own conception of itself"[74] is another matter. In such judgments a measuring rod is applied which has been acquired from Paul's supposedly purely eschatological thought about the Church, without inquiring whether the Paul of the epistles to the churches envisaged more clearly the external aspect of the Church, its constitution and order of ministries, the authority of the men who presided over it, in short its earthly form, than perhaps people are ready to admit (cf. above, Part One, §4). In that case the development historically speaking not only took place with a certain inevitability in the direction of so-called "early Catholicism", but also with inner justification and logic, though the danger bound up with this for the religious spirit and the deeper mission of the Church must be recognized.

Where and how is this picture of the Church (quite apart from the question of its author) to be fitted into the theological development that has been followed until now? E. Schweizer links the pastoral epistles in the structure of his work with "the conception of the primitive Church and its consequences", after the view of the Church of Matthew and Luke[75], but things can scarcely have been so continuous. Paul intervenes as an important link; according to the pastoral epistles, filled with the same consciousness of his grace-given vocation as in the chief epistles (cf. 1 Tim 1 : 12–16), he ascribes to his office a fundamental significance for the Church: "he is herald and apostle ... teacher of the gentiles in faith and truth" (1 Tim 2 : 7). He guarantees the message and doctrine and transmits it to his pupils as a precious deposit (see above). Schweizer

101

himself emphasizes that "the apostle and he alone is guarantor of the tradition"[76]. Now of course the primitive Church also persevered "in the doctrine of the apostles" (Acts 2 : 42); but even apart from the strong link with the apostle to the gentiles, the message itself, as we observed, shows unmistakable Pauline features. Pauline influence is difficult to dispute, therefore. This has been perceived more acutely by M. Goguel when he regards this ("deutero-Pauline") picture of the Church as a mixture of the Jerusalem and Pauline conceptions and as the result of a development that was necessary from both sides: the officials appointed as representatives and equipped with the charisma of office became necessary for the Jerusalem community, because the direct contact with the time and person of Jesus came to an end, and for Paul because the freely given (exceptional) charismata became rarer and disappeared[77]. Certainly it is doubtful whether such a deep cleavage existed between the Jerusalem and Pauline conceptions (in particular of the apostolic office) as Goguel assumes, if for no other reason than that both sides sought and found contact and agreement. The original apostles recognized the apostolate of Paul (Gal 2 : 8 f.), and Paul joined their ranks as the last witness of Jesus' resurrection (1 Cor 15 : 8–10), submitted his gospel to them (Gal 2 : 2; cf. 1 Cor 15 : 3, 11), and maintained connection with Jerusalem. Nevertheless as regards the conception of office, it is in fact possible to say that the institutional and charismatic components have fused into an organic unity in the pastoral epistles in as much as in them the "imposition of hands" confers the Spirit. The ecclesiological conception of the pastoral epistles must then represent a more advanced stage in accordance with historical and theological development and one which presupposes both the old Palestinian as well as Pauline Christianity; at the same time it must be again remarked that by the whole nature and purpose of these writings, their picture of the Church remains, and probably could not but remain, one-sided.

102

7. The Church in the Johannine writings, including the Apocalypse

At first sight the Johannine theology expounded in the Gospel according to John and in the "great epistle" (1 John) does not seem to recognize the Church as a theological factor (the term ἡ ἐκκλησία does not occur). It is different, of course, with the Apocalypse, which will be included here among Johannine writings in the wider sense, but its whole nature requires it to be envisaged separately, and consequently it is treated last here. For a long time John's Gospel was considered evidence of an individual, spiritualized, even "mystical", Christianity. The "religious individualism" expressed in the call "he that believes in the Son has eternal life", or other such statements (3 : 16, 36; 5 : 24 etc.), the "mysticism" that appears to lie in expressions denoting union (". . . abides in me and I in him", 6 :56; 15 :5 etc.), the wrongly interpreted statement concerning "worship in spirit and truth" (4 : 23), all contributed to such a distortion. Nor is R. Bultmann's existential interpretation, which regards the Gospel according to John as the chief witness on behalf of an already "demythologized" gospel message, capable of grasping the eminently ecclesiological aspect of Johannine theology. Where everything is aimed solely at the "eschatological", concrete decision of the individual in regard to the "revealer" and his word, no place remains for the reality and operation of a redemptive society equipped for, and charged with conveying the light and life brought into the world by the divine envoy. It is also insufficient to form the link with the community only by the requirement of brotherly love comprised in the moral summons; for then the movement is again solely from individual to society and it is not evident that the individual can realize his Christian life only on the basis of the redeemed community to which he is subordinated. In fact, the idea of the Church is much more deeply rooted in Johannine thought, and indeed is indispensable to this independent, magnificently devised theology, with its concentration on the essential. That has been convincingly shown by recent investigations[78], and will be confirmed by examination from the ecclesiological point of view.

There can be no doubt that the chief interest of the fourth evangelist is in Christology. The impelling motive for the composition of this late gospel (the traditions of which it is true must go back very far) certainly lies in the author's intention to provide the Church of his time and surroundings with a picture of Christ corresponding to the Church's spiritual condition, but which, in the evangelist's view, was already perceptible in Jesus' words and work (cf. 1 : 17 f.; 17 : 3; 20 : 31). But is it not inevitable that readers and faithful who were already living at a considerable distance from the historical events should raise the question of the relation in which they stood to the Christ who had brought revelation and salvation to the earth, and ask what function was assigned to the community which they acknowledged? Was the Church only the recipient of Christ's gospel and saving gifts; was it not also the administrator of his bequest, and the executor of his intentions? Closer penetration into John's gospel shows that the Church in fact is assigned a quite definite position in the work of salvation.

In the soteriological revelation saying: "He that believes in the Son has eternal life", the gift from God's envoy appears in the first place to be one made there and then. Yet it is only the Spirit sent from the exalted Christ who confers the divine life to the faithful in a definite and real manner. At the beginning of the individual's way of salvation there is needed in addition to faith, a "generation from on high", that is to say, baptism, in order to enter at all into the sphere of God's life (cf. 3 : 3, 5), and this at the same time places the individual, even when this is not expressly stated, in the array of the other children of God (cf. Jn 1 : 12 f.; 1 Jn 3 : 1 f.), who in the First Epistle of John are recognizable as the orthodox community (cf. 2 : 20, 27 f.; 3 : 9 f.; 5 : 1 f.). In defence against the "anti-Christs" the profoundly rooted community-consciousness appears: "They went out from us but they were not of us. For if they had been of us they would have remained with us; but it was to be made manifest that they all did not belong to us" (2 : 19). If W. Nauck is right in thinking that the basis of the epistle is an exhortation written in connection with baptism and its obligation[79], the significance of baptism becomes quite clear; but even without this the theological lines are plainly recognizable: baptism is the generation by God which produces children of God[80]; it implants in the believer the "seed of God", that is to say, the Holy Spirit, for a life without sin (cf. 3 : 9) and administers to him the "unction" for perseverance in correct doctrine (2 : 20, 27). But by the behaviour of the children of God, by their true confession of Christ (2 : 22; 4 : 2 f.; 5 : 1) and their fraternal love (2 : 9 ff.; 3 : 14, 23; 4 : 20 f.; 5 : 2), it is then recognized whether they are really such, or not rather "children of the devil" (3 : 10). The community represented by the author (cf. also 3 : 14) makes the claim to be the true children of God, to possess communion with God (1 : 3, 6; 2 : 3 etc.), and refers in this regard to its possession of the Spirit (3 : 24; 4 : 13). Spirit and life are only conveyed and preserved, are only operative and fruitful in the community.

That is not, however, as it were a subsequent, supplementary conviction formed in controversy with teachers of false doctrine. The same fundamental theological ideas are already expressed in the Gospel according to John, which is not dominated by this polemic. It is only since Jesus has been raised up that the Spirit has been there for the faithful as life-giving power (7 : 39). He is released in "streams of living water" which (so verse 37 f. should no doubt be interpreted)[81] flow from Jesus' body. This metaphor immediately recalls the scene in John 19 : 34 f., where blood and water come from the open side of the Crucified. If the cognate passage in

1 John 5 : 6 f. is compared with this, the assumption will probably be justified that the evangelist also sees in it a symbol for the sacraments of baptism and eucharist; for according to the passage in the epistle, Spirit, water and blood all become perpetual witnesses whose testimony converges (in favour of Jesus Christ) [82]. The death of Jesus becomes effective for salvation by means of the Spirit in the sacraments of the Church. For the holy eucharist we have another passage which fits into this group of ideas. At the end of the discourse on the bread of life in chapter 6, Jesus says: "If then you shall see the Son of man ascend up where he was before (will you be scandalized even then)? It is the Spirit that gives life, the flesh profits nothing" (6 : 62–63 a). This must certainly be interpreted as follows: a Son of man who comes from heaven (cf. however v. 42), returns there once more and shows by that that he is not confined to the sphere of the "flesh" (the earthly human sphere); he also gives his flesh and blood (v. 53), not in the manner of his earthly, natural existence, but after his return to heaven in a way in which his life-giving Spirit is at work. Both sacraments, but similarly the forgiveness of sins as well (20 : 22 f.), are effective through the Spirit proceeding from the exalted Lord [83]. In fact the thought is fundamental for the whole picture given by the gospel that the earthly Jesus continues and only then really fulfils his saving work when he is raised on high [84]. Consequently he asks his Father to be glorified; only when glorified will he be able to use the "power over all flesh" given to him, in order to bestow eternal life on all those "given" to him by the Father (17 : 2). Only when he is exalted will he "draw all to himself" (12 : 32) and only after his departure to the Father will the disciples accomplish "even greater works" than himself, clearly in winning over men (14 : 12). There is also for John a "time of Jesus" and a "time of the Church" characterized by the Spirit, but he does not present them as Luke does in a double work, but views them together in the very words

106

of his Christ. Jesus' gaze is already perpetually turned towards the future in which when glorified he will make his work, completed on earth (19 : 30), fruitful for all men (cf. 12 : 24, 32; 17 : 2, 21), through the Holy Spirit (cf. the sayings regarding the Paraclete) and through the activity of his disciples (15 : 27; 17 : 18; 20 : 21).

That this gaze of the Johannine Jesus, fixed on the future, is directed towards the Church, is clear from various sayings and metaphors with which he defines his work. The chief image is that of the flock which not only occurs in the discourses and imagery of chapter 10 but exercises a pervasive theological influence. The faithful, in Jesus' time the disciples assembled around him, are those whom the Father has "given" to the Son and brings to him, and whom the Son does not "cast out" but rather accepts and keeps and does not allow "to be lost" (cf. 6 : 37–39; 17 : 6, 9 f., 11 f.). If this mode of speech is compared with the pictures of the shepherd in chapter 10 a complete system of thought can be recognized which has also shaped that terminology. God is the real owner of the sheep but he has entrusted them to the shepherd Jesus so that the sheep belong to both, just as, in general, there is a complete community of property between the Father and the Son (cf. in particular 10 : 26–29; 17 : 10). The true and good shepherd, Jesus, in contrast to the hirelings (the Jewish leaders), knows and loves his sheep, cares for them and gives his life for them (10 : 11–15); the sheep who know him follow him and he gives them eternal life (10 : 10, 27 f.). On departing, however, he gives them back again to his Father's immediate care; above all he prays that the Father will preserve them in perfect unity (17 : 11 ff., 22 f.). By this metaphor light is thrown on other questions too, such as the call to faith, which results from the Father's free power over grace (cf. 6 : 44, 65); in the present connection, however, it is important that the image of the flock is also maintained for the future. "I have other sheep that are not of this fold; them

107

also I must bring and they will hear my voice and there will be one flock and one shepherd" (10 : 16). There the perspective opens out to the one Church composed of believing Jews and gentiles. The question regarding the old "Israel" and the call of the gentiles is, therefore, perceptible in John too. "Israel" is still a title of honour (cf. 1 : 31, 50; 3 : 10; 12 : 13); only the unbelieving Jews are depreciated, even verbally (οἱ Ἰουδαῖοι is used mostly in a negative sense for the leading Jewish circles), for as the representatives of the "world" hostile to God, they have become haters of Jesus and persecutors of Christians (cf. 2 : 18; 5 : 16, 18; 7 : 1 etc.; cf. also 15 : 8–16 : 4). Non-Jewish mankind already meets Jesus in very promising representatives (the Samaritan woman 4 : 39–42; the "Greeks" 12 : 20 ff.), and wait as it were to be incorporated in God's flock. Then all national or other modes of thought disappear; Jewish modes of thought are radically broken. The chosen children of God (not even: the children of Israel dispersed among the gentiles) are scattered all over the world and are to be gathered together into a unity by Jesus' redemptive death which avails for all (11 : 52). It is solely a question of faith in Jesus the Christ and the Son of God; the departing Lord prays for all who will believe in him through the word of his disciples (17 : 20 f.).

Finally the image of Christ's flock also appears in the "supplementary chapter 21", in the words of the risen Christ to Simon Peter: "Feed my lambs, feed my sheep" (21 : 15–17). Even if this chapter perhaps did not belong to the original plan of the gospel, it certainly belongs to the evangelist's tradition[85]. The conferring of pastoral ministry on the disciples whose position in the rest of the gospel (perhaps precisely on account of the rivalry with the "disciple whom Jesus loved", cf. 20 : 6 ff.) is not in doubt (cf. 1 : 42; 6 : 68 f.), cannot be dismissed with a remark that the Johannine picture of the Church is not interested in a constitution, for even in that scene after Easter, it is not the constitution which is the decisive viewpoint, but care for the guidance of the sheep which are deprived of their true and abiding shepherd (cf. 10 : 16). The heavenly protection of the Father, preservation from evil, sanctification (17 : 11–19), do not exclude earthly direction by a representative of Christ. For John, too, the Church is a reality both of the present world and the next, a society existing in the world but of a kind that is not of this world (cf. 17 : 14 f.).

The Johannine picture of the Church is enriched not only by the image of the flock but also by that of the vine and the branches (15 : 1–8), which concerns as it were the very sanctuary of the Church, its nature and mystery, that is to say, the living union of the faithful with Christ. In this sense it is a parallel to the Pauline idea of the Body of Christ. The Johannine picture, however, has a different basis and depth. If it was borrowed from the imagery of the Old Testament, and there is much in favour of this supposition[86], it is linked with the idea of God's chosen people; for in the Old Testament Israel is regarded as God's vineyard (Is 5 : 1–7; 27 : 2–6), or choice vineyard (Jer 2 : 21; Ps 80[79] : 9–16), which God himself has planted. In that case Christ himself first of all would take the place of Israel as the authentic vine on which believers in him would blossom like living vine branches, bear fruit and glorify the Father. This thought is not of course worked out because it is the need to "abide" in Christ which is to the fore. Nevertheless such an identification of Christ with the "true Israel" and such a concentration of eschatological thought on him as the representative and foundation of the life of the new people of God would certainly be possible, for in him the eschatological hour and salvation are already present (4 : 23; 5 : 25), and he has only gone on ahead of his own, where he intends to bring them themselves (cf. 14 : 2; 17 : 24, and the passages that refer to the Son of man). In the same way he could represent the new "temple", for the logion regarding the building up of the Temple in

2 : 21 is interpreted as referring to the body of the risen Christ, and the "adoration in Spirit and truth" is fulfilled (4 : 23 f.[87]) from now on (in the Church). But again the identification of Israel and vine, worshipping community and Temple (and certainly the interpretation of the Son of man in a collective sense[88]) is not at all so certain. It remains open to question whether the Johannine Christ may be regarded as a corporate personality (in the sense of the Pauline Body of Christ), who even in his historical work of salvation comprised in himself the society of believers. The Johannine Christ in fact makes a markedly exclusive claim. He, and he alone, is the divine revealer and bringer of salvation (cf. the ἐγώ εἰμι sayings); he is the Son; he demands adherence, by faith, to his person, in order then to give life to the believer and to lead those who are joined to him in that way into the heavenly world. Yet even if the "corporative" interpretation is not insisted on, the eschatological significance of the allegory of the vine remains. For what Jesus here says to his band of disciples in view of his departure is after all only realized in the Church. Only in the Church is the abiding in Christ and the promise of Christ's abiding in them possible; the disciples and the later believers could not have understood this in any other way (even as regards the supplementary exhortation "to remain in his love" and as regards brotherly love). Whether there is also a reference to the holy eucharist, as many commentators suppose, need not be inquired here. It is sufficient to recognize the Johannine Church's conception that in it the most profound communion with Christ is accomplished and that this alone permits any fruit to be borne. The Old Testament metaphor of the vine is then transferred to another, the Christian, plane; it is the new people of God which is the fruitful vine, by its union with Christ who gives it life and strength just as God's flock, led by its shepherd Christ stands in a new light: by its inner connection with him it attains true and full communion with God.

It is for that reason that the Church is so insistently called to unity. Unity is impressed on the Church as an essential characteristic, for Christ draws the Church into the existing indissoluble communion between Father and Son (cf. 10 : 14 f.; 17 : 21); consequently unity must also take effect perfectly and distinguish the Church (17 : 23), so that the world may believe in the divine mission of Jesus Christ. This idea of unity is hardly derived merely from topical reasons of polemic through the danger of heretics, but belongs to a profound Johannine grasp of the essence of the Church. God's love, which is wholly directed to the Son, also comprises all who are in communion with the Son (cf. 16 : 27) and is, therefore, also to overflow as a unifying force to all who are united with Christ (cf. 17 : 26).

This picture of the Church, however, also reveals some focal points of church life in the Johannine communities or, to put the matter in another way, shows us something of the functional context of John's exposition. They were churches in which liturgical and sacramental life was flourishing.[89] They understood their worship of God as "adoration in Spirit and truth" and themselves as true worshippers filled with the Holy Spirit; their worship was the eschatological culmination of all worship practised until then, transcending even the Jewish service of the Temple (which in the meantime had disappeared) (cf. 4 : 21–23). Their Pasch replaced and fulfilled the Pasch of the Jews (cf. 2 : 13; 6 : 4; 11 : 55), for they possessed the true paschal lamb, Christ (cf. 19 : 36; 1 : 29). They had already inwardly withdrawn themselves from the "festivals of the Jews" (cf. also 5 : 1; 7 : 2), even though they did not deny the historical origin of the redeemer of the world from Judaism (cf. 4 : 22). In the sacraments they possessed testimonies and vehicles of the continuing redemptive act of Jesus Christ (cf. 1 Jn 5 : 6 f.), and obtained living and abiding union with the Son of God and through him perfect communion with God (cf. Jn 6 : 56 f.)[90]. Whether divine service was celebrated only as celebration of

111

a meal or of baptism[91], or whether "the community at divine
service finds expression as body of the crucified and risen
Christ", as O. Cullmann seeks to infer from John 2 : 18, 22[92],
must remain doubtful; but it cannot be disputed that the
Johannine Church experienced the word of Christ (cf. Jn
6 : 63b; 8 : 31, 51; 14 : 23f.; 17 : 14, 17) and the person of
Christ (cf. 6 : 57) as present in its solemn worship (comprising
word and sacrament) and was even more consciously to
experience it through the Johannine writings.

A strong interest was also felt in the Johannine Church for
the mission. As well as what has already been quoted, two
further scenes may be indicated. The detailed account given
of the episode in Samaria (c. 4) culminates in the conversion
of the inhabitants of Sychar. These Samaritans, cut off from
Judaism and regarded as half pagans, make a full profession
of faith in the "saviour of the world" (4 : 42). The intervening
missionary discussion of Jesus with his disciples (4 : 31–38)
is noteworthy. The people of Sychar, approaching over the
fields are a harvest full of promise, and Jesus' gaze moves
prophetically into the distance to the day when he will have
sent out his disciples. They will harvest where they did not
labour; others have already laboured before them and they
have entered into their labours (v. 38). This vista which is no
longer fully intelligible to us, must have had a concrete
meaning for the evangelist, perhaps in relation to the mission
in Samaria[93]. The "Greeks" who shortly before the Passion
came to Jesus and wished to see him (2 : 20f.), are a sign
that the grain of wheat when it dies does not remain alone but
brings forth much fruit (v. 24) and that when Christ is lifted
up he will draw all things to himself (v. 32). Though the
Gospel according to John is not expressly a missionary work,
its missionary interest is nevertheless unmistakable.

Finally, the Johannine Church is engaged in a stern defensive
battle against an unbelieving hostile world, but is certain of
victory (cf. 16 : 33). It carries on the struggle not with weak

human powers but in the might of the Holy Spirit: The Paraclete will "convince the world of sin, of justice and of judgment" (16 : 8, cf. 9–11). How else is sin as such, unbelief in regard to the eschatological envoy of God, revealed than by the Church's preaching and its inflexible faith? How is "justice", the entry of Jesus into the heavenly world of his Father, made plain if not through the testimony of the Church to the resurrection? And how is it disclosed that "the prince of this world" is already judged, except by the triumphant existence of the Church in the midst of a world hostile to God? The testimony of the Holy Spirit is perceptible in the testimony of the disciples (cf. 15 : 26 f.). The same conviction that Jesus' victory is continued in the faithful and manifested before the world is expressed in 1 John 5 : 4–8 and, similarly, that this is only possible by virtue of the sacraments and of the Holy Spirit.

This should be the point from which the shortest way leads to the Church of the martyrs in the Apocalypse. This prophetic book was intended of course less to offer apocalyptic revelations about conditions and events in the future than to confer strength of faith and confidence to the contemporary Church. In the visions of the seer of Patmos the Church not only appears under various figures, but a spiritual picture of the Church emerges which eminently serves that purpose. For the oppressed believers, it must already have meant a great deal to be reminded of their dignity: Christ has made them "kings and priests" (1 : 6, cf. 5 : 10; 20 : 6; 22 : 5); those redeemed and sanctified by Christ (cf. 1 : 5 b) inherit these titles of honour of the old people of God (cf. Exod 19 : 6)[94]. The Church is the true eschatological Israel; that is shown in the great vision of the 144,000 "marked with a seal" in chapter 7. The enumeration of the twelve tribes (vv. 4–8) does not refer to the children of Israel according to the flesh, that is, to Jewish Christians, and the "great multitude which no man could number" of all nations and peoples (v. 9 f.) the

113

gentile Christians who are associated with them; it is rather a matter in the first and second sections of the same people and the new start in verse 9 (μετὰ ταῦτα εἶδον) marks a change of scene: the Church equipped for the eschatological battle with God's protecting seal, now appears in this new vision as the perfect and triumphant society. Its faithful are dressed in the white robes of conquerors, carry palms of victory in their hands and sing with loud voices rejoicing in victory the song of thanksgiving of the redeemed. In the image of the 144,000 marked with a seal it is perhaps symbolically indicated that the eschatological "Israel" is built up on the old Israel and is its true fulfilment. At all events there is only a single community of the elect and redeemed which is first represented under the figure of the eschatological Israel, then under that of the universal people of salvation composed of all nations and tongues. Only by this interpretation (according to which v. 99 ff. is a scene anticipating the perfect fulfilment)[95], can a connection be made leading to the later vision of the assembly on Mount Sion (14 : 1–5) and the Jerusalem which descends from heaven (c. 21, especially v. 12). Those who are saved "on the sea of glass" also sing "the canticle of Moses, the servant of God" which at the same time is the "canticle of the Lamb" (15 : 2 f.). The people of God of the Old Testament is fulfilled and transcended in the eschatological people of God of the New.

That a genuine continuity exists between the old Covenant and the new, and that fundamentally there is only a single people of God, also emerges from the most magnificent ecclesiological vision, that of the heavenly "woman", the great adversary of the dragon Satan (c. 12). In this, idea and reality, majesty and lowliness, unconquerable strength and earthly distress of God's Church have been focussed as they are nowhere else. The ecclesiological interpretation may be regarded as certain in view of the recent lively discussion[96]. According to it, the woman who bears on her head a "crown

of twelve stars" (12 : 1) signifies in the first place the old
people of twelve tribes which gave the world the Messias[97].
According to the intervening picture of the battle of Michael
with the dragon (vv. 7–12), however, the woman who has
to flee to the desert where she is miraculously protected,
unexpectedly assumes the features of the Christian Church;
for the rest of the woman's offspring against whom the dragon
wages war, are those "who keep the commandments of God
and have the testimony of Jesus" (v. 17). In the following
chapter where Satan's accomplices appear, the "beasts from
the sea" and that "from the land" (the anti-Christ and pseudo-
prophet), the contemporary historical background of the
persecution of Christians (under Domitian) becomes even
clearer. Consequently the woman in the vision concerns the
allegorical figure of God's Church of the old Covenant
and the new viewed as a unity, — a fact full of importance for the evaluation of the old Israel and for thought
in terms of sacred history, even if membership of the
eschatological Israel is only decided by confession of faith
in Jesus.

God's earthly community, however, also lives in mysterious
connection with the host of the redeemed and God's court
in heaven, and receives from this association strength and
confidence in victory. In 14 : 1–5 the afflicted Church (on
earth) is characterized as the followers of the Lamb. Something
of their interior glory already shines from them; for the
faithful and pure members of it hear a call from heaven
which sings a new song before the throne of God, the "four
living creatures" and the "ancients" (cf. c. 4), and only those
"who were purchased from the earth" can "learn" that hymn
of praise and victory. There is for the Church in the world
as it were an inner holy precinct ("Mount Sion"), a spiritual
protection in communion with the Lamb which makes it strong
and unconquerable. The same idea is probably expressed by
the figure of the measuring of the Temple, in which the inner

115

sanctuary with the altar remains reserved and protected while the outer court is abandoned to the gentiles who lay waste the holy city (11 : 1 f.). God provides that the Church, despite all Satanic seduction, remains incorrupt and that despite violent persecution it continues to exist. The time of Satan and his satellites is limited; the devil knows "that he has only a short time" and consequently rages with fearful but ultimately powerless anger (cf. 12 : 12). In heaven, however, the songs of victory are already ringing out (11 : 15, 17 f.; 12 : 10 ff.; 15 : 3 f.; 19 : 1 f., 6 ff.), and special jubilation prevails over those who have conquered Satan "by the blood of the Lamb and by the word of their testimony" and who "did not love their lives unto death" (12 : 11). The whole Church of Christ on earth is a Church of martyrs (cf. 7 : 14 f.; 13 : 7–10; 20 : 4), but in union with its already perfected brothers, strong and confident, for the victory of the Lamb is already decided (5 : 9 f. – 12, *passim* down to 19 : 11–16). There is only one Church in heaven and on earth which is journeying towards its victory and accomplishment at the marriage of the Lamb.

That is the last impressive metaphor: the Church as the bride of the Lamb. The more the end approaches, the more the Church prepares for this joyous festival. In heaven they sing, "Let us be glad and rejoice and give glory to him (to God); for the marriage of the Lamb has come and his wife has prepared herself. And it was granted to her to clothe herself with fine linen, glittering and white" (19 : 7 f.). But when this long-awaited event occurs (21 : 2, 9) the picture which so excellently expressed the close union of the Church with Christ and its eschatological longing is exchanged for that of the new Jerusalem. This is a significant proceeding, for it indicates that the Church has now attained its real destination and is taken up into a reality of another order: the perfected Church enters into the eschatological kingdom of God and becomes the company of the blessed in the future city of God, the new creation, the goal of the whole divine plan for the world and the economy of salvation.

If the picture of the Church given in the Apocalypse is compared with the others already described, it perhaps chiefly recalls that of the Epistle to the Hebrews. In both theological writings the earthly Church is journeying, in conflict and trial and yet in close connection with heaven and striving towards the eschatological goal. Yet the Apocalypse retains its special features in imagery and conceptual structure. In the Apocalypse, in a way quite different from that of the Epistle to the Hebrews, the Church has undergone suffering and persecution and become the Church of the martyrs; the word that is addressed to it is not simply doctrinal discourse and exhortation, but prophetic proclamation with sure anticipation of the end and insuperable certainty of victory. This prophetic character markedly distinguishes the Apocalypse from the Johannine writings in the narrower sense, although in fundamental religious attitude as well as in various particular theological ideas, threads of connection link them. But the confidence in salvation and victory, which is powerfully displayed in both, derives in the gospel and epistles of John principally from reference back to the salvation brought by Christ and which from that time onwards can never be lost; but in the Apocalypse it is also attained by gazing ahead to the irresistibly approaching end. The writings which seem so different, meet, however, in the "ecclesiological centre": the Church in this world stands firm on the foundation of Christ's saving work, inviolable in its possession of salvation; rich in its liturgical life, firmly confronting the world hostile to God and unswervingly bearing its witness. It only needs to hold fast to the gifts bestowed in order to be certain of the future victory.

PART THREE

The Essential Features of the Church

If, despite all the differentiation and development in the Church's life and despite the variety of ecclesiological views and guiding ideas, the Church in the New Testament can nevertheless be regarded as a unitary reality, the task now confronts us of attaining a deeper grasp of this one nature of the Church. For this purpose it is not a question of distinguishing marks, but only of characteristic features which permit the essential nature to be perceived more clearly. Some features of that kind have already stood out in what has been presented so far. These must now be brought together and also have more light thrown upon them. For this purpose a comparison may suitably be established with the old Jewish religious society from which the primitive Church emerged and with particular groups within that society, especially with the Qumran community, which is now known to us from original documents.

1. *The eschatological redeemed community*

In the first place the fundamentally eschatological attitude of the primitive Church is to be noted; it is conscious of being God's eschatological redeemed community, and of being this because the promised Messias has appeared in Jesus of Nazareth, because he has been raised up by God to his right hand and has sent the Holy Spirit to his Church. Down to this day that is the distinctive Christian confession of faith as compared with orthodox Judaism: in Jesus Christ the Messias has already come. But all the same cannot the primitive Church be understood as a manifestation in a modified form of the apocalyptic movement which was so powerful in the time of Jesus, inasmuch as the Church entertained and cultivated the intense eschatological expectation that its Messias Jesus Christ would soon return in glory? This question has to be raised and answered nowadays, it would seem, for two reasons. On the one hand some would like to claim that something similar happened in the Qumran community, that they too regarded their "teacher of righteousness" as a Messianic figure, but modified their eschatological attitude after his death and waited for his return and that they too believed in a present possession of the Spirit and yet still looked for the plenitude of the Spirit and perfect fulfilment in the future that still delayed to come; in other words, that they possessed an eschatological attitude of being between two ages and of living in the tension between possession of salvation and expectation of salvation. On the other hand it is asserted that the first Christians were filled with an extremely intense feeling of close expectation and that it was only the "delay in the Parousia" which, not without considerable difficulties and crises, caused the apocalyptic trend gradually to recede. It is also said that the theology of redemptive history that extended and made room for the "era of the Church", Lucan theology in particular, as well as Pauline theology which stressed in a different way present communion with Christ, together with the Johannine theology which, it is said, reduced and re-interpreted the futuristic eschatology, in conjunction with external factors such as its taking root in the Hellenistic world, placed the primitive Church in a position to overcome the internal danger

119

of a fatal shock to faith. In view of these and similar conceptions, it is important to bring out what was characteristic and distinctive in the eschatological attitude of the early Church.

As regards the Qumran community in the first place it is extremely doubtful whether they attributed a Messianic significance to their "teacher of righteousness",[1] and none of the sources so far available provides any proof that his return was awaited[2]. The conception they formed of the (Holy) Spirit will be examined below (Part Three, §2). It can be recognized positively that despite a consciousness of their purity and holiness and despite their opinion that they were living in the "last age", they nevertheless regarded the decisive turning-point towards eschatological deliverance as being still in front of them. The term "end" (kes) or "end of days" is not uniformly used in the texts[3]; that is clearly connected with the perpetually postponed expectation of the "fullness of time" (1 QpHab VII, 2 and VII, 1–14). The actual contents of statements must also be examined and once again as for Judaism generally the Messianic question is the decisive criterion. According to all the texts, the coming of the two "anointed (Messiases) from Aaron and Israel" still lies ahead (1 Qs IX, 11; 1 QSa I, 4; II, 11–14; cf. CD XIV, 19; XIX, 10 f.; XX, 1). In contrast to this the early Church had already crossed that eschatological dividing line: "But when the fulness ($\tau\grave{o}$ $\pi\lambda\acute{\eta}\rho\omega\mu\alpha$ = fulfilment) of time came, God sent his Son" (Gal 4 : 4). Jesus Christ has become the turning-point of the ages, so that the whole of time after him (even though the "end", namely the Parousia with the other cosmic events of the end of time, is still ahead) has a fundamentally different character. It is genuinely the time of salvation.

The new eschatological attitude of the early Church clearly appears particularly in the different content of its concept of the situation in regard to salvation (whatever the fluctuations of terminology), as opposed to the whole of Judaism including the Qumran community. Leaving out of account for the moment John, with whom the present possession of salvation receives every emphasis ("He who believes in the Son has eternal life"), even the early Christian theologians who are particularly attentive to the eschatological future sufficiently stress what has already happened and has been bestowed. Paul formulates the revolutionary statement: "If any one is in Christ, he is a new creation; the old has passed away; behold new has come to be" (2 Cor 5 : 17). The author of the Epistle to the Hebrews who urgently exhorts God's pilgrim people that none of them should be left behind while the promise of entering into rest is still open (cf. 4 : 1), nevertheless in another passage reminds the same recipients of his letter that they "were once illuminated, have tasted the heavenly gift and were made partakers of the Holy Spirit, have tasted the good word of God and the powers of the future aeon" (6 : 4). Behind this and precisely in the Epistle to the Hebrews[4] there also certainly stands the experience of early Christian worship, of which "gladness" was a fundamental element, as Acts 2 : 46 already testifies. The same "exultation" (ἀγαλλιᾶσθαι) is also spoken of in 1 Peter 1 : 6, 8, where "inexpressible and glorified joy" bursts forth on account of the experience of deliverance in baptism (cf. v. 3), as well as from the prospect of "the goal of (your) faith, the salvation of souls" (v. 9). Christian life is inevitably suspended between the two poles of the deliverance already attained in Christ and the deliverance still awaited but which is well-founded and awaited with certainty because of the grace already experienced. Jewish hope also held fast of course to the promises and the fidelity of God, but did not yet stand on the foundation of the salvific facts brought about by God in Christ and of the redemption now present in Christ in which every believer shares in the Christian community. That created a fundamental difference in eschatological attitude.

If this is clearly accepted a critical attitude will be adopted to the theses of "eschatologism". Has it really been proved that the early Church was dominated by an imminent expectation in the sense of one with a fixed date? As well as expressions that seem to suggest it, there are others which emphasize or presuppose the temporal indeterminacy of the end, in the gospels as well as in the other New Testament writings. It is sufficient to compare Mark 9 : 1; 13 : 30 with 13 : 32; 1 Thessalonians 4 : 15 with 5 : 1 f.; 1 Peter 4 : 7 with 2 : 11 f.; 5 : 6; Acts 1 : 3; 3 : 11; 22 : 7, 10, 20 with 6 : 10 f.; 7 : 9; 14 : 13; 20, 7–10. There is an early Christian "imminent expectation", but one which as well as from the sayings of Jesus that are to be interpreted in that sense, draws its strength from the knowledge that God has already inaugurated the eschatological time of salvation and consequently will also "soon" bring it to its fulfilment, that the fundamental events of redemption have already occurred in Christ and are now calling for their ultimate accomplishment in accordance with the promise they imply. So the characteristic early Christian imminent expectation was (unlike Jewish apocalyptic feeling) not orientated by the short space of time still to elapse but by the certainty of the ineluctably approaching end and at bottom (to the extent that human longing and curiosity did not find their way into it) was only interested in that. This kind of imminent expectation is rather "perpetual expectation" (H. Schürmann), as is shown in the exhortations moulding the eschatological attitude, which call to vigilance (Mk 13 : 34–37; 14 : 38; Lk 12 : 35 f.; Mt 25 : 13; 1 Thess 5 : 6; 1 Cor 16 : 13; Apoc 16 : 15), preparedness (Lk 12 : 40; Mt 24 : 44), sobriety (1 Thess 5 : 6, 8; 1 Pet 1 : 13; 4 : 7; 5 : 8) and steadfastness (ὑπομονή, Lk 8 : 15; 21 : 19; Rom 5 : 3 f.; 8 : 25; 1 Thess 1 : 3; Heb 10 : 36; 12 : 1; Acts 13 : 10; 14 : 12), virtues which also call for prayer and gain strength from it (Mk 14 : 38; 1 Thess 5 : 17; Eph 6 : 18). It is only such an eschatological attitude which excluded any apocalyptic calculation of the end and disregarded the question of the date of the Parousia that explains why no mention is heard of any real crisis provoked by the alleged "delay of the Parousia" (which is itself a dubious expression)[5]. It is only later and marginally that scoffers appear and are rebutted (2 Pet 3 : 2f.). Scarcely anything can be detected in the New Testament regarding a diminution of eschatological tension. Even Johannine theology does not alter the perspective on the last events and fulfilment, even though it perceives more clearly that since Jesus and in him, the eschatological "hour" of the revelation of salvation and the awakening of life is present (cf. Jn 4 : 23, 26; 5 : 25). In this eschatological time, since Christ's exaltation, the Church is at work, bearing fruit through her communion with Christ (cf. Jn 15 : 1–6), gathering together all who belong to God into itself as Christ's flock (cf. Jn 10 : 14–16; 11 : 52), conquering the world hostile to God by the powers conferred on it (Jn 16 : 33; 1 Jn 5 : 4f.). In it the light of divine truth, divine life and divine love which has come with Christ, advances in the darkness of the fallen cosmos (cf. 1 Jn 2 : 8).

2. *Filled with and guided by the Spirit*

The early Church's conviction of the eschatological outpouring of the Spirit and the operation of the Holy Spirit above it and in it is so apparent from various points of view, that this bond with God's Spirit must be regarded as another essential feature of the Church and one which is very closely connected with its eschatological character. Once again the question arises whether a similar view of a possession of the Spirit conferred on the community is not also found in Qumran. It cannot be denied that, as well as believing in an eschatological outpouring of the Spirit (*1 QS* IV, 20f.), they also believed in an endowment by the Spirit which occurs even now. The Spirit of God not only enlightens the prophets (*1 QS* VIII, 16) as in the Old Testament and among them in particular the "teacher of righteousness" (cf. *1 QpHab* VII, 4f.), in order

123

to recognize and announce God's will as well as his decrees and mysteries (cf. *1 QH* XII, 11 f.; XIII, 18 f. etc.), but he also purifies those who enter the community of the Covenant of God from all wicked deeds (*1 QS* III, 6 f.; cf. *1 QH* III, 21; XVII, 26)[6]. The Spirit of truth and holiness is given to the community as such, so that it becomes a stronghold of the holy Spirit of eternal truth, "in order to atone for guilt of sins and for guilty defection" (*1 QS* IX, 3 f.). We do not seem far from the view that the community is "a temple of the Holy Spirit" (1 Cor 3 : 16; Eph 2 : 22); the ideas of 2 Corinthians 6 : 16 or 1 Peter 2 : 5, 9 bear unmistakable resemblance to *1 QS* VIII, 5 f.

There are, however, characteristic differences. (1) In Qumran the Spirit who purifies, strengthens and enlightens is not regarded as the eschatological earnest or gift of first fruits, as was the case in the early Church, even if diverse operations of this Spirit were recognized, whether they were mainly exceptional phenomena (glossolalia, prophecy, miraculous powers), as in Acts, or saving works and moral powers as in Paul (cf. Rom 8 : 15, 23, 26 f.; 2 Cor 1 : 22; 5 : 5; Eph 1 : 13 f.). According to the Qumran conception, those who join the community are only cleansed from the stains which the divine spirit given them from birth has incurred through the seduction of the evil spirit (cf. *1 QS* III, 21 f.; IV, 23–26), and are then purified and strengthened by the Spirit of God (cf. *1 QH* VII, 6 f.; XVI, 11 f.; XVII, 26)[7]. The Christian on the other hand receives (sacramentally) the "earnest" of the Spirit in view of future glory (cf. passages quoted above), and bears "fruits" of the Holy Spirit (cf. Gal 5 : 22 f.) which by their very nature ("love, joy, peace") are already signs of the coming kingdom of God (cf. Rom 14 : 17). (2) The Spirit sent down on the primitive Church (Acts) and "dwelling" in the faithful (Rom 8 : 9–11) is the Spirit of Jesus Christ, and in actual fact the Spirit of the risen Lord who as lifegiving strength (1 Cor 15 : 45; cf. Jn 6 : 63) enters into the faithful and continues in them the work of redemption even to the raising from the dead of their mortal bodies (Rom 8 : 11). Because the Qumran community did not know of the raising from the dead of a redemptive leader (and perhaps not even the resurrection of the dead), its view of the gift of the Spirit remains far behind that of the Christians. The power of the Spirit to kindle life and the overcoming of death by the Spirit remain at the least obscure. (3) As a result in Qumran the community as "temple of the Holy Spirit" is very far from being the same as in the Christian perspective. According to the latter, the Church is filled with the eschatological Spirit of God (1 Cor 3 : 16f.), as is each individual member (1 Cor 6 : 19), and its "adoration in Spirit and truth" (Jn 4 : 23)[8], and "spiritual" sacrificial service (1 Pet 2 : 5), rests on the fact of the reception of the Spirit, understood in a very real (sacramental) way, which was only possible in this reality and plenitude through Christ's glorification (cf. Jn 7 : 39; 1 Pet 2 : 3f., 6; 3 : 18). The living Christ is its foundation and corner-stone and works in the Church through the Holy Spirit as principle of its life and its building up (cf. Eph 2 : 20–22). (4) The Qumran community has nothing comparable to set beside the guidance of the Holy Spirit as the early Church experienced it in its own regard. Through the Holy Spirit sent "from above", the Lord directs his earthly community, sends it preachers and pastors, effects its building up and growth, gives it freedom and unity, strength in persecution and strength for victory, in short, leads it through the ages into the perfect kingdom of God (cf. Acts 9 : 31; 20 : 28; Eph 4 : 11–16).

Despite all similarities, therefore, profound differences can be perceived and in the concept of the Spirit the dividing line between Qumran and the early Church is clearly apparent. The Church of Jesus Christ knows by reason of the resurrection of its Lord and the sending of the Spirit that it is in possession of the eschatological Spirit sent by the exalted Christ. This Spirit fills and guides all its members in a varying manner

125

which never excludes human co-operation, but nevertheless in such a way that the Church is his work and instrument, the sign and testimony to the Spirit of God bestowed on it[9].

3. *Hierarchical in structure*

The fundamental structure of the Church was seen above (Part One, §4) to be an order given by God, and based on the principle of mission. Here, too, a comparison with Judaism assists greater clarity. The hierarchical direction of the primitive Church can·in no case be mistaken for the Jewish hierarchy. In the latter after the end of the Monarchy, the high priest occupied the summit as representing God's authority and under him the chief priests held the leading offices in the Temple[10]; he was also president of the Sanhedrin which represented the assembly of the people as highest council and court of justice and in which once again the Scribes occupied a prominent position as professional interpreters of the Torah. In contrast to this what is new in the Christian community is the absolute authority of Christ. For the primitive Church it is basic that Jesus as God's eschatological envoy authoritatively proclaims the will of God and that with his exaltation to the right hand of God all power was conferred on him (Mt 28 : 18). Every exercise of office or service in the Church only takes place in virtue of the power (Mt 16 : 19; 18 : 18; Jn 21 : 15, 17) given to those he sent (Jn 20 : 21). For this there is no privilege of birth (as with the high priest), or of intellectual formation (as with the Scribes), but vocation, mission and endowment with grace from on high are alone decisive. Christ "gives" his Church the various men who are entrusted with services, who work together in building up "his body" (Eph 4 : 11 f.). In contradistinction to the Jewish hierarchy, no one of himself has any claim to an office and no suitability based on human qualities is decisive, but all qualification comes from God

(2 Cor 3 : 5 f.). In the early Church this qualification is often actually produced by the Holy Spirit (extraordinary charismata) and sometimes made known by prophecy (cf. Acts 13 : 2; 1 Tim 1 : 18; 4 : 14); but even with the imposition of hands (cf. 1 Tim 4 : 14; 2 Tim 1 : 6) it is always conferred by the Holy Spirit (charismatic grace of office). "This observation is very important in comparison with Jewish ordination in which the teacher handed on to the pupil the wisdom received from Moses. In the primitive Christian ordination, the man ordaining cannot transmit to the ordained a quality as if he himself possessed it, but God alone confers the χάρισμα." [11]

The Qumran community does not diverge from the rest of Judaism in its fundamental conception of order; only rule does not lie in the hands of the official priesthood officiating in the Temple of Jerusalem, whom the Essene dissidents rejected as unfaithful to the Law, but in the hands of their own priests who alone were regarded as sons of Zadok and conscientious observers of all the prescriptions of the Torah. "As for the liberal Sadducees, so also for the priests of Qumran, their genealogy had to be drawn from Zadok the priest." [12] So here, too, there was a nobility of birth, a prerogative of leadership based on ancestry. Priestly direction of the community is apparent in some particular precepts (cf. 1 QS VI, 3–5; VIII, I; IX, 7), which are not important for our purpose. For comparison with the original Christian community, however, there is something significant which is not found in the same way in official Judaism: the strict order of rank regulated down to the smallest detail; "The priests enter into order first, following one another in the rank corresponding to their spirits; after them the Levites are to come in and thirdly the whole people is to come in to order, one after the other in groups of a thousand, a hundred, fifty and ten, so that every Israelite may know his place within the community of God..." (1 QS II, 19–22). This gradation of rank and strict assignment of places, which also applies to the other assemblies, reveals a mode of thought that is completely alien to the Christian community. Here the law of service forbade any presumption; Paul is concerned in 1 Corinthians 12 precisely to overcome any attributing of different values to the various charismata, and in the next chapter he praises the sublime path of love (cf. as opposed to this the strict code of punishments in Qumran). Consequently if much in the external constitution of the original church of Jerusalem may suggest Qumran[13], the underlying conception is fundamentally different. Even the disciplinary case of Ananias and Saphira (Acts 5 : 1 to 11) must not be judged externally by the severe punishment: the hypocritical couple deceived by Satan have lied to the Holy Spirit and Peter is only announcing God's judgment. So even in ecclesiastical discipline,[14] which in any case seems to be restricted to exceptional instances, the law of guidance by the Holy Spirit holds good (cf. also 1 Cor 5), and the apostles only act as God's delegates. If later a hierarchy of offices developed, that does not represent a relapse into Jewish modes of thought or abandonment of the fundamental New Testament idea of church order, as long as rule by the heavenly Lord, the origin of authority in God, and the obligation to service of the Church were not forgotten. The gospels testify in their fashion, for example through the putting together of the "rules for the Church" in Matthew 18 or the recognizable intention of applying some words and parables of Jesus (such as Lk 12 : 42–48; 22 : 24–27) specially to the overseers, that the primitive Church was mindful of the new order given it by the Lord himself and of the responsibility springing from it.

4. *United and pursuing unity*

The concord and fraternal spirit of the first Christians is strongly emphasized by the author of Acts, and the voluntary community of goods is certainly idealized in the "summaries"

(2 : 44 f.; 4 : 32, 34 f.; 5 : 12; cf. above, Part One, § 3). Yet there must in fact have been considerable willingness to support one another, as the examples of Barnabas (4 : 36 f.) and the daily provision for widows (6 : 1 f.) show. All the epistles testify to the profound response evoked by Jesus' call for love[15]. The great collection which Paul organized as he had promised (Gal 2 : 10) in his churches for the "poor" or "saints" in Jerusalem (cf. 1 Cor 16 : 1–4; 2 Cor 8–9; Rom 15 : 25–27) was a work of mercy to provide relief; in addition, however, it became a recognition of Jerusalem as the point of origin of the message of salvation and the chief centre of the Christian churches (cf. Rom 15 : 27). The collection meant for the Pauline churches "a grace to take part in the service done on behalf of the saints" (2 Cor 8 : 4) and causes the "saints" in Jerusalem to praise God "for the obedience of your profession of the gospel of Christ and for the sincere giving to them and to all" (2 Cor 9 : 13). But it was a significant gesture of Paul to take that great collection to the Christians in Jerusalem himself, although danger threatened (cf. Rom. 15 : 25, 28; Acts 21 : 4, 10–13, 15 ff.). He wished to demonstrate the unity between his gentile Christian churches and the Jewish mother church. In this way, brotherly fellowship becomes a more profoundly comprehended unity, that of all the "churches of Christ" (Rom 16 : 16).

Now such fellowship was also cultivated among the Essenes (cf. Fl. Josephus, *Bellum Iud.* II, 122), and in Qumran, despite the strict differences of rank there (cf. "brethren" *1 QS* VI, 10, 22; *1 QM* XIII, 1; XV, 4, 7; fellowship *1 QS* V, 25 f.; VI, 2 f.; VIII, 2). The question arises, in what did the deeper ties and ultimate ground of unity among believers in Christ consist? The answer appears in the motives put forward in exhortation (cf. 1 Cor 1 : 10–13; 3 : 4 f.; 12 : 4–6, 12 f.; Rom 12 : 4 f.; 15 : 5 f.; Phil 2 : 1; Eph 4 : 1–6; Col 3 : 14 f.): it is the one God who has called all, the one Lord Jesus Christ to whom all belong, the one Spirit who fills all and unites them

129

in the one Body of Christ, the one baptism in which all become "one in Christ Jesus" (Gal 3 : 27 f.; cf. 1 Cor 12 : 13), the one bread of the eucharist in which all share (1 Cor 10 : 17). These motives show the unmistakable Christian element in the idea of unity, even though it is only with the advance of theology that it crystallizes more fully and becomes more profound. Ultimately what binds the Christians together is the common confession of their Lord and Messias, expressed in the formula which was already known from the Old Testament (and its Greek Septuagint translation)[16], but which was now transferred to Jesus Christ: "those who call on the name of the Lord" or its equivalents (1 Cor 1 : 2; Rom 10 : 13; Acts 9 : 14, 21; 22 : 16). The sign and seal of this, however, is baptism "in the name of the Lord Jesus" at which this "good name" was also invoked upon the baptized person (cf. James 2 : 7).

Although the tensions between the "Hebrews" and "Hellenists" (Acts 6 : 1–6) and the various different views regarding the Law which Matthew's gospel may indicate[17] are not to be minimized, it is nevertheless far too bold to claim to detect "a conflict in the oldest Christian community which cannot be described as anything else but a denominational one"[18]. It would be a mistake to think of the primitive Church merely as an ecumenical alliance of various "denominational churches". It was not only profession of faith in Jesus Christ in the form in which the apostolic proclamation presented it and as it found expression in early formularies of belief[19] that linked the communities and ecclesiastical regions but also the common worship and association in the eucharist which as far as we know was never attacked or abolished. The Antioch incident (Gal 2 : 11–14) in which the withdrawal of the Jewish Christians must have in fact led to something of that kind, was obviously settled quickly and involved no lasting split. There was only a real division in regard to false teachers who did not accept the common faith in Christ (cf. 1 Jn 2 : 19); they certainly, according to 2 John 10 f., were to be refused entrance to the house and denied a greeting.

The inner bond between the physically scattered faithful and churches probably finds its finest expression in the salutation of the First Epistle to the Corinthians, where Paul presents his greetings "to the Church of God that is in Corinth, to them that are sanctified in Christ Jesus, called to be saints, together with all who invoke the name of our Lord Jesus Christ in every place, theirs and ours" (1 Cor 1 : 2)[20]. It is precisely before the eyes of the Corinthian community which was divided into various rival groups (cf. 1 Cor 1 : 10–13 etc.), that the apostle places the greater unity of all "who call on the name of our Lord Jesus Christ" and reminds them of the obligation to the unity of those "sanctified in Christ Jesus". "It is notable in the apostle that he does not regard the dissensions in Corinth merely as problems of a single congregation, but rather considers the fate of the whole of Christendom to be at stake in this Greek port."[21] On this basis it can be said therefore that the idea of unity and also all later theology concerning the one Church, the Pauline notion of the Body of Christ, the Johannine teaching about the union of the faithful with Christ and between one another according to the union between the Father and the Son (Jn 17 : 21, 23), the conviction of the Epistle to the Hebrews regarding the union of the earthly people of God with the festive gathering in the heavenly Jerusalem (Heb 12 : 22 f.), and similarly that of the Apocalypse regarding the bond of the Church of the martyrs on earth with the triumphant band of Jesus' witnesses in heaven (cf. Acts 6 : 9–11; 7 : 1–8, 9–17; 19 : 6–9; 20 : 1–6), all ultimately rest on this fundamental conviction regarding the Church of God of the new Covenant formed into one by confession of faith in Jesus Christ and by the Spirit sent by him.

This unity in Jesus Christ is enjoined on the Church and has to be manifested more and more strongly and realized in practice in perpetual endeavour and the overcoming of human

131

weaknesses and differences. Jesus intended and founded only one Church, his own (Mt 16 : 18), and the heavenly Christ possesses only one body, his *ecclesia*. Its unity must therefore become visible in every respect: in doctrine, profession of faith, worship, and rule. This unity may still have been to some extent concealed in apostolic times by the varied theological development, the freedom in shaping the liturgy, the still fluid organization and the unsettled missionary conditions. A deeper scrutiny is called for to discern the essence of the Church behind the sometimes confusing appearances on which, from the sources available, judgment cannot always be passed with certainty. The Epistle to the Ephesians is an example where the unity formed of Jews and gentiles is termed the "mystery of Christ" which is revealed in the apostolic teaching (Eph 3 : 4 ff.). Consequently, unity in faith and love is always at one and the same time a task and a goal which can only be approached on earth, more by the grace of God than by human endeavour (cf. Eph 4 : 3, 13, 15 f.; Col 3 : 14).[22]

5. *Made holy and pursuing holiness*

In their striving after holiness the Essenes of Qumran and the Christian believers appear at least outwardly very close. The very expression used by both to designate themselves, "the saints", draws attention to this[23]. Moral rigour, a radical attitude in fulfilling the word of God, is to be found in Qumran as in early Christianity. For Christ's disciples the Sermon on the Mount (Mt 5–7; Lk 6 : 20–49) became the obligatory rule of their moral conduct; there is no doubt of the "intensification of the Torah" in Qumran: all the precepts are to be kept and that in accordance with the strict interpretation of the Qumran teachers of the Law[24]. A meticulous code of punishments (*1 QS* VI, 24–VII, 25) maintained discipline among the "men of holiness". In the Damascus Rule a whole section is devoted to legal casuistry (CD IX–XII), in which the strict Sabbath precepts, going even further than the Pharisee exegesis (X, 14 – XI, 18), and commands regulating ritual purity (XI, 19 – XII, 18) are particularly striking. But precisely the casuistical narrowness and rigorous discipline exhibit the profound difference between Essene and early Christian holiness. Jesus separated himself from the whole of Judaism of that time by his alarming attitude to the Law[25]. Characteristic of him was his liberty in relation to precepts concerning the Sabbath and ritual purity, his going back to "purity of heart" (Mk 7 : 18–23 parallel in Mt), and also his intensifying and making more radical the moral commandments (cf. the antitheses of the Sermon on the Mount), the summing up of all commandments in the great commandment of the love of God and the neighbour, and finally the requirement of the love of enemies, after the model of the heavenly Father ("perfection" according to Mt 5 : 48, an idea that is completely contrary to Qumran thought)[26]. Consequently his radical attitude has different aspects and reasons from the radicalism of Qumran.[27] It derives from his eschatological message which in the first place announces salvation, the limitless mercy of God, precisely to sinners, prostitutes and those who were despised as "unclean", but which also demands the answer of a loving heart, undivided devotion to God, untiring search for the kingdom of God and love of fellow-men carried to the utmost. Even if individual human beings and groups in the early Church formed an inadequate or false conception of this revolutionary message (and Matthew is not a leading witness for a "re-Judaizing" mode of thought),[28] on the whole those who confessed Jesus Christ regarded the moral instruction of their Lord as well as his religious teaching as something new, special and inseparable from the belief in Christ and in so doing clearly marked the dividing line separating them from Judaism. Early Christian ethics in content and motive had an eschatological orientation and was bound up with

Jesus' words, his example and the requirements of imitating him[29].

The difference between early Christian holiness and that of Qumran has even deeper roots, however, than the nature of their moral endeavour. It is only when attention is given to the process of sanctification which occurs in man, with its origin in God, that it is possible to recognize how intrinsically alien that Jewish sect was from the Church of Jesus Christ and at the same time what characterized and distinguished the latter. All remission of sins and sanctification in the early Church not only derive from God, but also take place through Jesus Christ and in union with him. The Qumran texts of course have taught us the surprising fact that a strict religious devotion to the Law need not exclude the idea of a "gratuitous justification"; in the *hodayot,* those psalms of praise and thanksgiving in which the speaker manifests his absolute dependence on God, his human nothingness and sinfulness, in an often moving way, the thought often recurs that God must make man righteous (cf. *1 QH* IV, 30 f.; VI, 8 f.; XI, 10 f., 30 f.; XIII, 16 f.; XVI, 11 f.; XVII, 20 f.); similarly in the final psalm of the Community Rule (*1 QS* XI, 2–5; 10–14)[30]. In the early Church, however, a concrete way of justification on the ground of God's mercy is taught: men must believe in Jesus Christ and be baptized in his name (summarized in the shortest formula in the canonical concluding chapter of Mark, 16 : 16). So all sanctification occurs "in Christ Jesus" (1 Cor 1 : 2) in the bath of baptism by the intermediary of the Holy Spirit (1 Cor 6 : 11). The whole Church is only without blemish and splendid because Christ "loved it and delivered himself up for it in order to sanctify it, cleansing it in the bath of water by the word" (Eph 5 : 25 f.). The ritual immersion baths and purifications in Qumran, to which no one has ascribed any sacramental efficacy[31], did not possess that significance as a means of salvation which belonged to the primary Christian sacrament through which the believer receives a share in the redemption established in the blood of Jesus (cf. Rom 5 : 9; Eph 1 : 7; Heb 9 : 11–14; 10 : 19 f.; 12 : 12; 1 Pet 1 : 2, 18 f.; 1 Jn 1 : 7; Apoc 1 : 5). Far less could the ritual common meals of the Essenes convey God's vital powers as is the case in the Christian celebration of the eucharist through partaking in Christ's blood and body (1 Cor 10 : 16), through receiving the flesh and blood of the glorified Son of man (Jn 6 : 53–58, cf. 62; above, Part One, § 6). The fundamental difference once again consists in the fact that the Essenes of Qumran did not know of an historical redemption through the vicarious atoning death of the Messias,[32] and their means of sanctification do not draw their power and efficacy from it. So they remain liturgical rites, anchored, by their very meaning, in the Law, ultimately only legal exercises intended with their other heroic endeavours to make atonement for themselves and the land (cf. *1 QS* VIII, 6, 10; IX, 4; *1 QSa* I, 3; *1 QM* II, 5). Believers in Christ on the other hand know they are saved solely by God's grace in the blood of Jesus Christ (Rom 3 : 24 f.; 2 Cor 5 : 18 f.; Eph 2 : 5; Tit 2 : 14; 3 : 7) and sanctified by the Holy Spirit in order then to lead a holy life, thankfully and obediently (cf. 1 Thess 4 : 3–8; Rom 6 : 12 f., 19). This kind of holiness bestowed by God and imposing obligations is an authentic feature of the Church of Jesus Christ.

6. *Universal and missionary*

Even in its greatest missionary period (which was the age in which Jesus appeared)[33], Judaism could not overcome a certain particularism and narrowness; even less in Palestine than in the diaspora. This is shown by the question to whom participation in the future aeon, that is, the attainment of salvation, was to be conceded. It is true that the answers given varied according to the various trends and groups and also according

135

to the personal standpoint of the teacher[34], yet Jesus' breadth of judgment and attitude was nevertheless unique and is an integral part of the ineffaceable picture of the historical Jesus. It is only necessary to recall his attitude to publicans and sinners, to the "multitude that is ignorant of the Law" which the Pharisees despised and condemned (cf. Jn 7 : 49) and also his attitude to the gentiles to whom he opened in principle the door to the kingdom of God (cf. above, Part One, § 7). In his proclamation of salvation, Jesus did not know of or recognize any limit imposed by nationality (cf. Mt 8 : 11 f.; 25 : 31–46), origin or intellectual formation. He turned to all and asked the same of all: conversion and faith, moral purity and love. In late Judaism the question really at issue was, "Where is the true Israel?" Different answers were given by the different groups, quite often with a stubbornness which excluded the others (Qumran!)[35]. In Jewish Hellenism the attitude, for missionary reasons, was more open-hearted and made the concept of the people of God less rigid and less tied to the nation. "The Jewish community was a missionary one and many proselytes became members of the people of God." Real equality of rights was, however, only to be had by such incorporation in Israel. "A certain 'universalism' was certainly present, but the centre of the universe was occupied by the people of Israel."[36] Jesus' message on the contrary possessed from the start the tendency to a genuinely universal spirit which opened the door of salvation to all equally.

Jesus' fundamentally universal attitude must be distinguished from the question how in God's salvific plan the gentiles were actually to attain a share in salvation. For Jesus' whole earthly activity it remains true that he knew that he was only sent to the "lost sheep of the house of Israel" (cf. Mt 10 : 6; 15 : 24). After Easter the apostles, too, at first only turned to Israel (cf. Acts 2 : 36; 3 : 17–26), and the transition to the gentile mission caused quite considerable difficulties to the original Jewish Christian community (cf. Acts 10–11). It has been indicated that this did not reveal any fundamentally different concept of the significance of the Church for salvation or of its work (cf. above, Part Two, §1). It is in any case a fact that the whole primitive Church then recognized the mission to the gentiles as willed by God and based on the command of the risen Lord (Mt 28 : 18 ff.), promoted it zealously, or at least (in Jewish Christian circles, cf. Matthew's gospel), acknowledged it and so fused the missionary tendency into its essence. The universalism which had its ground in Jesus' mission manifested itself as it were gradually. At first it showed itself and was realized in the Jewish domain itself; the community of the Messias Jesus addressed itself without distinction to the whole people of Israel and recruited adherents from all circles of that nation, and then disclosed itself to the world, too, by bursting the bounds of the old chosen people in an intrinsically inevitable and God-guided process. This universal spririt must now be further examined in comparison with the Judaism of that time and in the theological reflection which was soon undertaken in the Church itself.

The community of Qumran made great demands on its novices. Making no attempt at recruitment or mission they required that everyone who voluntarily sought admission to their ranks should spend a period of probation (postulancy) before he was accepted and even then he had to submit to a two year novitiate (in two stages of a year each) until he entered into full fellowship "in the Torah, in judgment, in purity, and in property" (*1 QS* VI, 22 f.) cf. also *1 QS* VI, 13–23). In contrast to this, acceptance into the Christian Church took place without further ado, precisely in the earliest days, provided a person professed belief in Jesus the Messias and Lord and was willing to be baptized (cf. Acts 2 : 38, 41, 47 etc.); there was no other impediment (cf. Acts 8 : 36). Priests (Acts 6 : 7), Pharisees (Acts 15 : 5), "Hebrews" and "Hellenists" (Acts 6 : 1), natives and foreigners (Acts 8 : 26–40) finally Samaritans (Acts 8 : 4–8) and gentiles (Acts 10; 11 : 19–24), were received in the same manner. The question whether special "burdens" (circumcision and the Jewish Law) were to be imposed on the gentiles streaming into the Church received in principle a reply in the negative at the "Council of Jerusalem" (Acts 15).

The congregations which came into existence in this way were often of motley composition. The Pauline missionary churches, especially, not only comprised former Jews but also brought together on equal terms men and women of the most varied social origins, in particular masters and slaves, which was not a simple matter in the social structure of those times as can be seen from the pastoral difficulties of the apostle. But the great missionary and theologian also based this openness of the Church to all who wished to be saved and this bringing together of natural contraries in the one community of belief and love on ideas which he derived from the concept of the Church's nature. He himself wished "to become all things to all men" and he made little account of external manner of life, whether according to Jewish Law or without it, adapting himself to the mentality of as many as possible (1 Cor 9 : 19–22). He took the idea seriously that in Christ a new man comes to be, with whom neither circumcision nor uncircumcision is of any importance (Gal 6 : 15) and there is no longer any question of social position. He even advises every believer to remain in the condition in which he was called to be a Christian, whether as free man or as slave; "for the slave who is called in the Lord is a freedman of the Lord, similarly the free man who was called is Christ's slave" (1 Cor 7 : 17–22)[37]. External differences lose their importance and the Christian Church combines all into a unity on a higher level: "For you are all by faith sons of God in Christ Jesus. For all you who have been baptized into Christ have put on Christ, so there is neither Jew nor Greek, neither slave nor free, neither male nor female; for you are all one in Christ Jesus" (Gal 3 : 26–28; cf. 1 Cor 12 : 13; Col 3 : 11).

The universality of the Church was not therefore promoted merely on missionary or opportunist grounds but was profoundly rooted in its essential idea. The Church speaks to all because it must incorporate in itself all who are called by God and cannot turn away anyone whom God leads to it, as the Johannine Christ also says of himself (Jn 6 : 37 ff.; 10 : 14 f.). Such an intention is there in the primitive Church from the very beginning (cf. Acts 2 : 39), even if in fact the mission to the gentiles was only undertaken with some hesitation. In order to reach all whom God summons, the Church must also turn to those who are "far off" (cf. Acts 2 : 39; 22 : 21; Eph 2 : 13, 17), must gather together the children of God scattered throughout the world (cf. Jn 11 : 52), and so its universality imperatively demands the mission. The Church does not become universal (or "Catholic") because it engages in missionary activity but engages in missionary activity because by nature the Church is universal.

The intrinsic missionary obligation marks another considerable difference from similar Jewish activities. The latter sprang from personal initiative not from official duty[38]. In the gentile Christian metropolis Antioch, on the other hand, the Holy Spirit himself imposed the task (by the voice of prophecy): "Separate me Barnabas and Saul for the work for which I have taken them" (Acts 13 : 2 f.). The mission is an official function of the Church (cf. also Gal 2 : 7); if the redeemed community of Jesus Christ wills to remain faithful to its task in the world it must keep on sending messengers of faith to those who are "far off". Their dispatch takes place in the perspective of Christ's mission which it continues and is carried on by his command (cf. Mt 28 : 19 f.; Jn 17 : 18; 20 : 21). As an extension of Christ's mission the ecclesiastical mission becomes an instrument of God himself, who by it fulfils his salvific will and saving work for mankind. As a permanent task of the Church, the mission is also a continuous action beginning with the dispatch of the envoys by the risen Lord

139

in virtue of the authority given him, right down to the full harvest on the last day.

In a missionary discourse in the Gospel of John, Jesus says to his disciples: "I have sent you out to harvest what you have not toiled for; others have toiled and you have entered into their toil" (4 : 38). Each missionary builds on the work of earlier envoys (cf. also 1 Cor 3 : 10), but all build on the work of Christ. Jesus himself began the eschatological missionary harvest (Jn 4 : 35 f.). That signifies, however, that the whole mission stands in an eschatological light. The image itself (probably also in Matthew 9 : 37 f. = Luke 10 : 2) suggests the interpretation: in the mission God's final success, that even gentiles are converted to him, is in a certain way anticipated; temporarily and in a way full of promise the blessing which derives from Jesus' atoning death "for many" becomes visible and the new Covenant becomes reality. For the success of the mission is the fruit of Jesus' death (cf. Jn 12 : 24) and the "works" of the disciples of Christ who are sent ("the greater works" which Jesus promises at John 14 : 12) are only possible through the powerful saving rule of the exalted Christ (cf. Jn 12 : 32)[36]. And so the mission itself is an eschatological event in the same sense as the authentic life of the Church is eschatological (cf. above. Part Three, §1). That shows that the universal mission belongs to the pilgrim Church journeying through the ages towards its perfect accomplishment just as in general all the essential features of the Church that have been mentioned combine to form a single picture.

PART FOUR

The Mystery of the Church

There are certainly various ways of approaching the mystery of the Church, the centre of its nature and life. Here the attempt will be made in the first place to suggest as it were the Church's inner dimensions, which exceed any earthly measure and are ultimately unfathomable. Then positive inquiry will be made into the theological statements that essentially concern the Church, trusting for this to the chief biblical concepts. Those that suggest themselves are, people of God, building in the Holy Spirit and Body of Christ. In the choice of these we are also guided by recognition of the fact expressed by N. A. Dahl at the end of his book on *Das Volk Gottes:* "The idea of the Church therefore has roots in the Old Testament, grew up on Jewish soil and in the Hellenistic atmosphere, yet is non-Jewish and non-Hellenistic, a new formation, Christian and solely Christian" (page 275). The idea of the people of God or God's Church or community, goes back to the beginnings of biblical revelation and sacred history and receives in the new Covenant a new interpretation but preserves the continuity of the divine thoughts developed and more precisely determined in the course of redemptive history. The activity and efficacy of the Holy Spirit in the eschatological redeemed community marks the new, progressive, transforming element that emerges in the new Covenant. What is really Christian, characteristic and distinctive, in the Church, however, is determined by the relation of the eschatological people of God to Christ and the wealth of relations between Christ and his Church finds strongest expression in the Pauline concept of the Body of Christ. Finally, the special position and function which belong to the Church in the course of its historical existence and its period in sacred history must then be dealt with in two sections, on Church and world, and Church and kingdom of God. The non-worldly existence of the Church in the midst of this world and at the same time its claim on and orientation towards the whole cosmos must be made clear, as well as its function in relation to the kingdom of God, in which it attains its goal but also the end of its "ecclesiastical" existence and in which it is perfectly accomplished and raised to merge into the higher unity to which it aspires.

1. *Unfathomable aspects*

The Church may be regarded as a unity in tension combining what is human and divine, earthly and heavenly, temporal and eternal; all these categories unite in the Church and link the various contrasted elements in its life to produce its characteristic appearance and efficacy.

A. A divine but human institution

Human and divine elements interpenetrate in every respect in the Church of God of the New Testament. It is presided over by men yet they act with divine mandate and divine authority. God's word is proclaimed in human language (1 Thess 2 : 13), not with the persuasive skill of human wisdom, yet powerfully, through the Spirit of God (cf. 1 Cor 2 : 4, 13). The heavenly Lord is encountered and closest union with him is realized within the framework of a simple meal; the spiritual gifts which convey the divine life have the form of bread and wine. Fleeting human words become bearers of the divine power of forgiveness (Jn 20 : 23). The voice of the prophet brings edification, exhortation and consolation, reveals what is hidden in men's hearts and announces the future, because God's Spirit is in him.

But the mystery of how what is divine is linked to what is human in the Church goes even deeper. The human life of the preachers is a poor and terrifying one (cf. 1 Cor 4 : 9–13; 2 Cor 4 : 7–12), and what they have to announce is folly and a scandal (1 Cor 1 : 21–23). Similarly those called are for the most part anything but high-born (1 Cor 1 : 26–31). But the paradox that God condescends to the weakness and inadequacy of men is willed by him and continues what happened on the cross in another way during the era of the Church: "It pleased God through the folly of the proclamation to save those who believe" (1 Cor 1 : 21); the preachers who cause "the light of the gospel of the glory of Christ" to shine forth, "have this treasure in earthen vessels so that the excellence may be of the power of God and not of us" (2 Cor 4 : 7). The human yet divine form of the Church is part of the mystery of the cross. Johannine theology which looks back more insistently to the incarnation of the Logos sees this mystery of the "veiled glory" still continuing in the Church, however much it emphasizes the Church's powerful testimony (which is linked with the testimony of the Holy Spirit; cf. Jn 15 : 26 f.; 16 : 8–11; 1 Jn 4 : 5; 5 : 4); for the separation between Church and world is great, the disciples continue to suffer affliction and persecution in the world (Jn 15 : 18 ff.; 16 : 33) and the world listens to others rather than to them (cf. 1 Jn 4 : 5). The sight of God's power in human weakness comes fully to the fore in the Apocalypse. On earth the Church is oppressed and persecuted, a Church of the martyrs which is only strong and triumphant in the blood of the Lamb and in testimony to him (cf. Apoc 7 : 14; 12 : 11).

It also belongs to this mystery that among the "saints" there are still failing and sinful men. Throughout the New Testament the Church is conscious of this. The parable of the cockle in the wheat is clearly applied by Matthew to their own ranks (Mt 13 : 37–43), and similarly the saying about the evil prophets, casters out of devils and miracle workers in the name of Jesus (Mt 7 : 22 f.); the parable of the shepherd who goes to seek the lost sheep is applied to the Church's leaders (Mt 18 : 12 f.), the admonition is addressed to catechists not to make themselves out to be masters (Mt 23 : 8–12). But Paul's epistles also indicate that he still had to fight against pagan vices among the baptized and a deficiency of Christian consciousness in the churches (1 Thess 4 : 3–7; 1 Cor 5; 6 : 1–11, 12–20 etc.), and that even the wonderful gifts of the Spirit, especially glossolalia, were misused out of vanity and egotism. The Epistle to the Hebrews aims at overcoming the weariness of good people, the state of weakness of those at rest after earlier testing in the battle of suffering (10 : 32–36; 12 : 12 f.) and has to warn them lest among them "any bitter root springing up should be troublesome and by it many be defiled" (12 : 15). Tepidity and abuses in the churches of Asia Minor are relentlessly laid bare in the seven circular letters of the Apocalypse (cc. 2–3) and censured by the heavenly Lord through the mouth of the prophet and seer. Yet the Church remains delivered from the power of darkness (Col 1 : 13), God's holy people which proclaims the powerful works of him who has called them from darkness into his wonderful light (cf 1 Pet 2 : 9).

B. A supra-mundane yet earthly reality

If the Church is examined as it were spatially, its mystery chiefly consists in the fact that it is a totality transcending particular localities yet presents itself in each local church as "the Church of God". Otherwise Paul's mode of expression in 1 Corinthians 1 : 2; 2 Corinthians 1 : 1, "the Church of God which is in Corinth" will not be intelligible; the individual church is "the eschatological people of God inasmuch as it is present in a place"[1]. The same idea is implied when the presbyters assembled in Miletus are admonished to care for themselves and the whole flock in which the Holy Spirit has placed them as overseers to pasture the Church of God (Acts 20 : 28); or when other presbyters in 1 Peter 5 : 2 are to pasture God's flock which is among them. Christ is here called the chief shepherd (1 Pet 5 : 4), which recalls the command of the risen Lord to Simon Peter: "Feed my lambs ... Feed my sheep" (Jn 21 : 15–17). The Church is the flock of the heavenly, exalted Messias which is led by human pastors in his name, whether these are the apostles with a mandate extending to the whole Church or local church leaders who in a limited way share in this pastoral function (cf. also Eph 4 : 11). Rule by Christ as chief shepherd guarantees the unity and uniformity of God's or Christ's whole flock which is manifested in the individual churches. Consequently the individual church or congregation is not merely a unit cell in the structure of the Church as a whole, but also represents, and is the concrete form of life of, the great "Church of God". The New Testament of course has only one word for both (ἡ ἐκκλησία), so that our division into "church" and "Church" does not fit if pressed too strictly. In 1 Corinthians 12, Paul first addresses the church of Corinth with the metaphor of the Body of Christ, but with the greater society of all the baptized in Christ in mind (v. 13), and finally widens the perspective to include the whole Church, in which God has placed apostles, prophets, teachers and other bearers of charismata (v. 28)[2].

The close connection of the earthly Church with its heavenly Lord leads, however, to a further mystery. The Church cannot be regarded merely as an earthly reality but extends into the heavenly world. This supra-mundane dimension of the Church is indicated in particular in the epistles to the Ephesians and

145

the Colossians. It is true that the Body of Christ is found on earth but it appears extended to cosmic dimensions (cf. Eph 1 : 10 with 23; Col 1 : 17 with 18; 2 : 19), and through its head Christ, it also has a heavenly presence. The more developed baptismal doctrine supports this idea: God has "vivified us together in Christ, raised us up together and placed us together in heaven in Christ Jesus" (Eph 2 : 5 f.). He has "delivered us from the power of darkness and transferred us into the kingdom of his beloved Son" (Col 1 : 13). The development of this Pauline theology of the Church is to be examined presently (cf. below, Part Four, § 4); here it is sufficient to observe that the idea that the Church belongs to the heavenly sphere is not found only in the two epistles quoted. The same idea is found in Philippians 3 : 20: "the city of which we are citizens is in heaven", so that "here on earth we are a colony of citizens of heaven" (M. Dibelius on the passage). We are only "strangers and pilgrims" on earth (1 Pet 2 : 11; Heb 11 : 13; cf. also 2 Cor 5 : 6). All this follows from our union with Christ who has already entered the heavenly domain. Those who have fitted like living stones into the Church have "approached" Christ, the living corner-stone chosen by God (cf. 1 Pet 2 : 4 ff.), and have also approached "Mount Sion, the city of the living God, the heavenly Jerusalem, and thousands of angels, the festive gathering and assembly of the first-born who are written in heaven" (Heb 12 : 22 f.). In the Apocalypse the Church of the martyrs on earth is intrinsically united with "brethren" who have gone on before to the Lord (cf. 6 : 11; 14 : 13); the Lamb will one day lead home his "bride" the Church, but no distinction is yet drawn between earthly and heavenly Church (19 : 7 f.; 21 : 2). The communion of saints inevitably strengthened even more the bridge between earth and heaven, and the period of persecution also gave wings to the aspiration "on high". What the Church was already aware of through Christ's ascension (cf. Eph 4 : 8 ff.), namely that it is a community whose home is in heaven, and which of its very nature belongs more to heaven that it does to earth, was even more intensely realized in the days of the first sufferings and persecutions. From this mystery the Church drew much consolation but also courage and strength to affirm itself in the world and to fulfil its earthly tasks.

C. An eschatological but also historical phenomenon

Finally the *complexio oppositorum* in the Church is also recognizable from the temporal point of view: the Church stands in the midst of time and yet has already overcome time. In a typological comparison with the forefathers of the desert generation, Paul regards Christians as those "upon whom the ends of the aeons have come" (1 Cor 10 : 11). The people of God of the New Testament stands at the end "of this aeon" and has already been delivered by Christ from it as from a situation of perdition, an impending domain of evil (cf. Gal 1 : 4), but is still as regards actual existence, maintained in it (cf. 1 Cor 3 : 18; Eph 1 : 21) as in a reality which continues provisionally to endure in the cosmos even though it is rapidly passing (cf. 1 Cor 7 : 31). The thoughts of those who are not receptive to the message of redemption and who are moving towards perdition have been blinded by "the god of this aeon" (2 Cor 4 : 4). Paul's particular eschatological yet interim awareness of time[3] leads with him to powerful exhortations not to be "conformed to this aeon" (Rom 12 : 2), not to devote oneself without reserve to the things of this world (cf. 1 Cor 7 : 29–31), making the most of time "as the days are evil" (Eph 5 : 16). Such admonitions, however, not only concern the situation of eschatological decision of the individual, but even more that of the Church to which the individual belongs, and in which he has to fulfil his authentic Christian life as is shown particularly in the First Epistle to the Corinthians (cf. 1 : 5–8; 5 : 2, 6–8; 11 : 30–32).

Even where the Church as a whole comes theologically to

147

the fore as an ideal entity, the thought of its still historically conditioned existence immersed in this evil aeon is not absent. However high and broad the dimensions of the Church of the Epistle to the Ephesians may extend, however unshakable its foundations and however certain its perfect accomplishment may appear, it is still nevertheless exposed to the onslaught of the deceptive opinions of men (cf. 4 : 14) and even to powerful attacks by diabolical powers (6 : 11 f.). The Johannine churches despite their awareness of belonging to God (1 Jn 18 : 20) and their already eschatologically decided victory (1 Jn 5 : 4; note the use of the aorist νικήσασα), are still disturbed by antichrists (2 : 18) and false prophets (4 : 1). Those to whom the First Epistle of Peter was addressed, who were rejoicing with inexpressible gladness over their deliverance (1 : 8) are not to be surprised by the "burning heat" which has broken out among them to try them, but also glad to share in the sufferings of Christ (4 : 12 f.) and remember that "the same sufferings befall your brethren in the (whole) world" (5 : 9).

The tension between already and not yet which marks the eschatological existence of the Church is most prominent in the Epistle to the Hebrews. If it is envisaged from the point of time (as well as what was said above in Part Two, § 5) it is said of the Son that he is "perfected for evermore" (7 : 28), but in his perfection[4] the "sons" also share (2 : 10). They are "sanctified once and for all by the oblation of the body of Jesus Christ" (10 : 10) and taste "the powers of the future aeon" (6 : 5). The "once and for all"[5] of Jesus' atoning death (7 : 27; 9 : 12; 10 : 10) determines a "for all time" of the redemption (7 : 25), an "eternal redemption" (5 : 9), an "eternal covenant" (13 : 20), an "eternal inheritance" (9 : 15). The "accomplishment of the aeons" was introduced by the sacrifice of Christ (cf. 9 : 26); but the people of God of the new Covenant has not yet entered into the Sabbath rest (4 : 9) and its path is marked by trials and sufferings (cf. 6 : 12; 10 : 32–39; 12 : 4–11). Only by zeal (4 : 11; 6 : 11) and endurance (10 : 36; 12 : 1) can it reach the goal and receive the "immovable kingdom" to which it already belongs (cf. 12 : 28).

All these metaphors and forms of statement whether they are spatial in orientation (from below to above) or temporal (from present to future), ultimately remain insufficient and cannot adequately represent the unity and tension of the Church's existence which comprises earth and heaven, eschatological present and the future; precisely this inexpressibility points to the unfathomable mystery of the Church in the world between time and eternity.

2. People of God

If an attempt is to be made to say something more positive about the meaning of the mystery of the Church, the first concept that presents itself is that of the people of God which has already been referred to several times[6]. According to Hebrew ways of thinking, the people forms a whole, a corporate personality and as such takes part in the events of history so that the individual is involved in the destiny of the whole, even in a supra-temporal way. Israel, however, became the people of God because Yahweh chose it to be his own possession (cf. Exod 19 : 5; 23 : 22 [LXX]; Deut 7 : 6; 14 : 2; 26 : 18). This thought was present from the time when Israel learnt to regard itself as a national and religious unity, and that occurred after and because of its merciful deliverance from Egypt by Yahweh. Moses proclaims to the Israelites in the name of Yahweh: "I am the Lord. I will free you from the oppression of Egyptian forced labour, deliver you from your bondage, redeem you with outstretched arm and powerful judgments. I will choose you for myself as my people and will be your God" (Exod 6 : 6 f.). Then the idea of the Covenant is linked to this: "I will turn to you. I will make you increase and multiply and will maintain my covenant with you...

149

I will establish my dwelling in your midst and will not turn against you but live among you and be your God and you shall be my people" (Lev 26 : 9–12). The theology and terminology of the people of God are systematically developed in Deuteronomy. The choice of this small nation to be God's possession in preference to other great nations is a favour and takes place purely from love: "It is you that the Lord your God has chosen among all the nations on earth to be a people that belongs to him alone. It is not that you are more numerous than other nations that the Lord turned to you and chose you, for you are the smallest of all the nations, but because the Lord loves you and is keeping the oath which he swore to your fathers" (Deut 7 : 6 f.).

The subsequent history of the Old Testament people of God, important as it is, (for its historical behaviour is part and parcel of its idea and gives further development to it), need not be gone into here. It is sufficient to recognize that out of it the eschatological concept of the people of God emerges, especially in the preaching of the prophets. After all Israel's breaches of faith and all Yahweh's judgments, God of his free grace and goodness is willing to re-establish the old relationship, undisturbed and indissoluble, new and definitive. "They will be my people and I will be their God ... I will make an everlasting covenant with them and will not cease to follow them to do them good" (Jer 32 : 38 ff.), such is the fundamental import of the prophetic promises (cf. Jer 24 : 7; 30 : 22; 31 : 1, 33; Ezek 11 : 20; 14 : 11; 36 : 28; 37 : 23, 27; Hos 2 : 3, 25; Zech 8 : 8; 13 : 9). Similarly in the view of late Judaism it is true that "at all events only the Israel of the eschatological future is the 'people of God' in the full sense of this term"[7].

Now it is evident from a number of passages in the New Testament that the Church knew itself to be this eschatological people of God. This is probably clearest in 1 Peter 2 : 9 f., where various Old Testament passages are combined and applied to the people of redemption, the Church. Four expressive predicates outline its splendid vocation and unique status: "chosen race, kingly priesthood, holy nation, purchased people". The continuation "so that you may proclaim the great deeds of him who has called you out of darkness into his wonderful light" refers to Isaias 43 : 20 f., where the prophet after recalling God's great deeds in the journey out of Egypt, promises a new Exodus. In doing so he calls Israel (according to the LXX): "My chosen race, my people that I have acquired for myself in order to tell of my great deeds." The epistle sees this eschatological Israel as realized in the Church. The expressions "kingly priesthood" and "holy people" derive from Exodus 19 : 6 (LXX) that beautiful passage which expresses both the sharing in God's kingship and also the priestly service of the people of God in the world [8]. That the primitive Church transferred these distinctive attributes and functions to itself and its members is shown by Apocalypse 1 : 6 and 5 : 10. The "purchased people" is frequently mentioned in the Old Testament. Finally in 1 Peter 2 : 10 another passage is also quoted, Hosea 2 : 3, 25, and the reference back to this old prophecy has already (cf. Part Two, § 5) been pointed out as particularly significant, because here the saving promise made to the old Israel that one day it would no longer be "not a people" and one that had "not obtained mercy" but would be granted mercy again and declared to be God's people, appears as applied more particularly to the gentiles who formerly sat in darkness but now have been called to God's wonderful light. There is no doubt that in this magnificent passage the Church is intended to be understood as the eschatological people of God in which the old promises for Israel are fulfilled in God's purchased people which he has newly acquired for himself through the redemptive action of his Son.

The fundamental Old Testament formula "I will be their God and they shall be my people" is quoted several times in the New Testament and applied to the eschatological community of redemption. Paul quotes it in 2 Corinthians 6 : 16

151

from Ezekiel 37 : 27 in order to distinguish the Church, this "temple of the living God" from the unbelievers. In Hebrews 8 : 10 it occurs in the lengthy quotation from Jeremias 31 : 31–34 in order to show the accomplishment of this great prophecy concerning the new Covenant. Finally the formula also appears in the Apocalypse 21 : 3 in the vision of the future Jerusalem. It is evident how deeply rooted was the primitive Church's conviction that it was the eschatological people of God. The idea is the guiding theological theme of the Epistle to the Hebrews (see above, Part Two, § 5). What, however, is the significance for the Church of Jesus Christ of this adoption of a fundamental concept of the Old Testament and of Israel's view of itself which it expressed? Is deeper insight to be had by it into the nature and mystery of the Church?

One essential factor of the Old Testament conception of the people of God still retained its force and validity for New Testament thought: God's gracious preferential love. Even before the foundation of the world he chose us in Christ that we might be holy and undefiled in his sight (Eph 1 : 4). It is from him that the call comes which leads to incorporation in the holy people of God (cf. 1 Pet 2 : 9), and those who belong to him are simply those who have obtained mercy (2 : 10). God even calls to it precisely those who in the eyes of the world are regarded as inferior and foolish (1 Cor 1 : 26–31). The reception of the gentiles is the work of God. He himself has undertaken "to take of the gentiles a people to his name" (Acts 15 : 14). Paul too is only a chosen instrument of God (cf. Acts 9 : 15); after the failure in Athens God encourages him for the beginning in Corinth: "Do not fear but speak and do not be silent for a numerous people belongs to me in this city" (Acts 18 : 10). In view of the hardening of the greater part of the Jewish people in unbelief, the willing acceptance of the gospel by the gentiles can even become a problem; but Paul in the Epistle to the Romans justifies God's providence by the grace of his vocation and the free disposition of his mercy and quotes as

a proof the same passage of Hosea 2 : 25 as 1 Peter 2 : 10:
"I will call the people that is not my people to be my people
and her that is not loved to be loved" (9 : 25). This new
people of God, formed of the remnant of Israel and many
gentiles has, like the old, only come to be because of the freely
given love and grace of God.

Something new and special, however, also contributes to
constitute it, Christ's saving action. God has acquired his
eschatological community for himself through his blood (or the
blood of his own, that is to say, of his Son?) (Acts 20 : 28).
The Greek expression for acquired (περιεποιήσατο) recalls
Isaias 43 : 21 (LXX): "my people which I have acquired",
and the image of the shepherd recalls Psalm 74 (73) : 1 f.:
"Why is thy wrath enkindled against the sheep of thy pasture?
Be mindful of thy congregation ('ēdah, LXX συναγωγή which
you acquired (ἐκτήσω) of old". God once chose and acquired
his people by the deliverance from Egypt, now he acquires his
community or Church (ἐκκλησία), namely the eschatological
one that belongs to him definitively, in a new way, as it were
by a new legal title, through the redeeming blood of his Son. All
the guilt incurred by the previous people of God disappears;
God makes a new beginning in grace. That also makes it clear
that for early Christian thought the "Church of God"
(ἡ ἐκκλησία τοῦ θεοῦ) is nothing else but the people of God,
so that Church and people of God in this perspective are
identical. This is confirmed by Titus 2 : 14: Christ Jesus "has
given himself for us in order to redeem us from' all iniquity
and cleanse for himself a people of his own". The passage
alludes to Ezekiel 37 : 23, a reference to the eschatological
people of God in which the old formula is found: "they shall
be my people and I the Lord will be their God". Instead of
this, of course, the expression known from Exodus and Deuter
onomy "people belonging to him" is used. Now all redeemed
by Jesus Christ have become God's own people. Significant
in this respect too are the supplementary expressions that are

sometimes added in Paul's epistles to ἡ ἐκκλησία. The apostle greets "the church of the Thessalonians in God the Father and the Lord Jesus Christ" (1 Thess 1 : 1; cf. 2 Thess 1 : 1). He praises the same persons as "imitators of the churches of God which are in Judaea in Christ Jesus" (1 Thess 2 : 14; cf. Gal 1 : 22). All the "churches of Christ" send greetings in Romans 16 : 16.

In this way, however, a new element makes its appearance against the background of the Old Testament concept of the people of God. The people of God of the new Covenant is no longer in any respect the same as in the old, even though fundamental ideas of gracious election to be God's possession, of Covenant and of God's community are preserved. It is true that nowhere in the New Testament is a "new" people of God mentioned, but the new Covenant is (Lk 22 : 20; 1 Cor 11 : 25; 2 Cor 3 : 6; Heb 8 : 13 cf. 6–12; 9 : 15; 12 :24), and if the close connection with the new Covenant, the idea of the people of God in Jeremias 31 : 31–34 (quoted in Hebrews 8 : 8–12) is remembered, then in fact a new and eschatological people of God is envisaged. It is true that the prophet was still thinking of the old Israel, simply renewed by grace. That the new people of God was also to extend beyond the bounds of the nation only became a certainty through the atoning death of Jesus "for many" (Mk 14 : 24), that is to say, for the gentiles too. The originality of the eschatological covenant of grace and of the eschatological people of God is seen in the fact that it is no longer the old sign of the Covenant, circumcision, but faith in Jesus Christ and the "circumcision of Christ" (Col 2 : 11), that is to say, baptism, which is decisive for admission into the people of God and membership of God's Church. Jews and gentiles have equal access if they take this new way of salvation opened up by God.

From this there also arises a certain difficulty, however, about the relation between the old and the new people of God, which probably no one felt more strongly than Paul. In his reflection on this question (cf. above, Part Two, § 4), in his answers, which can scarcely hide the fact that a certain tension remains, an important dual aspect of the people of God of the New Testament emerges. On the one hand, it is the legitimate heir, the continuation in sacred history, the true fulfilment of the Old Testament people of God, and forms an integral part of the continuous divine action which began with the election of Israel. On the other hand, it is an eschatological new creation, a new foundation built on the saving work of Jesus Christ, opposing the Spirit to the letter of the Law (cf. 2 Cor 3 : 6), and a discontinuity exists inasmuch as the old Israel in great part no longer belongs to this new people of God by reason of its unbelief. N. A. Dahl pertinently describes the dialectic of the Pauline statements: "Paul can therefore regard the relation between Church and Israel in two different ways. On one hand the Church is 'Israel κατὰ πνεῦμα', the Jewish people only 'Israel κατὰ σάρκα'. On the other hand there is only one people of God, Israel, and the gentiles have been incorporated into this one people as proselytes". The opposition between the two views must not of course be exaggerated. For Paul, Dahl holds, the Church is "the one Israel in the new eschatological age; the first view emphasizes the eschatological new creation, the second, the continuity within sacred history"[9]. In fact it is only under this dual aspect which is evident with Paul that justice can be done to the various points of view and shades of meaning found in the different books of the New Testament concerning the precise position of the Church in relation to Israel. The Church is sometimes more the true Israel, then again the new Israel; at one time the gentiles are regarded as "those added", at another, as called at once with the rest in the blood of Christ. It is instructive, however, that even the Apocalypse, despite its bitterness with the hostile because unbelieving Jewry as a "synagogue of Satan" (cf. 2 : 9; 3 : 9), can regard the people of God before and after Christ as a single reality which appears to the seer in the form of the heavenly woman (c. 12; cf. above, Part Two, § 7).

This finally brings us to the nature of the New Testament people of God. By its idea and existence it represents a mystery of divine election by grace, love and solicitous care. It gives shape to the divine economy of salvation and a testimony to God's immutable thoughts which develop in history in a multiplicity of outward forms and also permit transitions into a new order on a higher level. Even for the definitive eschatological order in the new Covenant, certain divine provisions are to be observed which follow from the character of our present eschatological interim period. Even the New Testament people of God as it is assembled in the Church, and continues to assemble, is not yet identical with the community of the elect which enters into the perfect kingdom of God; it is still subject to test and will be scrutinized and separated at the judgment. The evangelist Matthew in particular, on the basis of many sayings of Jesus, brings out the fact that one day all evil-doers will be cast out of the "kingdom of the Son of man" and only the "just" will shine like the sun "in the kingdom of their Father" (Matt 13 : 41–43). Even in the Church there are false prophets, those who drive out devils and work wonders and appeal falsely to their activity in the name of Jesus, but are then turned away by the Lord at the judgment (cf. 7 : 22 f.; cf. also above, Part Two, §3). On the other hand, people who, externally, clearly did not belong to the Church, are recognized by the Son of man as his brothers and sisters on the ground of their acts of charity (cf. 25 : 31–46). Consequently it is not surprising that at the Parousia the "elect" are to be gathered by the angels from the four winds (Mk 13 : 27 parallels). The Jewish people was rejected to the extent that it shut itself against Jesus in unbelief (cf. Mt 21 : 43a; Lk 13 : 69; Mk 11 : 13 f.); God's reign is to be given to a people which brings forth the fruits which are made possible and demanded by it (Mt 21 : 43b).

Precisely these fruits, however, are required from the newly formed people of God redeemed and sanctified by the blood of

Jesus. As a whole it will no longer disappoint God; that is guaranteed by the universal saving power of Jesus' death and the Holy Spirit bestowed on it. But that does not exclude that individual members fail and are turned away from the door of the kingdom of God; no one can take part in the marriage feast without a wedding garment (cf. Mt 22 : 11–13). This conviction filled the whole early Church and found expression in a variety of ways: in the thought of the pilgrim people of God which has not yet entered into Sabbath repose (Epistle to the Hebrews), that of the earthly exile which imperatively demands abstinence from carnal desires (First Epistle of Peter), that of enmity towards the world which still exercises its pernicious influence (cf. 1 Jn 2 : 15–17; James 4 : 4); that of wrestling with the diabolic powers which still threaten even Christians (Eph 6 : 10-17), that of the necessity of turning aside from all evil deeds and of perpetual conversion (Acts 2–3). Yet it is John the seer who gives particularly powerful expression to it, convinced as he is that the Church as a whole is a bride splendidly adorned, to whom it was granted by God "to clothe herself with fine linen shining and white; the linen signifies the just deeds of the saints" (Apoc 19 : 8). Perhaps in this view the nature of the eschatological people of God is most clearly revealed; as a whole it is holy by the grace of God because it unites within it "those who have washed their robes and have made them white in the blood of the Lamb" (Apoc 7 : 14), but now also themselves willingly "follow the Lamb wherever he goes" pure, truthful, undefiled (cf. Apoc 14 : 4 f.). As a whole it possesses the certainty of perfect fulfilment, victory and future blessedness within it; but earthly care, suffering and trial are not yet taken away. It stands on the threshold of the promised land, sees in faith the future glory, experiences even now something of this, particularly in its worship, but must still nevertheless bring the earthly journey to an end and bear the hardship of the road.

3. *Building in the Holy Spirit*

The image of the building or temple filled by the Spirit of God opens out further important perspectives in a view of the Church. It not only permits a better grasp of the eschatological nature of the Church, but permits a more penetrating view of its inner structure and life.

In the first place, what the New Testament has to say about the connection between the divine Spirit and the Church, completes what has so far been observed regarding the eschatological people of God, the new Covenant and God's community of the new Alliance. Ezekiel already ascribed a special eschatological function in the redeemed people of the last days to the Spirit of God, that of purifying and sanctifying: "I shall put my Spirit within you and cause you to walk in my commandments . . ." (36 : 27). It is only a continuation of the thought of holiness when Paul writes to the Corinthians: "Know you not that you are a temple of God and that the Spirit of God dwells in you? But if any man violate the temple of God, God will destroy him; for the temple of God is holy, which you are" (1 Cor 3 : 16 f.). We take that as a proof of the eschatological consciousness of the early Church (cf. above, Part Two, §§ 1 and 2); but that is only an aspect of the bond between the Spirit and the Church. Even more important seems the fact that Paul in 2 Corinthians 3 : 6–18 characterizes the new Covenant in general by the presence and operation of the Spirit. He concedes to the old Covenant which was dominated by the Law, only a temporary, transitory gleam of God's glory (on the face of Moses); for the rest, it holds good that "the letter kills but the Spirit vivifies" (v. 6). The power of the Spirit creating life and giving glory is reserved for the new Covenant. In it the Spirit proceeds from the "Lord of the Spirit", that is to say, from the risen Lord Jesus Christ who for us has become "a life-giving Spirit" (cf. 1 Cor 15 : 45)[10]. That means that it is only possible to speak of the eschatological people of God if and when the Spirit of God as a life-giving power has been freely bestowed. This conviction, however, is present in the whole early Church, even if the functions of the Spirit are variously viewed or differently emphasized (cf. above, Part One, § 2). The baptism conferred after Pentecost was everywhere understood to be the occasion for the reception of the Spirit and this eschatological gift of God was also understood to be the fruit of Christ's saving action. This thought is particularly clear in John's gospel: as long as Jesus was not yet glorified there was no Spirit, that is to say, for the faithful; but then all were to receive it (7 : 39; cf. also 6 : 63 a)[11].

The exalted Lord releases the Spirit and builds with him his Church. Through the Spirit and only through the Spirit which comes from the living Lord, does that holy building of God arise which is "built upon the foundation of the apostles and prophets", of which Jesus Christ forms the chief stone, which "grows into a holy temple in the Lord" and in which the gentile Christians too are "built together into a dwelling place of God in the Spirit" (Eph 2 : 20 ff.). The final phrase "in the Spirit" is not at all a chance or a superfluous one. If Jesus Christ is the "chief stone" in the sense of the corner-stone which holds all together, and gives the whole its line and strength[12], that is so precisely through the Spirit, just as ἐν κυρίῳ stands parallel to ἐν πνεύματι. Growth in the Spirit does not mean that the Spirit only comes as a supplement after the foundation of the Church by Jesus; it is rather that the community of Jesus' disciples only becomes the Church through the Spirit. Only after Jesus' earthly activity and departure is the service of the Church in the world necessary for the work of Jesus; only after the resurrection and exaltation of Jesus does it become possible, however, — through the Spirit sent by him. In the conception and language of the Epistle to the Ephesians this is expressed by saying that the two groups of men, Jews and gentiles, are reconciled (2 : 16) to one another

159

and with God in the Body of Christ ("in one body") but furthermore only have access to the Father "in one Spirit" (2 : 18). Christ's act of reconciliation only becomes effective and fruitful through the Spirit. So the Holy Spirit forms as it were a basis for the authentic life of the Church and makes it by its very nature pneumatic (a spiritual reality). That is extremely important for the concept of the Church. The Church is not understood if it is only regarded as an institution, even as one founded by Jesus, or as an association of Christian believers in the sense of an establishment or society willed by God. It is necessary to realize in addition to this that the Church owes to the divine Spirit of life and holiness its origin and existence, form and continuance, to that Spirit which since and through Jesus' glorification comprises and fills, unites and directs all who believe and are newly begotten in baptism. Through the Spirit of Christ the society of those who believe in him becomes the Church of Christ; through the Spirit, Christ becomes the Lord of his Church.

Consequently it is possible to gaze deeper into the inner life of the Church by means of the idea that the Church is a building in the Holy Spirit, than was possible with the concept of the people of God. It is true that the people of God can also be regarded as a "temple of the living God" in which God himself "dwells" and "walks" (cf. 2 Cor 6 : 16); but it is only the thought of the Holy Spirit filling every member that brings the picture of the New Testament people of God its full vividness. That occurs in 1 Peter 2 : 4 ff. Here Christ himself is first of all described as a "living stone" which "was rejected by men" but with God is "a chosen, valuable stone". Then it is said "Allow yourselves too to be built up as living stones into a spiritual house..." Through the baptism they have just received (cf. 2 : 1), these new Christians who are here addressed, have come to Christ the risen and living Lord (cf 1 : 3, 21), and by that very fact have entered into his "life in the Spirit" (cf. 3 : 18). By that too they have also become "living stones" in the spiritual house of the Church and as such must place themselves at the disposal of the edifice. It is clear that the Spirit constitutes the bond between Christ and the Christians united to him by baptism and between Christians themselves, just as Paul teaches with the concept of the Body of Christ (cf. below, Part Four, §4). In the baptismal paraenesis we are dealing with, however, it will be made even clearer what the service is that those incorporated into the spiritual building as living stones can perform. For that reason the image changes from that of "house" which is here understood as a temple, to that of the "holy priesthood" which performs its service in this holy place. Perhaps the influence of Isaias 61 : 6 is perceptible here: "You shall be called the priests of the Lord, you shall be named ministers of our God"; but the translation and interpretation of Exodus 19 : 6 in Hellenistic Judaism make it clear that "Jewish circles which used the Septuagint Bible were accustomed to apply to their nation simultaneously both the term temple and the term priesthood"[13]. As priests in the spiritual house of the community, the Christians are to "offer up spiritual sacrifices acceptable to God through Jesus Christ". It is evident how the spiritual sacrifices correspond to the spiritual house. What they consist in can be shown by a passage such as Hebrews 13 : 15: "Let us therefore always offer through him (Christ) a sacrifice of praise to God, that is to say, the fruit of lips confessing to his name. Do not forget to do good and to share; for God has pleasure in such sacrifices." In the concrete, therefore, what is meant are the fruits of piety and love which the young Christians are to bear in the Church and with the Church. Yet it would be false to interpret this only in the sense of a spiritualizing of the liturgical concepts of temple priests and sacrifices such as can be shown to have already taken place in late, and in particular Hellenistic, Judaism[14]. The qualification "spiritual" refers rather to the Holy Spirit through whom the "temple" of the Christian community is built up and through whose power the members bring forth moral fruits. Through the reality of the Spirit completely new Christian worship arises (cf. the "adoration in Spirit and in truth", Jn 4 : 23), and through his efficacy in Christians, quite different "fruits" are produced (cf. Gal 5 : 22 f.), from what were possible to all previous moral endeavour. The Church as spiritual house is a new reality and "stands in contrast to the stone temple in Jerusalem and the sanctuaries of the gentiles"[15]; the Holy Spirit enkindles in it a special life of worship and moral striving moved by divine impetus and divine power. Linked through the Spirit with Christ and his saving action, the Christians are in a position to offer to God truly pleasing sacrifices. Paul expresses this in another way when he admonishes the Romans to present their "bodies as a living sacrifice, holy and pleasing to God" and so to perform their "spiritual worship ($\tau\grave{\eta}\nu\ \lambda o\gamma\iota\varkappa\grave{\eta}\nu\ \lambda\alpha\tau\rho\epsilon\acute{\iota}\alpha\nu$)"[16]. Even though the expression may be borrowed from Hellenistic language, the "spiritualization" is to be understood in the same sense as in 1 Peter 2 : 5, that is, in the sense of a worship made possible by the Holy Spirit, in the eschatological community, which also manifests itself in moral fecundity.

A special effect of the Spirit in the early Christian, particularly the Pauline, churches are the charismata, which are also on one occasion called "gifts of the Spirit" ($\pi\nu\epsilon\upsilon\mu\alpha\tau\iota\varkappa\acute{\alpha}$ 1 Cor 14 : 1). In them the plenitude and variety of the eschatological Spirit conferred on God's Church is manifested, but also the help that he gives to its inner construction. "To each the manifestation of the Spirit is given to be useful", that is, to be useful to the Church (1 Cor 12 : 7). The various gifts of the Spirit are to serve "the building up of the Church" (1 Cor 14 : 12, 26). It is significant that even official ministries and auxiliary services are numbered among the charismata (cf. 1 Cor 12 : 28); not only divine service but the whole life of the Church is subject to the operation of the Spirit.

162

The Spirit cares for the order of the churches; they are completely under his direction. It is the Holy Spirit who, according to Acts 20 : 28, appointed the presbyters of the community as "overseers" to rule the Church of God. His guidance is clearly evident in the account of the Acts of the Apostles. By the dissimulation of Ananias and Saphira he is "lied to" (5 : 3); he is the "Spirit of the Lord" whom the deceitful couple have challenged (5 : 9). Again, the Church increases perpetually in numbers through the whole of Judaea, Galilee and Samaria, through the "consolation" of the Holy Spirit (9 : 31). The Holy Spirit sanctions the decision of the "Council of Jerusalem" (cf. 15 : 28). But the whole mission as Luke sees it is placed entirely under the impulse and guidance of the Holy Spirit[17]. Filled by him, Peter speaks to the Jewish people and its leaders (4 : 8), the apostles "with great power" bore their testimony to the resurrection of the Lord Jesus (4 : 33), and they spoke freely and confidently (2 : 29; 4 : 29, 31). The Seven also are men "full of the Spirit and wisdom" (6 : 3). None could withstand the wisdom and Spirit in which Stephen spoke (6 : 10). The Spirit leads Philip in the conversion of the Ethiopian chamberlain (8 : 29, 39); enlightens Peter when the baptism of the gentile Cornelius is to come about (10 : 19; 11 : 12); provides the impulse in Antioch to send out Barnabas and Saul on the mission planned by him (13 : 2, 4), and later directs Paul on a divinely-willed road to Europe (cf. 16 : 6 f.). This description is of course that of Luke; but he will certainly not be expressing purely personal ideas. The whole early Church was certainly convinced of the help of the Holy Spirit in the performance and preaching of the messengers of the faith and in his support of the mission by healings and miracles (cf. Acts 3 : 1–10; 8 : 13; 19 : 11–20). Paul, too, knew that his missionary preaching owed its success not to his human words but to the "demonstration of the Spirit and power" (1 Cor 2 : 4; 1 Thess 1 : 5; 2 Cor 6 : 6 f.; 12 : 12).

163

In Paul it is clearer that it is the Spirit of Jesus, of the exalted Lord, who in this way provides for the building up of his Church and rules it. The Lord himself gave his Church the charismatic bearers of office as "gifts" (Eph 4 : 11, cf. 8), and it is only a difference of point of view whether the charismata with their manifold services are traced back to the "Lord" or to God, "who works all in all" or to the visible manifestation of the Spirit (1 Cor 12 : 4–7). And so the Church's possession of the Spirit ultimately illustrates the decisive fact that existing and acting in the world, constituted in an earthly manner and directed by human bearers of office, the Church is nevertheless built up and led "from above". That happens continuously and permanently, even when the first witnesses and preachers died and the Church had to create services and ministries. The Spirit speaks to the churches through the mouth of the seer of Patmos (Apoc 2 : 7, 11, 17, 29; 3 : 6, 13, 22); but even where the direct "spirit of prophecy" (Apoc 19 : 10) does not present the testimony of Jesus, the Church is led by the Spirit. For even the official ministers appointed by imposition of hands receive a charism, an endowment with Holy Spirit which enables them to proclaim and teach, exhort and educate (cf. 1 Tim 4 : 13 f.; 2 Tim 1 : 6 f.). In the sayings about the Paraclete of the Johannine farewell discourses, the general principle is formulated: this assistance is to remain with the disciples for ever (Jn 14 : 16).

This life and enduring existence of the Church in the Holy Spirit is a mystery of which the Church itself is conscious, but which is hidden from those outside it. Paul indicates this in the case of the individual "pneumatic", that is to say, the Christian who is living in the Holy Spirit: "The natural man does not grasp what belongs to the Spirit of God; to him it is folly and he cannot understand it because it is only judged in the way of the Spirit" (1 Cor 2 : 14). John, however, widens out this perspective on to the life of the Church in the world: the cosmos which is far from God cannot receive the "Spirit of truth" given to the disciples "because it does not see him and does not know him" (Jn 14 : 17). Sharing in the Spirit and living membership of the Church is necessary in order to recognize with faith the mystery of the Church's pneumatic nature and the way it is permeated with divine forces.

4. Body of Christ

The innermost centre of the Church's life would be overlooked if its relation to Christ were passed over in silence. The question has occasionally been propounded whether for the ecclesiology of the New Testament the concept of people of God or that of Body of Christ should take precedence[18]. Anyone who attentively studies the New Testament documents and their theology will be inclined to use an "and" rather than an "or", for however true it may be that the idea of the people of God is everywhere retained (for Paul cf. "the Church of God" 1 Cor 1 : 2; 10 : 32; 15 : 9; the "Israel of God" Gal 6 : 16; and also Rom 9 : 25 f.; 15 : 9–12; 2 Cor 6 : 16), the Pauline concept of the Body of Christ nevertheless forcefully suggests itself as the most mature result of New Testament thinking about the Church. It remains of course distinctively Pauline in the particular form it takes but has unmistakable kinship with other images and statements in the rest of the New Testament, as for example with the Johannine allegory of the vine and the branches (Jn 15 : 1–8); with the spiritual house built on Christ as the corner-stone, where the holy priesthood offers its spiritual sacrifices once again through Jesus Christ (1 Pet 2 : 4 f.; cf. Heb 13 : 15); and even with the Church as the bride of the Lamb (Apoc 12 : 2, 9; 22 : 17 cf. 19 : 8). On a profounder view, that is to say, the basis of all these metaphors is the endeavour to express the inner bond of the New Testament people of God with Christ, its relation to God through Christ, the union of its members through

165

Christ, and its striving and journeying towards Christ as its goal. The Church in the New Testament remains God's people but it is a people of God newly constituted in Christ and in relation to Christ. Its new and unique form is most appropriately designated as Body of Christ; totality and membership, foundation and goal, life and growth of the Church can best be studied on that basis. Yet it would be a dangerous limitation if for that reason the concept of people of God were abandoned, and the idea of the Body of Christ were treated as absolute and made the sole basis of speculation. The Church is the people of God as the Body of Christ, in a sense which is determined by, or at least grounded on, the idea of the people of God.

That is most finely apparent in a consideration of sacred history in the Epistle to the Galatians, which leads to statements that are extremely close to those regarding the Body of Christ, without, however, mentioning the latter. After the apostle has described the change from the period of the Law to that of grace, from the pedagogue *nomos* to Christ our salvation (3 : 23–25), he recalls baptism in which all "in Christ Jesus" have become sons of God, by "putting on Christ" (3 : 26 f.). But in that it is not only the joyful experience of redemption by the individual that he is envisaging, but the Church as a whole: "There is neither Jew nor Greek, neither slave nor free, neither male nor female; for you are all one in Christ Jesus" (3 : 28). The final sentence too is important, in which the baptized are described as the descendants of Abraham and heirs of the blessing in accordance with the promise made to Christ (3 : 29). Here the new people of God as Paul sees it, is clearly apparent; at the same time, however, the passage is in complete agreement in form and content with 1 Corinthians 12 : 13 where the same statements occur under the metaphor of the "Body" (cf. v. 12). The terse formula "you are all one in Christ Jesus" can be directly compared with Romans 12 : 5: "So we being many are one body in Christ." The Church as presented in the passage in Galatians might be called a corporate personality, to which the individual baptized belong but which as a totality is superior to them — a way of thinking in terms of the whole. It is tempting to regard this collective personality as "the Christ" whom all in baptism have "put on" (cf. also 1 Cor 1 : 13; 12 : 12)[19]. However that may be, even here the relation between Christ and Church is viewed as being as close as can be conceived; the Church has become "in Christ Jesus" a unity which has no parallel in the natural realm, for in it all natural differences lose their validity. The new life of the individual "in Christ" (cf. 2 Cor 5 : 17) is at the same time life in a new society founded "in Christ Jesus". A separation of the individual and social aspects is not possible; the personal union with Christ also involves incorporation in the collective Christian society.

In this way we are already prepared when, in the First Epistle to the Corinthians, we find statements regarding the Body of Christ or the members of Christ[20]. In the first place it is the individual church here, the actual community of Corinth which is intended, as is shown particularly by the long passage in 12 : 12–27 addressed to the charismatics of Corinth; but the individual church nevertheless only appears as the representative of the whole Church (cf. 1 : 2), for in 12 : 28 the view opens out on to this and in principle, too, all the baptized belong to the Body of Christ (cf. 12 : 13, 27). The section is dominated by the *comparison* of the Church to a body which consists of many members and yet is one (cf. v. 12). With that Paul wants to illustrate the multiplicity and unity (vv. 14–20), the mutual dependence of the members (v. 21), the necessity and honour of all members (vv. 22–25), and their solidarity or unity of destiny (v. 26), in order to overcome a striving for particular favourite charismata that would endanger the community. It is a simile which has a variety of parallels in the ancient world (particularly the fable of M. Agrippa in Livy II, 32). On account of this general point of view, however, the relation of the community as Body of Christ (v. 27) to Christ himself is not very clear. That the expression was not coined simply for the sake of the simile seems plain from the very fact that, in earlier passages of the epistle, similar statements occur which cannot be explained in that way (cf. 6 : 15–17; 10 : 17 on which more below). The apostle was scarcely led to his manner of talking about the Body of Christ by the classical comparison of a society with an articulated organism but, rather, on the contrary, the former suggested the current simile which conveniently fitted the quarrels about spiritual gifts in Corinth. The already formed idea of the Body of Christ cannot, however, be clearly derived from 1 Corinthians 12, for the simile stands quite in the foreground. The mode of expression in v. 12 is concise: "so it is with the Christ". Does "the Christ" signify the (individual) exalted Lord or the (collective) Body of Christ?[21] How is the genitive case in v. 27 to be understood? From the reason given in v. 13 it can only be gathered that the baptized were incorporated by the *one* Spirit into the one Body (as in Gal 3 : 27 f.), and certainly into the Body of *Christ,* but the relation between Body and Christ remains unexplained or uncertain.

In 1 Corinthians 6 : 15–17, Paul provides motives against unchastity. The Corinthians must surely know that their bodies are "members of Christ". "Shall I therefore take the members of Christ and make them the members of an harlot?" The "members of Christ" immediately suggest the "Body of Christ" (cf. 1 Cor 12 : 27), although this expression is not used. By "Christ", by analogy with the members of a harlot, the personal Christ, the exalted Lord must be meant; that signifies that the Christians with their bodies belong as members of Christ to the Lord (cf. also v. 13) and suggests the inference that the whole Body of Christ is nothing but the body of the individual exalted Lord[22]. That is certainly correct in the sense that this Body belongs to Christ the Lord, but the relation of this "ecclesiological" Body to the body of the risen Jesus is nevertheless not yet made clear. Whether one may speak of a "mystical identification" (L. Cerfaux) remains disputable. At all events that "Body" is not yet placed (as it is in Colossians and Ephesians), in relation to Christ as its "heavenly head"; it should be noted that the exalted Jesus is always termed in these verses (13 f., 17), the Lord (ὁ κύριος). Another point, however, clearly emerges; the union between the latter and "members of Christ" is created by the Spirit. In the continuation of motives against unchastity it is said: "He who is joined to a harlot is one body (with her) ... But he who is joined to the Lord is one Spirit (with him)." The almost surprising expression draws attention to what is dissimilar within this analogy: the relationship with Christ despite the closest imaginable union is nevertheless of a different kind, a community which comes about and is characterized by the Spirit. For the Body of Christ, we realize, the πνεῦμα which proceeds from the Lord is the principle of unity (cf. 1 Cor 12 : 13); it links the baptized with Christ as well as the baptized with one another.

The eucharist as sacrament of unity appears clearly in 1 Corinthians 10 : 17, a verse which is also important for the concept of the Body of Christ. In the context Paul is concerned to keep Christians away from dinners connected with pagan sacrificial rites. By the eucharist the Christians really share in the blood and body of Christ (v. 16) and cannot at the same time be partakers of the "table of the Lord" and "the table of devils" (v. 21). Yet just as with baptism (cf. Gal 3 : 26 ff.), Paul is not only thinking of the individual's union with Christ, but his view extends to the unity among the participants themselves which is brought about by the sacrament. "Because one (and the same) bread (is), we, the many, are one body; for we all share in one bread" (v. 17). In itself "one body" could be a metaphor for the close unity of the congregation; but such a figure of speech would not fit the passage as a whole. The reason given for the unity is that all share in the one bread and that, according to verse 16 b, means the one body of Christ. The one body which the many form must therefore signify the Body of Christ. A profound relation exists between the body of Christ in the eucharist and the Body of Christ represented by the congregation. How Paul understands this relation is not immediately clear, for in v. 17 a new line of thought is present[23]. Not a few recent exegetes consider they must understand the apostle to be envisaging the ecclesiological Body of Christ only as a new mode of being of the crucified and risen body of Christ present in the eucharistic bread[24]. In view of the flexibility of Paul's language, however, it can scarcely be said that this conclusion is inescapable. Certainly the common sharing in the one eucharistic bread and so in the body of Christ, brings about the unity of the congregation as the one Body of Christ; yet Paul need not be speaking each time of the "body of Christ" (or as the case may be, "one body") in completely the same sense. Only one thing may be taken as certain: behind 1 Corinthians 10 : 17 also lies the idea that the congregation is the "Body of Christ" and this is brought out quite realistically. What it already is through baptism is given new ground and reality by the eucharist, and in particular in relation to unity: a single body, the Body of Christ.

Probably the apostle had already expressed his conception of the Church as Body of Christ by word of mouth (cf. 1 Cor 6 : 15: οὐκ οἴδατε) so that he was able to refer to it in his epistle just as he did to the metaphor of the "temple of God" (1 Cor 3 : 16), only that the Body of Christ is more than a metaphor. The term directly expresses something about the relation of Church to Christ, its profound union with him through the Spirit, indeed unity with him in the Spirit, the constituting of this unity by baptism and its renewal by the eucharist, and about the intrinsic union of the members among themselves, with the obligation of making this unity visible and fruitful. Yet this doctrine is more presupposed than developed in 1 Corinthians and Romans[25], and overbold inferences regarding the relation of Christ to this "body" of his will have to be avoided.

It is different in the Epistles to the Colossians and to the Ephesians, where we enter into the light of significant statements regarding the relation of the heavenly Christ to his Church — here in the sense of the Church as a whole. In particular in these epistles Christ is described as the head of his body the Church (Col 1 : 18; Eph 1 : 22; 4 : 15; 5 : 23); consequently it is possible to determine more precisely the relations between him and the Church. According to the view of the "body" which is basically implied[26], all life and growth, the whole building up of the body proceeds from the head (cf. Eph 4 : 12, 16; Col 2 : 19); the heavenly Christ builds himself up in the Church and through the Church itself, in love (Eph 4 : 16). As head, he possesses a sovereign position in relation to the Church his body (Eph 5 : 23 f); but he only uses this to distribute his gifts to it and these are viewed concretely in Ephesians 4 : 11 as the charismatic offices. So Christ rules (from heaven) his Church through the organs established and directed by him, which serve the good of the whole (4 : 12 f.). But the influence of the head is even more extensive. Christ as head causes his whole nature and life, the wealth of divine blessing to pour into the Church. The Church is the "plenitude" of him who "fills all in all" (or, who is filled by all) (Eph 1 : 23)[27]; that means, it would seem, that "with all the forces which derive from him, Christ sovereignly governs the powers which have become subject to him (v. 22 a), giving life to the whole Church (v. 22 b)"[28]. Consequently all the Christians in the Church through him and in him are "filled" (Col 2 : 10), endowed with every blessing of grace. This, however, can also be expressed as a prayerful petition that they may be filled in order to attain to the whole "plenitude of God" (Eph 3 : 19). The previous sentences show that in this "being filled" it is a question of the riches of

171

divine life, of "being strengthened with might in the inward man through his Spirit" (3 : 16), but also of fruitful knowledge and love. Once again it is ultimately the divine Spirit who, from Christ the head, flows with his vivifying power, strengthening, enlightening and impelling to good, into the body and all its members and who then is manifested in the spiritual intoxication of gladness and thanksgiving, particularly in divine worship (cf. Eph 5 : 18 ff.).

The "government" of the Church by Christ is therefore in reality a service, a perpetual care for the Church, as is clear in the "conjugal" considerations of Ephesians 5 : 22–23. Christ is head, yet also "saviour of the body" (v. 23). He has "loved his Church and delivered himself up for it, in order to sanctify it for himself..." (v. 25 f.). There the apostle is looking back at Christ's great act of redemption which was for the benefit of the Church and demonstrates its blessing in baptism; for the sanctification took place by his "cleansing it by the bath of water in the word, in order to present the Church to himself gloriously, without spot or wrinkle or any such thing, but that it should be holy and without blemish" (v. 26 f.). The Church, like the bride, goes through the water of baptism and becomes pure and radiant by the power of Christ's sacrificial death (cf. Eph 5 : 2). Here a close connection is apparent, but is not described in more detail, between the Church and Christ's redemptive act; it is made clearer in 2 : 14 ff. (see below). Baptism appears not only as the place where the faithful are united with Christ and (by the Spirit) are incorporated into his body (Gal 3 : 26 f.; 1 Cor 12 : 13), but also as Christ's solicitude for his (already existing) Church. Similarly, Christ continues to feed and cherish the Church (v. 29), — perhaps an allusion to the eucharist, so that here also the second "sacrament of the body of Christ" may be obliquely envisaged as well[29].

The "distance" between Christ and the Church disappears in this conjugal point of view, without their distinction becoming blurred, while in other passages the unity of Christ and Church is even more clearly recognizable. In Ephesians 2 : 5 f. it is stated with evident reference to baptism (cf. Col 2 : 11–13) that God "when we were dead by the transgressions, has given life to us also with Christ — it is by grace you are saved — and has raised us up also and placed us also in heaven in Christ Jesus". The compound verbs with συν- express in the strongest manner our link with what happened with Christ and at the same time our union with himself. We have even "in him" attained a presence in heaven. It is true that the apostle does not speak in this context of head and body; yet if the passage 1 : 20–22 is compared with this one, there can scarcely be any doubt that the idea is present. God has raised Christ "from the dead and set him in heaven on his right hand over every principality and power and virtue and dominion ... has subjected all things under his feet and has given him as the head (which is set) over all things, to the Church which is his body ...." Now if we were also raised up and also placed in heaven, that clearly took place by reason of our incorporation in the body of Christ through baptism. All the baptized, the whole Church, shares in the saving event and the heavenly sovereign position of Christ, precisely because he is its head and the Church is his body, both in indissoluble unity and solidarity. Certainly Christ in person remains the victor over the cosmic powers of perdition (cf. Col 2 : 14 f.); but as head he allows his body to share in his victory. He takes us in his body "also" up to heaven, although it is not forgotten that in our present life we are still bound fast on the earth and in this aeon must prove ourselves (Eph 2 : 7, 10; 4 : 14 f.) and fight against Satan and his diabolical powers (6 : 10–18). Consequently the Church as Body of Christ has a heavenly yet earthly appearance; it is his sphere of operation and instrument in this world (cf. below, Part Four, § 5), and nevertheless rises with him as its head and extends up into the heavenly sphere, — a dynamic polarity which springs from the particular character of this concept and cannot be resolved.

In addition to the "vertical" point of view, however, the reference back to the redemptive action accomplished once and for all by Christ on the cross gives rise to similar unfathomable statements regarding the Church as his "body". In Ephesians 2 : 14–18 the apostle is occupied with the main theme of the epistle: the unity of Jews and gentiles in the Church and precisely for this "mystery of Christ", the idea of the "body of Christ" is indispensable to him (3 : 4). He wishes to explain how the former gentiles who once were "far off" have become "near" in the blood of Christ (v. 13), that is to say, share in salvation on an equal footing with Israel, and how Christ has united both these formerly divided human groups and reconciled them with God. In order to describe this double establishment of peace, he accumulates a variety of expressions and imagery. Among these and of particular importance for the present purpose is the statement about Christ's purpose in his action: "That he might make the two in his person into one new man, making peace, and might reconcile both in one body with God, by the cross, so killing the enmity in himself" (vv. 15 ff.). By this one body in the first place only the body of Christ given up to the bloody death of the cross can be meant, his physical body (cf. v. 14 ἐν τῇ σάρκι αὐτοῦ, and also Col 1 : 22). Nevertheless, as we read further, precisely this body assumes a more comprehensive meaning. "Through him (Christ) we both (groups of men) have access to the Father in one Spirit" (v. 18). The "one Spirit" corresponds to the "one body" just as 4 : 4 reads "one body and one Spirit". It is the Spirit which fills and unites the ecclesiological Body of Christ. The apostle can therefore only be understood to be saying that the one physical body of Christ which bled on the cross for the two previously divided groups of mankind and which established reconciliation, then becomes after the resurrection in a new way through the Spirit the one "Body of Christ" which is the Church, so that ἐν ἑνὶ σώματι v. 16 perhaps itself is deliberately intended to have a double meaning. The same, however, follows from the previous equivalent statement that Christ "made the two in his person into one new man" (v. 15). This *anthropos* is nothing else than the whole Christ with head and body — probably the strongest indication that Paul is here in fact taking up old speculations regarding Adam and anthropos, perhaps even taking into account, and giving a Christian interpretation to, the gnostic anthropos myth as this can be shown to have existed in the Jewish and gentile sections of Hellenism[30]. Without going into the question, which at present is the subject of intense discussion, regarding the idea of the σῶμα in Colossians and Ephesians in relation to the background opened up by comparative religion[31], we note that that conception, which many exegetes consider is already to be seen in the First Epistle to the Corinthians and in the Epistle to the Romans, indubitably appears here: the body of the crucified and risen Lord expands into the ecclesiological Body of Christ by means of the Spirit; through the latter the Lord (the head) builds up his Church (the body) for himself and becomes with it a full unity. In this way the Church becomes a reality which is already present in Christ's body on the cross and which then is built up by inner and outer growth deriving from its head, Christ, and takes possession of the cosmos in order to achieve its perfect form. That may be alluded to in the pregnant statement of Ephesians 4 : 13 that we are all to attain "to the perfect man, to the full measure of the plenitude of Christ", whether ἡλικία is to be understood in a spatial or in a temporal sense. At all events the Church is regarded as a cosmic and eschatological reality which in its temporal and earthly existence only unfolds and strives after what in its head, Christ, is already a reality. Viewed from Christ, the Church as his body is his instrument for bringing the cosmos more and more under the blessing of

175

his rule, in order to make the universe (cf. 1 : 10) subjected to him share as far as possible in the graces of redemption. One sign of this eschatological saving event, however, is the fact that the gentiles are now "fellow-heirs and of the same body and co-partners of the promise in Christ Jesus by the gospel" (3 : 6). Consequently, however, it is also one of the most urgent exhortations of the apostle to preserve the unity given to the Church in Christ by the Spirit and to make it visible by brotherly love and concord and the bond of peace (Eph 4 : 1–7; Col 3 : 12–15).

For ecclesiology we may observe that it is on the heights of this theology of the Body of Christ that what is new, specific and unique in the Christian idea of the Church clearly emerges, even when the background of Old Testament thought regarding the people or community of God, the Covenant and eschatological promises is remembered or comparison is made with certain gnostic, Hellenistic conceptions. The further development of the ideas, their penetration by speculation and the Christian distinctions drawn, are guided by the revelation of Christ. The Church of Jesus Christ is only intelligible as a result of the saving event which took place in Jesus' crucifixion and resurrection and as a continuation of his activity in the Holy Spirit; its relation to the exalted Lord, however, its link with him and its dependence on him and union with him, its life deriving from him and striving directed towards him, cannot ultimately be further understood: that is the deepest mystery of the Church.

5. Church and world

The relation of the Church to the world was already touched upon in the previous section, but must be further examined, for it can throw more light on the Church's nature. A distinction must be drawn between "world" in the sense of the present world or the "aeon" which is still unfolding, and "world" in the sense of the universe or totality of all creation. In the earlier letters of Paul it is principally the former, dualistically coloured concept of the cosmos that is found, but in the Epistles to the Ephesians and Colossians not a few references to (τὰ) πάντα, all things, occur. According to the texts which refer to the world as a sinister reality, the Church stands in a condition of tension or even in antithesis to the domain in which its historical life takes place (cf. above, Part Four, § 1, c). Since the sin of man's first parents, this world, in the biblical perspective of the economy of salvation, has fallen into a calamitous situation and development; sin and death have made their entry into it like victorious powers (cf. Rom 5 : 12). The world is not regarded simply as God's creation, as the universe of created things and the abode of mankind, which he was meaningfully to transform with all his powers, but as a realm already darkened and occupied by the powers of evil, and which exercises its destructive influence on man. Through his physical existence man is bound up with this world and presents in his members, through the σάρξ and the desires and passions that inhabit it, a vulnerable point of attack by sin, in Paul's view, and of his own resources man cannot resist the onslaught of the sinister power of sin. The world for him has turned into a calamitous situation, so that he is not able to accomplish the good which, in itself, he wills (cf. in particular Rom 7 : 5, 14–20). It is not only by chance that in this perspective "(this) world" and "this aeon" are interchangeable expressions; it is no longer simply the world of God's creation but the world of historical human life in which evil works itself out and is powerful. This idea of the "world", deriving from the thought of later Judaism, is a guiding concept not only for Paul but to a large extent for the New Testament generally, and its special features must be distinguished from modern linguistic usage. It is an eschatological notion concerning the economy of salvation[32].

The position of the Church in regard to the "world" so understood is fundamentally determined by the fact that the world adopts an attitude hostile to God and is making towards an end in calamity. God has "made foolish the wisdom of this world" (1 Cor 1 : 20); the Christians have not received "the spirit of the world, but a Spirit which is of God" (1 Cor 2 : 12). For Paul (and for every Christian) through Christ, "the world is crucified" and he to the world (Gal 6 : 14). "This world" is a transitory thing (1 Cor 7 : 31; cf. 1 Jn 2 : 17). The term "aeon" is similarly used when "the wisdom of this aeon" and its "rulers" doomed to defeat is rejected (1 Cor 2 : 6; cf. 1 : 20; 3 : 18), and it is positively stated that Christ wanted to deliver us "from this present wicked aeon" (Gal 1 : 4). The Christians are admonished not to be "conformed to this aeon" (Rom 12 : 2). The world or this aeon appears particularly dangerous because Satan and the diabolical powers subject to him still have influence in it, and in fact are the real rulers everywhere where the blessed dominion of Christ is not operative (cf. 2 Cor 4 : 4; Eph 2 : 2; 6 : 12; Jn 12 : 31). It is true that the "prince of this world" has been "cast out" and "judged" by Christ's victory on the cross (Jn 12 : 31; 16 : 11); but this deprivation of power only benefits those who believe in Christ and allow themselves to be drawn to him. As long as Christ's victory has not universally prevailed, it remains true that "the whole world lies in the power of the evil one" (1 Jn 5 : 19). That is precisely what constitutes the eschatological situation of the Christians; for that reason they must separate themselves from "darkness", chose between Christ and Belial (2 Cor 6 : 14 f.), give up association with "the sons of perdition and walk as children of the light" (Eph 5 : 6 f.). It would be dangerous to love the world and all that is in it (1 Jn 2 : 15 ff.), for friendship with the world is hostility to God (James 4 : 4).

In such contexts the Church appears as a holy precinct, a temple of God (2 Cor 6 : 16), delivered by Christ from the sphere of corruption of this aeon (Gal 1 : 4). Instead of conforming themselves to this aeon, the Christians in the world are in a position, by renewal of spirit, to reform and cultivate a service of God of the kind he wishes (cf. Rom 12 : 1 f.). Christ himself has sanctified himself for them and sanctified them through the truth (Jn 17 : 17, 19). The new life "in Christ" is shown as contained for the faithful in the Church, strengthened by the community, facilitated by fraternal association. Hostility to the "world" does not, however, lead to an exclusion of what is outside, or to an attitude of flight from the world. The apostle opposes false conclusions drawn by the Corinthians from an earlier letter of Paul. He explains that he did not mean complete separation from the "fornicators of this world or the swindlers and thieves or idolators"; for otherwise they would of course have to "go out of the world" (1 Cor 5 : 9 f.). John tells us Christ prayed expressly before his departure: "I do not pray for you to take them out of the world, but to preserve them from (the) evil (one)" (Jn 17 : 15). Although the disciples are not of the same kind as the world, he nevertheless sends them into the world (Jn 17 : 16, 18). The Church, therefore, has to realize its eschatologically unworldly attitude in the midst of this world.

In this purely religious perspective which gave its character to paraenesis too, there never really was any confrontation of the Church as a community with an earthly constitution, or even of the local churches as groups in human society, with secular institutions and the various domains of civilized life[33]. The Christians of course had their daily life in society and it became necessary to give them exhortations and rules of conduct for this (cf. the "household codes" and the instructions for associating with pagan fellow-citizens as well as the exhortations to obedience towards the authorities, particularly in the First Epistle of Peter); but modern problems such as Church and State, the Church and civilization, were still remote, if for no other reason than that the churches still hardly represented any real factor in public life. Caution is therefore necessary in drawing conclusions from the negative view taken by the early Church of the "world" in that religious sense in the perspective of sacred history, when dealing with questions regarding the possibility of exercising a formative influence on the world as it exists in modern conditions. Only the reserve expressed in principle in regard to the "world" as a dangerous reality, and eschatological detachment (cf. 1 Cor 7 : 29 f.), should not be forgotten when Christians are urged to more energetic "secular" service.

The world appears in another light when it is regarded as the sum of things, the cosmos; for then the gaze goes right back to the creation and forward in anticipation to the eschatological new creation[34]. All is from God and "through Christ" (1 Cor 8 : 6); God is praised because "from him and through him and for him" all things are (Rom 11 : 36). This is the term, (τὰ) πάντα, preferred to denote all creation, the universe (Jn 1 : 3; Col 1 : 16, 17; Eph 3 : 9; 1 Tim 6 : 13; Heb 1 : 3; 2 : 10; Apoc 4 : 11); but at the end too, at the "restoration of all things" (Acts 3 : 21), "God makes all new" (cf. Apoc 21 : 5), creates a "new heaven and a new earth" (Apoc 21 : 1). This cosmic view remains faithful to the biblical manner of thinking in terms of redemptive history, only its span is wider than the concept of "this world" or "this aeon", and extends from the beginning of creation to its renewal and so it is impossible to forget that the whole world belongs to God, that as created it is good and that it has an eschatological purpose. In the calamitous period of sacred history in which the creation was drawn into the curse of sin and subjected to "vanity", it nevertheless waited in hope for the "revelation of the sons of God" and "groaned in pains also" in order one day to be delivered from the "servitude of corruption into the liberty of the glory of the children of God" (cf. Rom 8 : 19–22)[35]. The world as creation is therefore also implicated in the history of mankind's salvation and perdition and is waiting "even until now" (Rom 8 : 22) for redemption. The question therefore arises how Christ's universal saving action affects the universe and what part the Church has to play.

According to the Epistles to the Colossians and the Ephesians, the disturbed order of the cosmos, its state of contrariety to God, is determined by the fact that the created spiritual "principalities and powers" which under God ought to move and direct the world, have turned themselves in revolt into diabolical rulers[36]. Their might, tyrannical over man too, must be broken, the original order of the universe restored, the rule of God that brings peace and salvation must be renewed and eschatologically accomplished. This process, however, is introduced by Christ's victory on the cross and his exaltation and enthronement at the right hand of God. It will be carried on until the eschatological new creation and will then be concluded when God is "all in all", as is said as early as 1 Corinthians 15 : 28. The statements which because of this picture of the world have a "mythological" ring, regarding the dispossession of the powers hostile to God by the cross of Christ and the triumphal progress of the saviour, "above all the heavens" to the throne of God (cf. Col 2 : 15; Eph 4 : 8–10); his enthronement at the right hand of God "above all principality and power and virtue and dominion" (Eph 1 : 21), so that "all things are subjected under his feet" (so, with reference to Ps 8 : 7 or Ps 110 (109) : 1, a number of times: 1 Cor 15 : 25, 27; Eph 1 : 22; Heb 1 : 13; 2 : 8; 10 : 13; cf. Phil 3 : 21); the "fulfilment" of all things through Christ (Eph 4 : 10), and the "reconciliation" of all things (Col 1 : 20); all simply serve the purpose of describing the subjection of the irreconcilable powers and the bringing in of all creatures capable of redemption and willing to be saved into God's order. In Ephesians 1 : 10 a comprehensive expression is used for the full wealth of this idea: ἀνακεφαλαιώσασθαι τὰ πάντα ἐν τῷ Χριστῷ. In Christ, the cosmos once again becomes an ordered unity subjected to God[37]; in Christ, however, it also receives its head and is subjected to him[38], as it is said in Colossians 1 : 16: "All things were created by him and in him" and also in Colossians 2 : 10: "he is the head of all principality and power". This position as head and ruler was reached by Christ by his exaltation and became an irrevocable fact; yet we still hear of the struggle of the Christians "against principalities and powers, against the rulers of the world of this darkness, against the spirits of wickedness in the high places" (Eph 6 : 12). This struggle concerns men and Christians too as long as they are still in their earthly human existence. The two series of apparently contradictory statements about the subjection by Christ of the powers hostile to God and about their still continuing diabolical activity on earth agree in regard to the position of man in this aeon and reveal his situation in redemptive history. According to their decision for or against Christ, men can either "walk according to the aeon of this world, according to the prince of the (diabolical) power of the air" as "sons of disobedience" (Eph 2 : 2), or allow themselves to be delivered by God's mercy in Christ and obtain the superabundant riches of his grace if they walk in a way appropriate to their redeemed state (cf. Eph 2 : 4–10). In fact, therefore, the "mythological" manner of expression has an anthropological sense even when we firmly maintain the reality of created spiritual beings. "Since the exaltation of Christ Jesus 'above all the heavens' (4 : 10), the question is put to man whether he will decide for the 'rule' of Christ which in itself is 'superior' to 'all the heavens' or for one of the domains of life which these or those powers grant him ... As long as man is on earth, human existence is in dispute and therefore threatened, precisely in its transcendence."[39]

In this way the positive significance of the Church for the world and primarily and chiefly for the world of humanity, is clear. The Church, of course, as has been seen (cf. above, Part Four, § 4), is the Body of Christ, which is filled with the plenitude of his blessings; in it men are no longer helplessly exposed to the preponderant influence of powers hostile to God, the oppressive compulsion of the lower planes of the world, the tendency of a creature away from God. Instead, in the Body of Christ they are received into the divine domain, borne up into the heavenly regions, filled with God's plenitude in Christ and drawn into the process of growth into maturity of the whole Body to the "full measure of the plenitude of Christ". The Church is therefore the place of "deliverance from the world" as well as of "divinization". In the same proportion as it withdraws men from the false enslaving attachment to the empty condition of a creature cut off from God, it leads back to redemptive communion with God and fills men with the riches of divine life. The tendency of the Church operating against the world is in truth a movement raising them into God's order, bringing them back into union with God. In this the Church is the means or instrument of Christ who died "for the life of the world" (cf. Jn 6 : 51) and it accomplishes the will of God who sent his Son into the world not to judge it but to save it through him (cf. Jn 3 : 17).

How does the Church fulfil this task in the world? Above all by the proclamation by which the Church calls men from darkness into light (2 Cor 4 : 3–6) and reveals the hitherto hidden plan of salvation of God, the creator for his world (cf. Eph 3 : 9 f.). The human beings won over by the proclamation, however, are incorporated into the Church itself by baptism and saved in this way from "the power of darkness" and transported into "the kingdom of the beloved Son of God" (cf. Col 1 : 13; Eph 2 : 5 f.). Finally the Church admonishes and teaches every man "in all wisdom" in order to "present every man perfect in Christ Jesus" (Col 1 : 28). But the inner strengthening of its members in faith and love, in unity and concord implies a pushing back of the destructive powers in the world (cf. Eph 4 : 13–16; 5 : 10–12). And so outer and inner growth, missionary activity in the widest sense and the work of building up

183

within the Church, go together, mutually condition and complete one another, and only by their compenetration constitute the true and full way in which the Church takes possession of the world in order to make it the world of God[40]. A purely external mission would be just as false as a mere cultivation of inwardness; one would involve flight into worldly methods and so ultimately back into "this world", the other, flight from the world and from the task for the world.

When the Church remains faithful to its essential function of preaching the gospel, sanctifying its members, unshakable faith and universal love, it fulfils thereby its task in regard to the irreconcilable powers, the men who cannot be converted and the tendencies in the world that are hostile to God. In the language of the Epistle to the Ephesians, "the manifold wisdom of God" is to be "made known to the principalities and powers through the Church" (3 : 10), above all by the proclamation of the "mystery of Christ" (3 : 4–9). By the latter is meant primarily the unity of Jews and gentiles in the Body of Christ, but also reconciliation with God in the cross (cf. 2 : 16), and the victory of Christ over the powers (cf. 1 : 20 ff.). All this is announced by the Church as the previously hidden wisdom of God to the rulers of the world who are hostile to God, and is manifested at the same time by its own appearance. By the Church's drawing of Jews and gentiles into the Body of Christ as well as by its inner growth in strength in the world, and its holiness and unworldliness, its invincibility and indestructibility, it must become for them a sign of God's victory and their own downfall. The same teaching is evident in John's gospel, where it is said that the Paraclete will "convince" (confound, that is, by making plain) the (unbelieving) world (hostile to God) of sin, justice and judgment (Jn 16 : 8–11). The Paraclete will prove to the unteachable and unconvertible world that its unbelief in Christ is sin absolutely as such, but also that by it, it has pronounced judgment on itself, just as the "prince of this world" is already judged (by the cross of Christ, cf. Jn 12 : 31). This activity attributed to the Paraclete, however, takes place in fact through the Church's existence and testimony (cf. Jn 15 : 26 f.), its proclamation of the word and its mission. The Church of the martyrs in the Apocalypse is convinced of this, for even on its road to death it knows it is the stronger and soon to be victorious "through the blood of the Lamb and the word of their (the martyrs') testimony" (12 : 11). This is a mystery of the Church: without the means of earthly power it confounds and overcomes powers hostile to God and their human instruments by its word and its hidden power in the cross of Christ.

Finally, the Church acquires a significance not only for the world of man but also for the cosmos[41]. Since the whole creation was drawn into the curse of sin, yet also awaits and hopes for its "deliverance" together with the "sons of God" (Rom 8 : 29 ff.), it may be assumed from the start in this anthropocentric world-view, that the creation itself also has a share in a certain way in the redemption which has already begun. That is also suggested by the statements about "all things" in the Epistles to the Colossians and the Ephesians which it is difficult to interpret as referring solely to the human world. Christ wills to bring into unity the entire universe, "the things that are in heaven and the things that are on earth" (Eph 1 : 10; cf. Col 1 : 20), and lead them under his rule to God. To be sure as head in the Church he forms his Body, but he is also the "head of every (cosmic) principality and power" (Col 2 : 10), even though it is still disputed whether the world itself is ever regarded as his "body" (cf. Col 2 : 19)[42]. The Church is not indeed identified with the cosmos, but nevertheless acquires a cosmic aspect and a cosmic task: the more the Church as the domain of Christ's grace and as his Body grows in the cosmos, the more Christ bringing deliverance takes possession of the universe. His "filling of all things" (Eph 4 : 10) takes place in a double manner by his dominating

185

and subjecting the powers hostile to God and by building up with abundance of blessings his Body, the Church (Eph 4 : 11–16). Consequently the more he raises the Church up to himself, the more the Church approaches the full measure of his plenitude, the more strongly the universe is drawn into the blessed domain of Christ through the Church. As no other way is recognizable in which Christ causes the universe to share in his redemption, it must be concluded that the Church in addition to its missionary work for men, also fulfils a "mission" for the cosmos. The rest of creation is comprised in the Church's healing and sanctifying action, probably in particular by the sacraments and consecration, exorcisms and prayers, as well as by the right use of things to God's honour by the members of the Church (cf. 1 Tim 4 : 4 f.). The Church's service to men also becomes a service to the world which is given to man as his dwelling-place.

In this way the present world moves into a less gloomy light than when it was still considered as belonging to "this aeon"; it already stands in the first flush of the dawn of the coming aeon, of eschatological completion. Behind this thought which, it is true, is less prominent in the New Testament than the warnings against the dangerous and seductive world, and is implied rather indirectly by the statements regarding creation and all things, it is possible and right to give a more positive sense to the Christians' service of the world, earthly trades and professions, Christian influence on the world in politics, social work, cultural activity etc. The world that surrounds us, in other words the world in its ordinary sense, bears a double character for the Christian on account of his position in sacred history; on the one hand it is the place where the struggle against calamitous powers of sin and death is still taking place, on the other hand it is the creation, never rejected by God, which is to be saved by the powers of Christ's redemption and to be perfected one day in the "new creation" (cf. Apoc 21 : 5). Consequently the Christian will never attain rest in his relations with the world, will never be able one-sidedly to affirm the world and embrace it, but neither can he ever completely deny and reject it. The Church too stands in this situation in the world: turning away from the world in its transitoriness and vanity, yet turned towards the goodness it possesses in virtue of its creation and its eschatological purpose. In both these respects the Church has received a task from Christ: to confront the world in rebellion against God, but to draw the universe aspiring to salvation under Christ the head and under the universal rule of God.

6. Church and kingdom of God

In another study we were led by the idea of God's rule and kingdom to the Church in which God's eschatological rule is realized in a special way[43]. After his exaltation Christ, endowed with all authority in heaven and earth (cf. Mt 28 : 18) takes God's government in his hands and he "must reign until he has brought to nought all principality and power and virtue (hostile to God)" (1 Cor 15 : 24). This rule of Christ, however, is realized with abundant blessings in the Church for all who belong to it by faith and baptism; for it is said of them: "God has delivered us from the power of darkness and translated us into the kingdom of his beloved Son in whom we have redemption, the remission of sins" (Col 1 : 13 f.). At the end of our investigations into New Testament thought regarding the Church, we cannot omit to determine the relation of the Church to the kingdom of God which represents the goal of all God's saving works. From many passages and from many points of view it has become clear that on the one hand the Church is an eschatological reality, on the other that it is still God's pilgrim people, foreign to the earth, the growing house of God in the Spirit and the Body of Christ building itself up and striving to reach its full measure of the plenitude of

Christ. Despite the Church's perfect endowment, it is not yet perfectly completed; although its true home is in heaven it has not yet wholly entered heaven; despite its deliverance from this wicked aeon it is not yet entirely given over to the future aeon. Most light is thrown on this mystery if we think of the coming kingdom of God.

It is not the Church but the kingdom of God which is the ultimate goal of the divine economy of salvation and redemption in its perfect form for the whole world. That is what the great petition which Jesus taught his disciples in the Our Father refers to: Thy kingdom come (Lk 11 : 2; Mt 6 : 9). This kingdom of glory is what is signified by all the metaphors and parables with which Jesus indicated what was to come: the banquet prepared by God or the marriage feast, the abundant fruit, the tree overshadowing the earth etc. Until then, all is in movement and approaching; not, of course, as though we lived merely in expectation; rather is the kingdom of God in a certain way already there, namely as the eschatological rule of God which became present and operative in Jesus' person and work, and perceptible and tangible in his saving powers. It was then realized in a new way as the dominion of the exalted Christ through the mission of the Spirit and found its grace-abounding presence precisely in the Church. But the Church still belongs to the time of growth and maturation, and however much it is filled by the "powers of the aeon to come", it has nevertheless not yet attained the glory of the kingdom of God in its final perfection. If this is forgotten, there is the danger of glorifying the Church in a manner incompatible with much that is said in the New Testament about the Church and for the Church. The Church then becomes an *ecclesiae gloriae* in which all the promises appear to be fulfilled [44] and it is no longer seen that the ultimate promise, the glory of the kingdom of God, is still unfulfilled. Christ willed to present his Church "glorious (ἔνδοξον), without spot or wrinkle or any such thing" (Eph 5 : 27), but that refers to the interior sanctification of the Church which, when viewed in relation to Christ's work and intention (ἵνα), is a perfect one, to the Church's ideal as it were; but that does not exclude defilement in its earthly members. The passage alludes to the sacramental event in baptism (cf. v. 26), and in that we are in fact "raised up together and made to sit together in the heavenly places in Christ Jesus" (Eph 2 : 6), and so attain a share in the glory of Christ; but the preservation of this baptismal glory which certainly provides the basis of and anticipates the future glory, is a charge laid upon us and must prove itself by "walking in good works", even though it is God who has "prepared" these also "beforehand" for us (Eph 2 : 10). The splendour of the Church after the bath of baptism (which perpetually renews it) is in a similar case, therefore, to the Church's unity and holiness (cf. above, Part Three, §§ 4 und 5), which always remains at the same time a never completely accomplished task of the empirical Church and its members. It is not necessary, therefore, to regard the description in Ephesians 5 : 27 as applying to the "Church" in the coming kingdom of God as the later Augustine did, in contrast to his earlier view[45], and from the exegetical point of view that is not permissible[46]; yet it is a testimony to that Father of the Church's instinct for the faith when he remarks: "As the whole (Church) as long as it is here, says, Forgive us our guilt! it is not without spot or wrinkle or thing of that kind; yet by what the Church has received here, it is led to that glory and perfection which is not found here."[47] For the whole concept of the Church, it would be well with Augustine not to lose sight of the difference between the pilgrim Church and its perfection in the kingdom of God.

No less serious than to identify Church and kingdom of God would be to weaken or destroy the relationship of the Church to the future kingdom of God. The Church is not just an *ecclesia crucis* or a negative pointer to the kingdom of glory, which would intervene at the end as something quite new.

189

The Church in this world epoch not only experiences the Passion with its Lord, in order to attain to the resurrection in the kingdom of God; it already stands and works even now under the aegis of his resurrection. The Church shares with its Lord both Passion and glorification, death and resurrection. In its earthly life, the law of death and resurrection together with Christ works out in a way similar to what Paul can say of himself: "We also are weak in him (Christ), but we shall live with him, by the power of God towards you" (2 Cor 13 : 4); that is to say, "weakness" and "strength" of Christ are equally recognizable in the life of the apostle. The same is true of the Church. In many respects it suffers in its members, but there is also the life of the risen Christ in the Church and in very much stronger measure than was evident in the individual case of Paul.

The Church possesses strength and powers which belong to it from the present reign of Christ. Even by its very constitution as Christ established it the Church is endowed with powers which relate directly to the future kingdom of God. When Simon Peter receives the "keys of the kingdom of heaven" (Mt 16 : 19) he is given the function and authority to "open" (cf. Mt 23 : 13) access to the kingdom of God to the candidates for salvation who gather in the Church. If the Church is viewed as the eschatological people of God, then it is possible to express this as follows: Peter "is to lead the people of God into the kingdom of the resurrection"[48]. In order to be able to fulfil that function, that divine authority (ἐξουσία) is needed which Jesus himself exercised during his earthly life and work, and in particular by forgiving sins (cf. Mk 2 : 10 parallels). Consequently it is only logical if the power of binding and loosing is also conferred on Peter and, *mutatis mutandis,* on the other apostles (cf. Mt 18 : 18). What is decisive there is that the human word, the decision made on earth by those to whom his authority is given, is acknowledged by God in heaven and put into effect. The scope of this power extends, as investigation of the expression "binding and loosing" shows[49], fundamentally as far as Jesus' authority on earth extended, and consequently comprises, as well as the vital saving action of forgiving sins (cf. also Jn 20 : 23), authoritative teaching also (Mk 1 : 22, 27) and power over the devils (cf. Mk 3 : 15; 6 : 7). Precisely this last shows the deepest meaning of all Jesus' authority (cf. also Mk 11 : 28 f., 33 parallels): to break the rule of Satan (cf. Lk 11 : 20; Mt 12 : 28) and to establish the reign of God. It became a power of cosmic rule and deliverance, however, through the exaltation and heavenly enthronement of Jesus (cf. Mt 28 : 18) and this power is precisely what Christ wills to exercise through the Church by sending his disciples to all nations in order to call them all to discipleship, to subject them to his rule visibly and fruitfully, by baptism and to preserve them as his followers through the instruction and discipline of his representatives (cf. Mt 28 : 19 f.). Those are profound inner connections between the mission and rule of Christ and the constitution and endowment of his Church. In this way the *ecclesia* becomes the place where after Jesus' departure all must gather who are called for the kingdom of God and the divine institution through which they can reach their goal, in particular by forgiveness of sins and the gift of the Spirit. That is the dignity and joy of the Church, just as it is its shame and grief that not all who are called prove to be worthy and elect (cf. Mt 22 : 11–14 in the perspective in which the evangelist presents it).

Jesus' promise that "the gates of the realm of the dead will not prevail against it" implies, however, that the saving powers and forces of life in the Church are indestructible also because the exalted Lord is with his representatives. Therefore the Church will endure "even to the end of the (present) aeon", that is, until the coming of the kingdom of God in glory. The healings and overcoming of other ills can also be considered signs of the powers of the future aeon already present in the Church and of the life of the resurrection in the midst

191

of the present world still afflicted with suffering and death; they were granted to the disciples "in the name of Jesus" and promised for the future by the risen Christ (cf. Lk 10 : 17, 19; Mk 16 : 17 f.). "It is predicted for the *ecclesia* founded on Peter as the rock that it will indeed stand in the time where death still rules, in the present aeon, therefore, but it will nevertheless already have a share in the power of the resurrection which characterizes the kingdom of God."[50]

The orientation of the Church towards the kingdom of God is most beautifully revealed, however, in the central act of worship, the celebration of the eucharist. Jesus himself gave this meaning to his foundation of the Lord's supper: "Amen I say to you, that (from now on) I shall drink no more of the fruit of the vine until that day when I shall drink it (with you) new in the kingdom of God" (Mk 14 : 25; Mt 26 : 29; cf. Lk 22 : 16, 18, 30a). That is not only an eschatological outlook, but also implies deeper relationship: by his blood Jesus constitutes the new Covenant (cf. Lk 22 : 20; 1 Cor 11 : 25), that is to say, the eschatological order of God's grace for the whole of mankind; only by the universal atoning power of this blood of the Covenant (cf. Mk 14 : 24; Mt 26 : 28) can men share in the kingdom of God. To the new Covenant, however, belongs the eschatological people of God, the Church; it is the society of those who are redeemed by the blood of Jesus and experience the blessings of God's definitive Covenant of salvation of the last days — and in particular in the celebration of the eucharist. This is expressed in the Lucan account of the Last Supper by the fact that here the saving power of the blood shed by Jesus is directly imparted to those sharing in the meal (Lk 22 : 20: "for you"; similarly in the words over the bread, Lk 22 : 19; 1 Cor 11 : 24). And so all who in the congregation celebrate the eucharist with the Church are filled with the powers which make them capable of sharing in the kingdom of God and receive gifts which even by the earthly form of the bread and the wine recall to their minds the fellowship at table in the kingdom of God and at the same time confer on them a real candidature for it. The celebration of the eucharist becomes nothing less than a representation, a ritual anticipation and sacramental preparation for the "eating and drinking at Jesus' table in his kingdom" (cf. Lk 22 : 30a). Paul who in regard to the Corinthians had to put emphasis on commemoration of the Lord's death, nevertheless does not overlook the importance of the eschatological reference of the Lord's supper when he writes: "For as often as you shall eat this bread and drink the chalice of the Lord, you shall shew (you announce) the death of the Lord until he come" (1 Cor 11 : 26). With the expression "you announce", however, he indicates the participation of the Church (here, concretely speaking, the congregation gathered for divine service) in this holy event, in which the Lord is the one who is graciously acting (the "host", cf. 1 Cor 11 : 20 with 10 : 21). "The Lord's supper is the ritual meal of the Church, which knows that it is redeemed by the saving death of its Lord and understands itself to be a society awaiting the return of Christ and its own fulfilment. The congregation of the Lord's supper is itself a 'sign'."[51] It testifies to a vivid consciousness of these relationships in early Christianity that among the eucharistic prayers of the *Didache* the petition is found: "Be mindful, Lord, of your Church, to deliver it from all evil and to perfect it in your love, and gather it together from the four winds, the Church that has been sanctified, into your kingdom which you have prepared for it" (10 : 5).

Finally, therefore, we inquire how the Church will find its fulfilment in the coming kingdom of God. It should be clear from all that has been said that the Church does not simply cease to exist in order to make way for what is more perfect, that its road does not end on the threshold of the kingdom of God, because as an *ecclesia crucis* it has completed its course. But the New Testament does not really continue to use the term "Church" for the throngs of the blessed in the kingdom of God (cf. at most Heb 12 : 23); the concept of the New Testament "Church of God" is reserved for the eschatological interim period between the coming of Christ and his return. It is more the idea of the people of God which extends through all the periods of sacred history from the election of Israel to the "restoration of all things". The word once addressed to Israel: "You shall be kings and priests to me, a holy people" (Exod 19 : 6 — variant reading), is applied in the Apocalypse in the first place to the New Testament people of God (1 : 6; 5 : 10), but then finds its ultimate fulfilment only at the end. Of those who are permitted to share in Christ's "kingdom of a thousand years"[52], it is said that "They will be priests of God and of Christ and reign with him 1,000 years" (20:6), but finally it is said of all who dwell in the new Jerusalem that is to say those who share in the kingdom of God: "His servants shall serve him as priests (λατρεύσουσιν) ... and they shall reign for all eternity" (22:3, 5). The idea of the "holy people" in which all are "priests and kings" has reached its culmination. According to the Epistle to the Hebrews, the "pilgrim people of God" has then reached its destination, entered into the "Sabbath rest"; the worshipping community has followed its high-priest Christ definitively and perfectly into the heavenly sanctuary. The earthly Church is merged in the heavenly community, the "thousands of angels", the "festive assembly and community of the first-born" (Heb 12 : 22 f.) to which it already intrinsically belonged. It is a merging, a being received and raised up into a higher unity.

The same eschatological event is described perhaps even more appropriately by another metaphor, that of the marriage of the Church to her heavenly bridegroom. Paul tells the Corinthians that he has espoused them to one husband in order to present a chaste virgin to Christ (2 Cor 11 : 12). The Church is to preserve itself like a chaste virgin in order to celebrate a marriage with Christ at the Parousia — an old metaphor yet in its concrete application a completely Christian one[53]

194

which vividly expresses not only the eschatological vocation of the Church (for the individual congregation here can again stand as representative of the Church as a whole), but also the fulfilment of the Church's longing and the transition to a new life and the final condition striven for. The same metaphor is again met with in the Apocalypse where the marriage of the "Lamb" with his "wife" is greeted in anticipation in a heavenly song (19 : 7 f.). It does not matter to the seer that (following Old Testament custom in these symbols) he immediately links the metaphor of the bride adorned for her husband (21 : 2; Is 61 : 10) with that of the holy city, the new Jerusalem. And once again it is said: "Come and I will show you the bride, the wife of the Lamb" (21 : 9); but there at once follows the long description of the holy city of Jerusalem "coming down from God in the glory of God" (Apoc 21 : 10 ff.). This exchange of metaphors and also the preference given to that of the holy city, is characteristic and significant. Before the dawn of this new world, the Church has hastened like a bride towards her husband; she was already prepared for the marriage (Apoc 19 : 7; 21 : 2), and now takes the last steps in blissful joy. For the description of the perfect kingdom of God, however, the city of Jerusalem is more appropriate, filled with the radiance of God where the whole creation and particularly elect mankind, finds its place, salvation and blessedness. Yet this elect mankind is none other than holy Church, cleansed of all the unworthy, which has incorporated all those redeemed by the blood of Christ and has reached its destination.

Notes and Bibliography

The following abbreviations are used:

Bib	Biblica
BZ	Biblische Zeitschrift
EvTh	Evangelische Theologie
ExpT	Expository Times
IKZ	Internationale Kirchliche Zeitschrift
JBL	Journal of Biblical Literature
JThS	Journal of Theological Studies
LThK	Lexikon für Theologie und Kirche (Freiburg i. Br., 2nd ed. 1957 ff.)
MThZ	Münchener Theologische Zeitschrift
NTS	New Testament Studies
PL	Patrologia Latina, ed. J. P. Migne (Paris, 1878–90)
RAC	Reallexikon für Antike und Christentum, ed. T. Klauser (Stuttgart, 1941 ff.)
RB	Revue Biblique
RevSR	Revue des Sciences Religieuses
RGG	Die Religion in Geschichte und Gegenwart (Tübingen, 3rd ed. 1956 ff.)
RHPhR	Revue d'Histoire et de Philosophie Religieuses
RScPhTh	Revue des Sciences Philosophiques et Théologiques
RSR	Recherches de science religieuse
StTh	Studia Theologica, cura ordinum theologicorum Scandinavicorum edita (Lund, 1948 ff.)
TThZ	Trierer Theologische Zeitschrift
ThLZ	Theologische Literaturzeitung
ThQ	Theologische Quartalschrift
ThRv	Theologische Revue
ThRdsch	Theologische Rundschau
ThStKr	Theologische Studien und Kritiken
ThW	Theologisches Wörterbuch zum Neuen Testament, ed. G. Kittel — G. Friedrich (Stuttgart, 1933 ff.)
ThZ	Theologische Zeitschrift
TU	Texte und Untersuchungen zur Geschichte der altchristlichen Literatur (Leipzig — Berlin, 1882 ff.)
ZNW	Zeitschrift für die neutestamentliche Wissenschaft
ZThK	Zeitschrift für Theologie und Kirche

Introduction and Part One

[1] The distinction has been made between "church" (local congregation or community) and "Church" (as whole), to correspond to the German "Gemeinde" and "Kirche". In Greek and Hebrew, there is of course only one term for both. On theological grounds the distinction is maintained in the present work, but on the understanding that the relation between the two aspects, in view of the uniformity of the term used, will require elucidation (see Part Two, § 4 above. On linguistic usage in the matter see Part Two, § 1 above.

The almost inexhaustible literature on the subject can be found listed in the particularly full bibliographies of the following works: O. Linton, *Das Problem der Urkirche in der neueren Forschung* (1932); A. Médebielle, "Église" in *Dict. de la Bible*, Suppl. II (1934), 487–691; K. L. Schmidt, "ἐκκλησία" in ThW III (1938), 502–39, English translation "The Church", *Bible Key Words* (1950); N. A. Dahl, *Das Volk Gottes* (1941), 335–46; V. Warnach, "Kirche" in *Bibeltheologisches Wörterbuch*, edited J. B. Bauer (1959), 432–59; K. Stendahl in RGG 3rd ed., III, 1297–304.

[2] On this see K. Rahner, *Inspiration in the Bible*, Quaestiones Disputatae 1, 2nd rev. ed. (1964).

[3] See A. Wikenhauser, *Die Apostelgeschichte und ihr Geschichtswert* (1921); E. Trocmé, *Le "Livre des Actes" et l'histoire* (1957), 154–214; J. Dupont, *The Sources of the Acts* (1964); Dupont discusses the problems that have recently been raised.

[4] Cf. recently from the Catholic point of view: O. Kuss, "Bemerkungen zum Fragenkreis Jesus und die Kirche im NT" in ThQ 135 (1955), 28–55; J. Betz, "Die Gründung der Kirche durch den historischen Jesus" in ThQ 138 (1958), 152–83; A. Vögtle, "Jesus und die Kirche" in *Begegnung der Christen* (O. Karrer-Festschrift) (2nd ed. 1960); R. Schnackenburg, "Kirche" in LThK VI.

[5] Cf. H. Conzelmann, *Die Mitte der Zeit. Studien zur Theologie des Lukas* (3rd ed. 1960), especially 66–86, English translation, *The Theology of Saint Luke* (1960); W. M. C. Robinson, "The Theological Concept for Interpreting Luke's Travel Narration" in JBL 79 (1960), 20–31.

[6] On the problems connected with this, cf. R. Bultmann, *Die Geschichte der synoptischen Tradition* (3rd ed. 1958), 304, English translation, *The History of the Synoptic Tradition* (1963); V. Taylor, *The Gospel according to St Mark* (1952) on the passage; A. Deschamps in Bib 40 (1959), 738 f.

[7] Cf. W. G. Kümmel in ThRdsch 17 (1948–9), 7 (on M. Goguel): "It should be clear, however, that the sources on the contrary show that the appearances of the risen Christ, particularly those to James and Paul, compelled recognition of Jesus' resurrection from men completely unprepared for it, and it is both historically and theologically impossible to evade this fact by asserting in contradiction to the sources, the necessity of a development towards this belief; in this way violence is done to sources."

[8] Cf. E. Schweizer, *Gemeinde und Gemeindeordnung im Neuen Testament* (1959), 30 f.

[9] Cf. R. Schnackenburg, *God's Rule and Kingdom* (1963).

[10] Cf. C. H. Dodd, *The Apostolic Preaching and its Developments* (2nd ed. 1944); J. Schmitt, *Jésus ressuscité dans la prédication apostolique* (1949), 3–36; B. Rigaux, "L'historicité de Jésus devant l'exégèse récente" in RB 65 (1958), 481–522 (bibliography). A different view is given by U. Wilckens, *Die Missionsreden der Apostelgeschichte* (1961).

[11] Cf. Ph.-H. Menoud, "Les additions au groupe des douze apôtres, d'après le Livre des Actes" in RHPhR 37 (1957), 71–80. E. Haenchen, *Die Apostelgeschichte* (3rd ed. 1959), 128–30 stresses the redactional character of the presentation, but traces the concrete indication that Judas had Matthias as a successor by lot, and not Joseph Barsabbas, back to a tradition.

[12] On the Twelve, cf. J. Gewiess, "Die neutestamentlichen Grundlagen der kirchlichen Hierarchie" in *Zwischen Wissenschaft und Politik* (Festschrift für G. Schreiber) (1953), 1—24 and particularly 2–8; B. Rigaux, "Die 'Zwölf' in Geschichte und Kerygma" in *Der historische Jesus und der kerygmatische Christus* (collective work) (1960), 468–86.

[13] A few earlier hypotheses are dealt with by W. G. Kümmel in ThRdsch 17 (1948–9) 16 f., 22–26; the commentary of E. Haenchen on Acts; and E. Käsemann, "Die Anfänge urchristlicher Theologie" in ZThK (1960), 162—85.

[14] Cf. N. Adler, *Das erste christliche Pfingstfest* (1938); E. Lohse, "Die Bedeutung des Pfingstfestes im Rahmen des lukanischen Geschichtswerkes" in EvTh 13 (1953), 422–36; the same author in ThW VI, 50–52; E. Haenchen, *op. cit.* 135–9; A. Wikenhauser, *Die Apostelgeschichte* (3rd ed. 1956), 38–41.

[15] Cf. R. Schnackenburg, "Die 'Anbetung in Geist und Wahrheit' (Jn 4 : 23) im Lichte von Qumrân-Texten" in BZ N. F. 3 (1959), 88–94. On the meaning of "Spirit" cf. above Part Three, § 2, and Part Four, § 3.

[16] Cf. H. Zimmermann, "Die Sammelberichte der Apostelgeschichte" in BZ N. F. 5 (1961), 71–82 (with a discussion of the previous literature).

[17] On the concept of apostle, cf. among others E. Lohse, "Ursprung und Prägung des christlichen Apostolates" in ThZ 9 (1953), 259–75; J. Dupont, Le nom d'apôtres a-t-il été donné aux Douze par Jésus? (1956); E. M. Kredel, "Der Apostelbegriff in der neueren Exegese" in ZKTh 78 (1956), 169–93, 257–305; L. Cerfaux, "Pour l'histoire du titre Apostolos dans le NT" in RSR 48 (1960), 76–92; G. Klein, Die zwölf Apostel (1961), expresses radical theses.

[18] Cf. Ph.-H. Menoud, "Les Actes des Apôtres et L'Eucharistie" in RHPhR 33 (1953), 21–36; J. Gewiess, "Brotbrechen" in LThK II, 706 (with bibliography). See also note 76 below.

[19] Cf. P. Neuenzeit, Das Herrenmahl. Studien zur paulinischen Eucharistieauffassung (160), 69–76; H. Schürmann, "Eucharistiefeier" in LThK III, 1159–62 (with bibliography).

[20] Cf. as well as the commentaries, M. Simon, St Stephen and the Hellenists in the Primitive Church (1958); J. Bihler, Die Stephanusgeschichte im Zusammenhang der Apostelgeschichte (unpublished dissertation, Munich 1957); A. F. J. Klijn, "Stephen's Speech — Acts 7 : 2–53" in NTS 4 (1957–8), 25–31; P. Geoltrain, "Esséniens et Hellénistes" in ThZ 15 (1959), 241–54.

[21] Cf. H. Zimmermann, op. cit. note 16 above; S. E. Johnson, "The Dead Sea Manual of Discipline and the Jerusalem Church of Acts" in The Scrolls and the New Testament, edited by K. Stendahl (1957), 129–42, particularly 131 f.

[22] Cf. note 88 below.

[23] Cf. J. Dupont, Les problèmes du livre des Actes d'après les travaux récents (1950), 51—70; E. Haenchen, op. cit. 396–414; also P. Benoit, "La deuxième visite de s. Paul à Jérusalem" in Bib 40 (1959), 778–92.

[24] According to E. Peterson, "Christianus" in Frühkirche, Judentum und Gnosis (1959), 64–87, the name was officially given to the adherents of Christ by the Romans, and that as a group with messianic tendencies, separate from the Jews and without citizen rights (75). Against this, E. Haenchen, op. cit. 312.

[25] So among others, J. Kürzinger, Die Apostelgeschichte (1951); J. Dupont, Les Actes des Apôtres (Bible de Jérusalem) (2nd ed. 1958) on the passage. On the significance of the mission with imposition of hands, cf. D. Daube, The New Testament and Rabbinic Judaism (1956), 239 f.; E. Best, "Acts 13 : 1–3" in JThS 11 (1960), 344–8 (deliberate undertaking of the mission to the gentiles).

[26] On the Seven, cf. P. Gaechter, "Die Sieben (Apg 6 : 1–6)" in ZKTh 74 (1952), 129–66; H. Zimmermann, "Die Wahl der Sieben (Apg 6 : 1–6), ihre Bedeutung für die Wahrung der Einheit in der Kirche" in *Die Kirche und ihre Ämter und Stände* (Festgabe für Kardinal Frings) (1960), 364–78; also the literature listed in note 20 above.

[27] On Peter's pre-eminence in Acts, cf. 1 : 15, 2 : 14 and his other discourses; also 5 : 1–11; 8 : 20–23; 9 : 32–43; 10–11; 12 : 3–17. The following indications from the Pauline letters are important: 1 Cor 15 :5 first appearance of the risen Christ; 1 Cor 9 : 5 missionary; Gal 1 : 18; 2 : 9 position in Jerusalem; Gal 2 : 11–14 prestige in Antioch; 1 Cor 1 : 12; 3 : 22 a Cephas group in Corinth. On the meaning of the name Cephas (which Paul always uses, except in Gal 2 : 7 f.), cf. J. Schmidt, "Petrus 'der Fels' und die Petrusgestalt der Urgemeinde" in *Begegnung der Christen* (O. Karrer-Festschrift) (2nd ed. 1960), 347–59; J. Betz, "Christus — Petra — Petrus" in *Kirche und Überlieferung* (J.-R. Geiselmann-Festschrift) (1960), 1–21.

[28] The literature on the question of the Petrine primacy has swollen, particularly since O. Cullmann's book *Petrus, Jünger — Apostel — Märtyrer* (2nd rev. ed. 1960), English translation, *Peter — Disciple, Apostle, Martyr,* (2nd rev. ed. 1962). For a Catholic viewpoint, cf. among others O. Karrer, *Peter and the Church. An Examination of Cullmann's Thesis* (Quaestiones Disputatae 8) (1963), as well as the Festschrift dedicated to O. Karrer (previous note). Some new and not always convincing points of view are put forward in the studies of P. Gaechter, *Petrus und seine Zeit* (1958). A full account of Protestant scholarship is available in E. Dinkler, "Die Petrus-Rom-Frage" in ThRdsch 25 (1959), 189–230 (and 289–335 on the archaeological findings).

[29] R. Sohm, *Kirchenrecht I. Die geschichtlichen Grundlagen* (1892); cf. by the same author, *Wesen und Ursprung des Katholizismus* (2nd ed. 1912).

[30] H. von Campenhausen, *Kirchliches Amt und geistliche Vollmacht in den ersten drei Jahrhunderten* (1953), 69.

[31] Ibid. 71.   [32] E. Schweizer, *op. cit.* 186.

[33] Cf. P. Vielhauer, *Oikodome* (dissertation, Heidelberg 1939); O. Michel, "οἰκοδομέο" in ThW V, 142–5.

[34] Cf. H. Schürmann, *Der Abendmahlsbericht Lukas 22 : 7–38 als Gottesdienstordnung, Gemeindeordnung, Lebensordnung* (3rd. ed. 1960); also W. Trilling, *Hausordnung Gottes. Eine Auslegung von Matthäus 18* (1960).

[35] Cf. on this O. Linton, *Das Problem der Urkirche in der neueren Forschung* (1932), 36 ff.

[36] Cf. J. Brosch, *Charismen und Ämter in der Urkirche* (1951); E. Lohse, *Die Ordination im Spätjudentum und im Neuen Testament* (1951), 82 ff.; J. Gewiess, "Charisma" in LThK II, 1025–7; cf. also K. Rahner, "Das Charismatische in der Kirche" in LThK II, 1027–30.

[37] K. Holl, "Der Kirchenbegriff des Paulus in seinem Verhältnis zu dem der Urgemeinde" in *Gesammelte Aufsätze zur Kirchengeschichte* II (1928), 44—67. Holl's influence is perceptible in M. Goguel, *The Primitive Church* (1964), 37–64.

[38] Cf. W. Mundle, "Das Kirchenbewußtsein der ältesten Christenheit" in ZNW 22 (1923), 20–42; C. Michel, *Das Zeugnis des Neuen Testamentes von der Gemeinde* (1941), 31–33; E. Schweizer, *op. cit.* 43.

[39] Cf. however J. Munck, *Paulus und die Heilsgeschichte* (1954), particularly 61–78, 277–302; P. Gaechter, *Petrus und seine Zeit*, 155–212; 213–257; (the "limits to the apostolate of Paul" affirmed in the last section 338–450, do not however, according to the view held by most Catholic scholars, do justice to Paul's special vocation).

[40] H. von Campenhausen, *op cit.* 50.

[41] On Paul's ἐξουσία, cf. W. Foerster in ThW II, 567; O. Schmidt, ThW, V, 762: "For that matter, however, his instructions even in the question of women covering their heads at divine service have very definitely the character of authoritative apostolic precepts, with his full power conferred by Christ behind them."

[42] W. Doskocil, *Der Bann in der Urkirche* (1958), 64. (Cf. 64–67.)

[43] On the exegesis of this passage, cf. B. Rigaux, *S. Paul, Les Epîtres aux Thessaloniens* (1956), 499 f.

[44] Cf. A. von Harnack in ZNW 27 (1928), 7–10; A. Wikenhauser, *Die Kirche als der mystische Leib Christi nach dem Apostel Paulus* (2nd ed. 1940), 78 f.; B. Rigaux, *op. cit.* on the passage.

[45] Cf. H. Schlier, "Die Ordnung der Kirche nach den Pastoralbriefen" in *Die Zeit der Kirche* (1956); and also above Part Two, § 6.

[46] Cf. W. Mansion, *The Sayings of Jesus* (1949), 77 f. He would like to trace this back to the Aramaic *qabbel* which can mean both "accept" and "hear" (in the sense of "obey"). He interprets: "The disciple represents in the fullest sense Jesus, and Jesus represents in the fullest sense the Kingdom of God."

[47] Cf. J. Dupont, *Le nom d'Apôtres a-t-il été donné aux Douze par Jésus?* (1956).

[48] E. Schweizer, *op. cit.* 25.

⁴⁹ Cf. R. Schnackenburg, *God's Rule and Kingdom*, 225–34; A. Vögtle, "Jesus und die Kirche" (cf. note 4 above), 71 f.; B. Rigaux, "Die Zwölf in Geschichte und Kerygma" (see note 12 above), 475 f.

⁵⁰ Cf. J. Schmid, *Das Evangelium nach Matthäus* (3rd ed. 1956), on the passage; J. Jeremias in ThW III, 751.

⁵¹ Cf. A. Vögtle in LThK II, 480–2.

⁵² H. von Campenhausen, *op. cit.* 139.

⁵³ Cf. R. Schnackenburg, "Episkopus und Hirtenamt" in *Episcopus* (Festschrift für Kard. von Faulhaber [1949]), 66–88; on the further development of offices cf. J. Gewiess, *op. cit.* (note 12 above); and also M. Kaiser, *Die Einheit der Kirchengewalt nach dem Zeugnis des Testamentes und der Apostolischen Väter* (Munich 1956).

⁵⁴ Cf. A. Wikenhauser, *op. cit.* 77–81; 174 f.; H. Schlier, *Der Brief an die Epheser* (1947) observes on Eph 4 : 11 that the choice took place "in view of the sacred history of the emerging Church which already could be looked back over", 196.

⁵⁵ Cf. W. Nauck, "Probleme des frühchristlichen Amtsverständnisses (1 Petr 5 : 2 f.)" in ZNW 48 (1947), 200–20.

⁵⁶ Cf. the two articles of J. Schmid and J. Betz listed in note 27 above.

⁵⁷ Cf. P. Gaechter, "Das dreifache 'Weide meine Lämmer!'" in *Petrus und seine Zeit*, 11–30.

⁵⁸ Cf. E. Hirsch, "Petrus und Paulus" in ZNW 29 (1930), 63–76; J. Munck, *op. cit.* in note 39 above; O. Cullmann, *Petrus* (see above, note 28), 72–77.

⁵⁹ O. Cullmann, *op. cit.* 32 f., 44 f., 246–55.

⁶⁰ Cf. note 28 above.

⁶¹ Cf. R. Schnackenburg, *God's Rule and Kingdom*, 259–70.

⁶² G. Friedrich in ThW II, 717, 35 f.

⁶³ For a critique of present-day "Kerygma Theology", cf. P. Althaus, *Das sogenannte Kerygma und der historische Jesus* (Gütersloh 1958). H. Schürmann, "Kerygma" in LThK VI, 122–6.

⁶⁴ Cf. H. Schlier, "Die Verkündigung im Gottesdienst der Kirche" in *Die Zeit der Kirche*, 244–64; also the collection of articles *Im Dienst des Wortes* (1959).

⁶⁵ Cf. H. Schlier, *Worte Gottes. Eine neutestamentliche Besinnung* (1958).

⁶⁶ The thesis has several times been propounded that the four expressions used in Acts 2 : 42 describe the course of an early Christian divine service; cf. O. Cullmann, *Urchristentum und Gottesdienst* (2nd ed. 1950), 16 and 31, English translation, *Early Christian Worship,* and in particular J. Jeremias, *Die Abendmahls-*

worte Jesu (3rd ed. 1960), 111-14, English translation, *The Eucharistic Words of Jesus* (1955). Different views are expressed by G. Delling, *Der Gottesdienst im Neuen Testament* (1952), 124; H. Zimmermann in BZ N. F. 5 (1061), 75 f.

[67] Cf. K. Rengstorf in ThW II, 147–9.

[68] Cf. G. Delling, *op. cit.* (note 66 above), 89–91.

[69] Cf. H. Dodd, *According to the Scriptures* (1952); R. V. G. Tasker, *The Old Testament in the New Testament* (2nd ed. 1954); C. Smits, *Oudtestamentische Citaten in het Nieuwe Testament,* three volumes (1952–7); K. Stendahl, *The School of St Matthew* (1954).

[70] For more detailed exposition, cf. as well as the Commentators, H. Schlier in *Die Zeit der Kirche,* 258–64.

[71] So E. Käsemann, "Sätze Heiligen Rechtes im Neuen Testament" in NTS 1 (1954–5), 248–60, in particular 256–8; P. Vielhauer in *Festschrift für G. Dehn* (1957), 59 f.; E. Käsemann in ZThK 57 (1960), 170 ff., 176 ff.

[72] Contrary to A. Kragerud, *Der Lieblingsjünger im Johannesevangelium* (1959), *passim;* on this cf. R. Schnackenburg in BZ 4 (1960), 306.

[73] Many scholars would like to suppose there were Essene priests among them; cf. J. Daniélou, *Les Manuscrits de la Mer Morte et les Origines du Christianisme* (1957); less decidedly K. Schubert, *Die Gemeinde vom Toten Meer* (1958), 130; against it, E. Haenchen, *op. cit.* 222.

[74] Cf. H. Schürmann, *der Paschamahlbericht Lk 22 (7–14), 15–18,* (1953).

[75] Cf. H. Schürmann, "Die Anfänge christlicher Osterfeier" in ThQ 131 (1951), 414–25; J. Jeremias in ThW V, 900–3.

[76] Cf. above note 18. In the case of Luke 24 : 35 a reference to the eucharist is often assumed now; cf. J. Dupont, "Les Pèlerins D'Emmaüs" in *Misc. Bibl. B. Ubach* (Montserrat 1953), 349–74, especially 362–4; J. Jeremias, *Die Abendmahlsworte Jesu op. cit.* 113 f. note 4.

[77] Cf. J. Gnilka, "Das Gemeinschaftsmahl der Essener" in BZ N. F. 5 (1951), 39–55 (with bibliography).

[78] Cf. E. Schweizer in RGG 2nd ed., I, 10; P. Neuenzeit, *op. cit.* (cf. note 19 above) 220 f.

[79] Cf. H. Schlier, *Der Brief an die Epheser* (1957) on Eph 5 : 18 ff., in particular, page 248.

[80] Cf. H. Schürmann, "Abendmahl" in LThK I, 26–31, especially 29 f.

[81] Cf. K. G. Kuhn in ThW IV, 470–5.

[82] Cf. G. Bornkamm, "Das Anathema in der urkirchlichen Abendmahlsliturgie" in ThLZ 75 (1950), 227–31; J. A. T. Robinson, "Traces of a Liturgical Sequence in 1 Cor 16 : 20–24" in JThS 4 (1953), 38–41; a different view in C. F. D. Moule, "A Reconsideration of the Context of Maranatha" in NTS 6 (1959–60), 307–10 (The Maranatha belongs, he thinks, to the anathema).

[83] Cf. W. C. van Unnik, "Reisepläne und Amen-Sagen" in *Studia Paulina in honorem J. de Zwaan* (1953), 215–34.

[84] Cf. P. Neuenzeit, *op. cit.* (note 19), 175–83.

[85] So L. Cerfaux, *The Church in the Theology of Saint Paul* (1959), 95–114.

[86] Cf. R. Asting, *Die Heiligkeit im Urchristentum* (1930), 133–89, brings the expression into connection with the "holy assembly" (Exod 12 : 16 etc.), and observes, "It is clear that the expression designates the community of Israel just as it gathered on the Sabbath and on festivals for divine service" (p. 142). L. Cerfaux, *op. cit.* 118–45, would prefer to limit the title more strictly to the "authorities" in Jerusalem (apostles and other original disciples). Of late, comparison has been made in particular with the expression used by the Essenes of Qumran to describe themselves; cf. on this H. Kosmala, *Hebräer — Essener — Christen* (1959), 50–62; P. Nötscher in *Revue de Qumran 2* (1960), 326–32. See above, Part Two, § 1.

[87] Cf. on this, Part Four, § 4 above.

[88] E. Haenchen, *op. cit.* 218–22, considers that the "Hellenists" formed a community of their own under the direction of the Seven and that the "Hebrews" had presumably no objection to this (p. 222). Cf. on this H. Zimmermann's work listed in note 26 above.

[89] Cf. among others J. Gewiess, *Die urapostolische Heilsverkündigung nach der Apostelgeschichte* (1939), 116–32; W. F. Flemington, The New Testament Doctrine of Baptism (1948), especially 43 f.; O. Cullmann, *Die Tauflehre des Neuen Testamentes* (1948), English translation, *Baptism in the New Testament* (1951); F. J. Leenhardt, *Le baptême chrétien, son origine, sa signification* (1946); J. Schneider, *Die Taufe im Neuen Testament* (1952); 28 ff.; J. Jeremias, *Die Kindertaufe in den ersten vier Jahrhunderten* (1958) with bibliography, English translation *Infant Baptism in the First Four Centuries* (1960).

[90] Cf. N. Adler, *Taufe und Handauflegung* (1951), particularly 93–97. He seeks to explain the contrast between reception of the Spirit and baptism in the Acts of the Apostles by assuming that "by the Holy Spirit not only the gift of justification and sanctifi-

cation but his fullness ... the gift of the Holy Spirit κατ' ἐξοχήν" is to be understood (p. 195). Cf. also J. E. L. Oulton in ExpT 66 (1954–5), 236–40.

[91] Cf. O. Cullmann, *op. cit.* (in note 89 above), 7; J. Schneider, *op. cit.* (note 89 above), 29; R. Bultmann, *Theology of the New Testament*, I (1952), 40 ("eschatological sacrament which made one a member of the holy Congregation of the end of days").

[92] Cf. J. Leipoldt, *Die urchristliche Taufe im Lichte der Religionsgeschichte* (1928); E. Stauffer, *New Testament Theology* (cheap ed. 1963), 160: "How this Christian practice of baptism originated is a puzzle that only begins to be solved if we come at last once more to conclude that the tradition of the risen Lord giving a missionary charge is to be taken seriously"; J. Schneider, *op. cit.* in the same sense; N. A. Dahl, "The Origin of Baptism" in *Festschrift S. Mowinckel* (1955), 33–52 with bibliography; J. Jeremias, *op. cit.* (note 89), 34–44 (derives from baptism of proselytes).

[93] Cf. R. Schnackenburg, *Das Heilsgeschehen bei der Taufe nach dem Apostel Paulus* (1950); O. Kuss, *Der Römerbrief, Erste Lieferung* (1957), 307–19.

[94] Cf. J. Dey, Παλιγγενεσία (1937); R. Schnackenburg, *op. cit.* (previous note), 132–9.

[95] Cf. also "Le Baptême dans le Nouveau Testament" (various authors) in *Lumière et Vie* 26 and 27 (1956); on John, R. Schnakkenburg, "Die Sakramente im Johannesevangelium" in *Sacra Pagina* II (1959), 235–54.

[96] Cf. O. Cullmann, *Petrus*, 2nd ed. 45–62, English translation, *Peter, Disciple, Apostle and Martyr* (1953).

[97] G. Schille in NTS 4 (1957–8), 20.

[98] Cf. also W. Trilling, *Das wahre Israel. Studien zur Theologie des Matthäusevangeliums* (1959), 101–6.

[99] Cf. J. Jeremias, *Jesu Verheissung für die Völker* (1956), 16–33, English translation, *Jesus' Promise to the Nations* (Studies in Biblical Theology 24 [1958]); D. Bosch, *Die Heidenmission in der Zukunftschau Jesu* (1959), 84–86; W. Trilling, *op. cit.* 78–84.

[100] Cf. J. Jeremias' view (*op. cit.* previous note, 47–62), that in Jesus' perspective the gentiles would stream in at the end; on this the observations of A. Vögtle in BZ N. F. 3 (1959), 149–52; on the mission to the gentiles generally R. Liechtenhan, *Die urchristliche Mission* (1946); D. Bosch, *op. cit.* gives further bibliography; M. Meinertz "Zum Ursprung der Heidenmission" in Bib 40 (1959), 762–77; E. Neuhäusler in LThK V, 69–71.

[101] That is contested by E. Haenchen, *op. cit.* 314 f. He assumes

that Barnabas belonged more likely to "Stephen's Community". But is the existence of such an independent community (and its rivalry with the Twelve) really well-founded? Was not Barnabas in reality (not only in Luke's view) very likely an intermediary?

[102] H. Schlier in *Die Zeit der Kirche* (1956), 94. Cf. the whole essay, "Die Entscheidung für die Heidenmission in der Urchristenheit" (90–107).

[103] Cf. J. Gnilka, *Die Verstockung Israels. Isaias 6 : 9–10 in der Theologie der Synoptiker* (1961).

[104] Cf. W. Trilling, *op. cit.* 12–14.

[105] Cf. W. Bauer, *Griechisch-deutsches Wörterbuch zu den Schriften des Neuen Testaments und der übrigen urchristlichen Literatur* (5th ed. 1958), 1772 s. v. I.

[106] Cf. the missionary principle Rom 15 :20; but elsewhere too Paul acknowledges fellow-workers in the gospel, cf. 1 Thess 3 : 2; 1 Cor 3 : 5–15; 2 Cor 8 : 23; Phil 1 : 15–28; 2 : 22, 25; Col 4 : 11.

[107] As well as the commentators cf. F. W. Maier, *Israel in der Heilsgeschichte nach Rom 9–11* (1929), 138–50; H. M. Matter, "Aldus zal geheel Israel behouden worden" in *Arcana revelata*, Festschrift für F. W. Grosheide (1951), 59–68; J. Munck, *Christus und Israel. Eine Auslegung von Röm 9–11* (1956), 99–103; E. Dinkler, "Prädestination bei Paulus" in *Festschrift für G. Dehn* (1957), 81–102, especially 87–91, 96 f.; H. Schlier, "Das Mysterium Israels" in *Die Zeit der Kirche*, 232–44.

[108] Cf. H. Schlier, *Der Brief an die Epheser*, Excursus 159–66.

Part Two

[1] This is made clear by the work of E. Schweizer, *Gemeinde und Gemeindeordnung im Neuen Testament* (1959), which follows the "manifold character of the New Testament community" right down into the sub-apostolic age, but can only trace certain lines of development.

[2] Cf. E. Haenchen, *Die Apostelgeschichte* (3rd ed. 1959), 72–80; J. Dupont, *The Sources of the Acts* (1964); E. Grässer, "Die Apostelgeschichte in der Forschung der Gegenwart" in ThR 26 (1960), 93–167, especially 103 f., 115 f. (on E. Trocmé), 123–30.

[3] Cf. L. Cerfaux, *The Church in the Theology of Saint Paul* (1959), 95–114; see also above, Part Four, § 1 b.

[4] Cf. W. Michaelis in ThW V, 93 ff.

[5] Cf. O. Betz, "Felsenmann und Felsengemeinde" in ZNW 48 (1957), 49–77.

[6] Cf. K. L. Schmidt, in ThW III, 531, English translation, *The Church (Bible Key Words)* (1950).

[7] On the idea of the "people of God" cf. above, Part Two, §§ 3 and 4; Part Four, § 2.

[8] Cf. K. L. Schmidt in ThW III, 529, 20 f. and those named in note 80 there; English translation, *The Church (Bible Key Words)* (1950).

[9] Cf. O. Betz, *op. cit.* 57 f.

[10] Cf. H. Kosmala, *Hebräer — Essener — Christen* (1959), 63 ff. He says, "Despite all other attempts at explanation, there can be no doubt that the basis of the New Testament expression the *ecclesia* is to be found in the Essene term '*edah* and not in the word *qahal*" (65).

[11] H. Kosmala, *op. cit.* 65, thinks "that the first Christian communities had an inner kinship with them (the Essene Communities) and to a large extent grew on their basis."

[12] So to some extent J. Schmitt too, "L'Église de Jérusalem ou la 'Restauration' d'Israël d'après Actes 1–5" in RevSR 27 (1953), 209–18 (traditions from Deuteronomy).

[13] In that case, however, it would be remarkable that the Greek-speaking Christians did not choose the word that is by far the most frequently used for it in the Septuagint, συναγωγή (about 130 times). The reasons adduced by H. Kosmala (*op. cit.* 67 f.), are not convincing. The profoundest reason must after all have been that the Christians gave quite a new content to their ἐκκλησία Cf. also N. A. Dahl, *Das Volk Gottes* (1941), 8–11, 62–67, 164–6. K. Sten-

dahl in RGG III, 1298 concludes from linguistic observations, including ones made on the Qumran texts, "that the original community by the term ἐκκλησία consciously made the claim to be the true people of God."

[14] Cf. A. Vögtle, *Das öffentliche Wirken Jesu auf dem Hintergrund der Qumranbewegung* (1958).

[15] Cf. R. Schnackenburg, *God's Rule and Kingdom* (1963), 225–34; and also above, Part Four, § 6.

[16] Cf. J. Dupont, "Repentir et conversion d'après les Actes des Apôtres" in Sciences Ecclésiastiques (Montreal) 12 (1960), 137–73.

[17] H. Kosmala, *op. cit.* 65 f.

[18] *Op. cit.* 30.

[19] Cf. N. A. Dahl, "A People for His Name Acts (15, 14)" in NTS 4 (1957–8), 319–27.

[20] Cf. Conzelmann, *Die Mitte der Zeit. Studien zur Theologie des Lukas* (3rd ed. 1960), 89–127, English translation, *The Theology of St. Luke* (1960); E. Grässer, *Das Problem der Parousieverzögerung in den synoptischen Evangelien und in der Apostelgeschichte* (1957), 178–98; also J. Schmid, *Das Evangelium nach Lukas* (3rd ed. 1955) on Luke 21 (especially 301–3).

[21] E. Schweizer, *op. cit.* 60.

[22] E. Lohse, "Lukas als Theologe der Heilsgeschichte" in EvTh (1954), 256–75, and here, 266.

[23] *Op. cit.* 9 f.; this thesis is then developed in particular on pages 128–57.

[24] Cf. J. Gnilka, *Die Verstockung Israels. Isaias 6, 9–10 in der Theologie der Synoptiker* (1961).

[25] Cf. H. Schürmann, *Jesu Abschiedsrede Lk 22, 21–28* (1957); *Der Abendmahlsbericht Lukas 22, 7–38 als Gottesdienstordnung, Lebensordnung* (3rd ed. 1960).

[26] Cf. W. Foerster, "Lukas 22 : 31 f." in ZNW 46 (1955), 129–33.

[27] The "temptations" cannot be taken as referring to the Passion of Jesus now beginning or to the disciples' period of need and struggle which it implies, even in the view of the evangelist (as against Conzelmann, *op. cit.* 73 f.).

[28] H. Schürmann, *Der Abendmahlsbericht* (see above, note 25), 70.

[29] The attempt of P. Nepper-Christensen, *Das Matthäusevangelium ein judenchristliches Evangelium?* (1958), is on the whole not convincing. Cf. on the other hand G. D. Kilpatrick, *The Origin of the Gospel According to Saint Matthew* (1964), particularly 101–23.

[30] W. Trilling, *Das wahre Israel. Studien zur Theologie des Mat-*

thäusevangeliums (1959), 200: "If it is assumed, in accordance with the common opinion, that the readers in mind were Jewish Christians, this would only have to be understood in a restricted sense, for it can only have been a question here of a completely 'purified' Judeo-Christianity without any national or particularist alloy."

[31] On Matthew 23 cf. E. Haenchen, "Matthäus 23" in ZThK 48 (1951), 38–63. He says among other things, "The judgment of Matthew on the rabbis and Pharisaism draws no distinctions, has no shades, no exceptions. The opponents are one *massa perditionis*... The Jews are seen only as fanatical adversaries with whom friendly discussion is no longer possible and consequently no longer sought" (59).

[32] Hence the title of Trilling's work; on the picture of the Churc 1, cf. 101–37 in it.

[33] Cf. on Matthew 5 : 17–20, J. Dupont, *Les Béatitudes*, I, 2nd ed. (1958), 130–45 (with an abundant bibliography); W. Trilling, *op. cit.* 138–59.

[34] So W. Grundmann, "Die Arbeit des ersten Evangelisten am Bilde Jesu" in *Christentum und Judentum* (1940), 53–78, especially 63; cf. W. Trilling, *op. cit.* 117 f.

[35] Cf. J. Schmid, *Das Evangelium nach Matthäus* (3rd ed. 1956), 180: "The situation of the mission of the disciples is consequently abandoned here (from v. 17), and we have in this part of the Matthew discourse (and in the following verses up to v. 39) no longer a missionary discourse, but instruction of the disciples."

[36] Cf. E. Lohmeyer, *Das Evangelium des Matthäus*, edited by W. Schmauch (1956), 412–26; W. Trilling, *op. cit.* 6–36.

[37] Cf. I. Daumoser, *Berufung und Erwählung bei den Synoptikern* (1954), 186–212; for the redactional history, cf. W. Trilling, "Zur Überlieferungsgeschichte des Gleichnisses vom Hochzeitsmahl, Mt. 22, 1–14" in BZ N. F. 4 (1960), 251–65.

[38] Cf. also J. Jeremias in ThW IV, 751.

[39] Cf. G. Lindeskog, "Logia-Studien" in StTh 4 (1950), 129–89, especially 171–7.

[40] W. Trilling, *op. cit.* 86.

[41] Cf. the sources quoted in P. Billerbeck, *Kommentar zum Neuen Testament aus Talmud und Midrasch* (1922), I, 794 f.

[42] Cf. the monographs of A. Wikenhauser, *Die Kirche als der mystische Leib Christi nach dem Apostel Paulus* (2nd ed. 1940), and L. Cerfaux, *The Church in the Theology of Saint Paul* (1959), 95–114.

43 Cf. the works listed in note 107 of Part One, above; and also E. Peterson, *Die Kirche aus Juden und Heiden* (1933); K. L. Schmidt, *Die Judenfrage im Lichte der Kapitel 9–11 des Römerbriefes* (2nd nd. 1947); G. Schrenk, *Die Weissagung über Israel im Neuen Testament* (1951), 25 ff.; H. J. Schoeps, *Paulus* (1959), 248–59, English translation, *Paul. The Theology of the Apostle in the Light of Jewish Religious History* (1961).

44 Those who preferred the application of this to the Jewish Christians included T. Zahn, *Der Brief des Paulus an die Galater* (3rd ed. 1922), on the passage; E. de Witt Burton, *A Critical and Exegetical Commentary on the Epistle to the Galatians* (1921). Those favouring its application to the old people of God, Israel: G. Schrenke, "Was bedeutet Israel Gott?" in *Judaica* 5 (1949), 81–94; "Der Segenswunsch nach der Kampfepistel" in *Judaica* 6 (1950), 170–90; against this N. A. Dahl, "Zur Auslegung von Gal 6, 16" in *Judaica* 6 (1950), 161–70.

45 H. Schlier, *Der Brief an die Galater* (1949) on the passage (209).

46 Cf. A. von Harnack, *Die Mission und Ausbreitung des Christentums in den ersten drei Jahrhunderten* (4th ed. 1924), 259–67, 281–9; English translation, *The Expansion of Christianity in the First Three Centuries* (1904–5, 2 vols.).

47 Cf. H. Strathmann in ThW VI 535.

48 Cf. E. Schweizer, *op. cit.* 99.

49 On the question of the authorship, cf. A. Wikenhauser, *Introduction to the New Testament* (1963), 501–6; W. Michaelis, *Einleitung in das Neue Testament* (2nd ed. 1954), 285 ff.; J. Cantinat in *Introduction à la Bible*, sous la direction de A. Robert et A. Feuillet, II (Nouveau Testament) (1959), 583–6 (Silvanus as secretary).

50 Cf. J. Blinzler, 'Ιεράτευμα. Zur Exegese von 1 Petr 2, 5 und 9" in *Episcopus* (Festschrift für M. Kard. Faulhaber) (1949), 49–65.

51 Cf. T. Spörri, *Der Gemeindegedanke im ersten Petrusbrief* (1925), 218, "For him (the author) Christ represents the comprehensive basis and single and decisive beginning and ground, the only sociological point of reference of the community."

52 Ibid. 144.

53 Cf. W. Nauck, "Probleme des frühchristlichen Amtsverständnisses (1 Petr 5, 2 f.)" in ZNW 48 (1957).

54 So most recent Commentaries; cf. H. Windisch, *Die Katholischen Briefe* (3rd ed. 1951); J. Michl, *Die Katholischen Briefe* (1953) on the passage; also K. L. Schmidt in ThW II, 102–4. A different view is taken by E. G. Selwyn, *The First Epistle of Saint Peter* (1952), 42 f. and on the passage (118 f.).

[55] Cf. K. L. Schmidt and M. A. Schmidt in ThW V, 850 f.

[56] Ibid. 851, 2 ff.

[57] Cf. E. Käsemann, *Das wandernde Gottesvolk. Eine Untersuchung zum Hebräerbrief* (2nd ed. 1957); A. Oepke, *Das neue Gottesvolk* (1950), 17–24, 57–74 (yet against the "gnostic" thesis); F. J. Schierse, *Verheissung und Heilsvollendung. Zur theologischen Grundfrage des Hebräerbriefes* (1959); cf. also J. Cambier in *Introduction à la Bible* (cf. note 49 above) II, 552 ff. A different, more Christological view, O. Kuss, "Der theologische Grundgedanke des Hebräerbriefes" in MThZ 7 (1956), 233–71.

[58] Cf. O. Michel in ThW V, 128 f. — A different view, F. J. Schierse, *op. cit.* 108–12.

[59] Cf. F. Schierse, *op. cit.* "The Christian community, however, most clearly shows its otherworldly and future character in worship . . ." Cf. also 196–207, where it is pointed out that the liturgical imagery had its context and function in the life of the community, and that even the construction of the epistle fits early Christian divine worship very well. For a criticism of this, cf. O. Kuss in ThRv 53 (1957), 247–54.

[60] F. J. Schierse, *op. cit.* 137.

[61] The analogies adduced by E. Käsemann (*op. cit.* 124–40) overlook the fact that the author of Hebrews argues entirely on the basis of Scripture.

[62] In Kosmala's inquiries (*op. cit.*) the profound differences of content are taken too little into account. This is particularly true of the idea of "perfection" (which he does not deal with), and "enlightenment" (Heb 6 : 4; 10 : 32). In Qumran it is not a question in that respect of "initiation" but rather a metaphorical expression for illumination by God's revelation and truth, cf. *1 QS* 4, 2; 11, 3–6; *1 QH* 18, 19; similarly with the "knowledge of the truth" (Heb 10 : 26), cf. *1 QS* 9, 17; *1 QH* 9, 9 f.; 10, 20, 29 etc., cf. 1 Tim 2 : 4; Tit 1 : 1; 2 Tim 2 : 25; 3 : 7.

[63] As well as Kosmala, cf. C. Spicq, "L'Épître aux Hébreux, Apollos, Jean-Baptiste, les Hellénistes et Qumran" in *Revue de Qumran* 1 (1959), 365–90 (with more discriminating judgments).

[64] H. Kosmala, *op. cit.* 4.

[65] H. Kosmala translates: "the doctrine of the beginning of Messianic life" (30).

[66] C. Spicq in *Revue de Qumran* 1 (1959), 390.

[67] Cf. C. Spicq, *Les Épîtres Pastorales* (1947), XCV–CXXX;

A. Wikenhauser, *Introduction* (note 49), 445–52; L. Cerfaux in *Introduction à la Bible* (see above, Part Two, note 49), II, 523–9.

[68] That is done in Paul by the stress laid on the Spirit; cf. O. Michel in ThW V, 142–5.

[69] M. Dibelius — H. Conzelmann, *Die Pastoralbriefe* (3rd ed. 1955) bring out the "domestic society", while O. Michel, *op. cit.* 129 would prefer to omit this element of the *familia Dei*.

[70] Cf. *1 QS* 8, 5, 7 f., 9; 9, 6; *1 QH* 6, 28; *4 QpPs* 37, 2, 16; and also O. Betz in ZNW 48 (1957), 57 ff.; J. Maier, *Die Texte vom Toten Meer* (annotations) (1960), 93 f.

[71] O. Betz, *Offenbarung und Schriftforschung in der Qumran-Sekte* (1960), 54.

[72] On reconciliation cf. especially P. Galtier, "La réconciliation des pécheurs dans la Première Épître à Timothée" in RSR 39 (1951–2), 317–20; cf. also M. Dibelius — H. Conzelmann, *Die Pastoralbriefe* on the passage; on the contrary for ordination, among others, C. Spicq, *Les Épîtres Pastorales* (1947) on the passage; J. Freundorfer, *Die Pastoralbriefe* (3rd ed. 1959) on the passage; W. Doskocil, *Der Bann in der Urkirche* (1958), 90–3.

[73] Cf. C. Spicq, *Les Épîtres Pastorales*, 43–51; H. Schlier, "Die Ordnung der Kirche nach den Pastoralbriefen" in *Die Zeit der Kirche* (1956), 129–47.

[74] Cf. R. Bultmann, *Theology of the New Testament*, II, 111–18; also N. A. Dahl, *Das Volk Gottes* ("metamorphosis of Paul's concept of the Church").

[75] *Op. cit.* 67–79.

[76] Ibid. 70.

[77] "Le problème de l'Église dans le christianisme primitif" in RHPhR 18 (1938), 293–320, especially 300 and 313 f.

[78] E. Gaugler, "Die Bedeutung der Kirche in den johanneischen Schriften" in IKZ 14 (1924), 97–117, 181–219; 15 (1925), 27–42; D. Faulhaber, *Das Johannesevangelium und die Kirche* (1935); A. Corell, *"Consummatum est." Eschatology and Church in the Gospel of Saint John* (1958); E. Schweizer, "Der Kirchenbegriff im Evangelium und den Briefen des Johannes" in *Studia Evangelica* (TU 73, 1959), 363–81.

[79] *Die Tradition und der Charakter des ersten Johannesbriefes* (1957).

[80] Cf. R. Schnackenburg, *Die Johannesbriefe* (1953), 155–62; F. M. Braun, "La vie d'en haut (Jo 3 : 1–15)" in RScPhTh 40 (1956), 3–24; J. Guillet, "Baptême et Esprit" in *Lumière et Vie* 26 (1956), 85–104.

[81] Cf. especially M. E. Boismard, "De son ventre couleront des fleuves d'eau" in RB 65 (1958), 522–46; P. Grelot, M. E. Boismard, J. P. Audet in RB 66 (1959), 369–86; G. D. Kilpatrick, "The Punctuation in John VII, 37–8" in JThSt 11 (1960), 340–2.

[82] Cf. R. Schnackenburg, *op. cit.* on the passage; W. Thüsing, *Die Erhöhung und Verherrlichung Jesu im Johannesevangelium* (1960), 165–74.

[83] Cf. R. Schnackenburg, "Die Sakramente im Johannesevangelium" in *Sacra Pagina* II (1959), 235–54; and W. Thüsing, *op. cit.* 159–65.

[84] Cf. W. Thüsing, *op. cit.* 101–92.

[85] Cf. M. E. Boismard, "Le Chapitre 21 de saint Jean" in RB 54 (1947), 473–501; E. Ruckstuhl, *Die literarische Einheit des Johannesevangeliums* (151), 134–49.

[86] Cf. C. H. Dodd, *The Interpretation of the Fourth Gospel* (1953), 410 ff.; cf. also E. Schweizer, *Der Kirchenbegriff,* (cf. above, note 78), 369 and note 3 (contrary to his earlier derivation from Mandaean texts).

[87] Cf. R. Schnackenburg, "Die 'Anbetung in Geist und Wahrheit' (Jn 4 : 23) im Lichte von Qumrân-Texten" in BZ N. F. 3 (1959).

[88] For the application of John 2 : 21 to the community, cf. in particular O. Cullmann, *Urchristentum und Gottesdienst* (2nd ed. 1950), 72–6, English translation, *Early Christian Worship* (1953); A. Corell, *op. cit.* 49 ff. The "collective" interpretation of the "Son of man" was repeatedly proposed by T. W. Manson, last of all in *The Servant — Messiah* (1953), 72 ff., cf. also O. Cullmann, *Die Christologie des Neuen Testamentes* (Tübingen 1957), 157 ff., English translation, *The Christology of the New Testament* (1963). The (false) translation in the Septuagint in Ps 79 :16 to which C. H. Dodd draws attention (*op. cit.* 411), can hardly prove anything with regard to John.

[89] A. Corell, *op. cit.* 47: "It reflects the seething life of the early Christian Church, a life which found its main expression in liturgy and teaching."

[90] The section John 6 : 51c–58, the Johannine style of which cannot be disputed, also belongs by content to the "bread of life" discourse, cf. H. Schürmann, "Jo 6, 51c–58, ein Schlüssel zur grossen johanneischen Brotrede" in BZ N. F. 2 (1958), 244–62; the same author's "Die Eucharistie als Repräsentation und Applikation des Heilsgeschehens nach Joh 6, 53–59" in ThZ 68, 30–45, 108–18.

[91] O. Cullmann, *Urkirche und Gottesdienst* (2nd ed. 1950), 58, English translation *Early Christian Worship* (1953).

[92] Ibid. 75.

[93] Cf. O. Cullmann, "Samaria and the Origins of the Christian Mission" in *The Early Church* (1956), 183–92; the same author in NTS 5 (1958–9), 163 f.

[94] Cf. J. B. Bauer, "Könige und Priester, ein heiliges Volk (Ex 19, 6)" in BZ N. F. 2 (1958), 283–6.

[95] So most recent commentaries; cf. E. Lohmeyer, *Die Offenbarung des Johannes* (3rd ed. 1953); J. Behm, *Die Offenbarung des Johannes* (5th ed. 1949); J. Bonsirven, *L'Apocalypse de saint Jean* (1951); A. Wikenhauser, *Die Offenbarung des Johannes* (3rd ed. 1959); all on the relevant passage.

[96] Cf. the account of the literature by J. Michl, "Die Deutung der apokalyptischen Frau in der Gegenwart" in BZ N. F. 3 (1959), 301–10.

[97] An interpretation which seeks to refer Apocalypse 12 : 2 ff. to the birth of the Christ of the Parousia by the community (cf. E. Schweizer, *Gemeinde und Gemeindeordnung*, 119, note 485), breaks down over the "carrying off" of the child after the birth and the "flight" of the woman, into the desert.

Part Three

[1] On this controverted set of problems cf. particularly K. Schubert, "Die Messiaslehre in den Texten von Chirbet Qumran" in BZ N. F. 1 (1957), 177–97; A. S. van der Woude, *Die messianischen Vorstellungen der Gemeinde von Qumran* (1957); the same author's "Le Maître de Justice et les deux Messies de la Communauté de Qumrân" in *Recherches Bibliques* IV (1959), 121–34. On the well-known thesis of A. Dupont — Sommer and J. M. Allegro, cf. J. Daniélou, *Les Manuscrits de la Mer Morte et les origines du Christianisme* (1957).

[2] Cf. J. Carmignac, "Le retour du Docteur de Justice à la fin des jours?" in *Revue de Qumran* 1 (1958), 235–48.

[3] Cf. F. Nötscher, *Die theologische Terminologie der Qumran-Texte* (1958), 162–9; K. Schubert, *Die Gemeinde vom Toten Meer* (1958), 88–93.

[4] Cf. the work of F. J. Schierse referred to in Part Two, note 57 above, and also cf. note 59.

[5] Cf. E. Grässer, *Das Problem der Parousieverzögerung in den synoptischen Evangelien und in der Apostelgeschichte* (1957); for criticism cf. O. Cullmann, "Parusieverzögerung und Urchristentum" in ThLZ 83 (1958), 1–12; J. Gnilka, "Parusieverzögerung und Naherwartung in den synoptischen Evangelien und in der Apostelgeschichte" in *Catholica* 13 (1959), 277–90.

[6] On the concept of the Spirit in Qumran, cf. F. Nötscher, "Geist und Geister in den Texten von Qumrân" in *Mélanges bibliques rédigés en l'honneur d'A. Robert* (Paris 1957), 305–15; J. Coppens, "Le Don de l'Esprit d'après les Textes de Qumran et le quatrième Évangile" in *L'Évangile de Jean (Recherches Bibliques III)* (1958), 209–23; F. Nötscher in *Revue de Qumran* 2 (1960), 333–44.

[7] Cf. O. Betz in NTS 3 (1956–7), 324 f.

[8] Cf. above, Part One, note 15.

[9] Cf. P. Bonnard, "L'Esprit saint et l'Église selon le Nouveau Testament" in RHPhR 37 (1957), 81–90.

[10] Cf. J. Jeremias, *Jerusalem zur Zeit Jesu* (2nd ed. 1958), IIB, 2–59.

[11] E. Lohse, *Die Ordination im Spätjudentum und im Neuen Testament* (151), 84.

[12] K. Schubert, *Die Gemeinde vom Toten Meer* (1958), 30.

[13] Cf. S. Johnson, "The Dead Sea Manual of Discipline and the Jerusalem Church of Acts" in *The Scrolls and the New Testament* edited by K. Stendahl (1957), 129–42; B. Reicke, "The Constitution

of the Primitive Church in the Light of Jewish Documents" ibid. 143–56; J. Schmitt, "L'organisation de l'Église primitive et Qumran" in *Recherches Bibliques* IV (1959), 217–31; F. Nötscher, "Vorchristliche Typen urchristlicher Ämter? Episcopos und Mebaqqer" in *Die Kirche und ihre Ämter und Stände. Festgabe für Kardinal Frings* (1960), 315—38.

[14] Cf. R. Bohren, *Das Problem der Kirchenzucht im Neuen Testament* (1952), also W. Doskocil, *Der Bann in der Urkirche* (1958).

[15] Cf. R. Schnackenburg, *The Moral Teaching of the New Testament* (1965), 217–25.

[16] Cf. K. L. Schmirt in ThW III, 500; N. A. Dahl, *Das Volk Gottes* (1941), 206, stresses (as against W. Bousset): "As 'those who call upon the name of the Lord', the Christians are the members of the people of God."

[17] Cf. E. Haenchen, "Matthäus 23" in ZThK 48 (1951), 38–63; also G. Barth, "Das Gesetzesverständnis des Evangelisten Matthäus" in *Überlieferung und Auslegung im Matthäusevangelium* (1960), 54–154, especially 149–54; E. Käsemann, "Die Anfänge christlicher Theologie" in ZThK 57 (1960), 162–85. But this is mostly conjectural.

[18] E. Käsemann, *op.cit.* 166.

[19] Cf. O. Cullmann, Die ersten christlichen Glaubensbekenntnisse (1949); J. N. D. Kelly, *Early Christian Creeds* (2nd ed. 1960), 6–29.

[20] On the *crux interpretum* αὐτῶν καὶ ἡμῶν cf. now U. Wickert, "Einheit und Eintracht der Kirche im Präskript des ersten Korintherbriefes" in ZNW 50 (1959), 73–82. [21] U. Wickert, ibid. 82.

[22] On unity of the Church cf. H. Schlier in LThK III, 750–4 (bibliography). Lutheran (Evangelical) view: E. Kinder, *Der Evangelische Glaube und die Kirche* (1958), esp. pages 44–50, 199–209.

[23] Cf. above, Part Two, § 1 and note 86 to Part One.

[24] Cf. H. Braun, "Beobachtungen zur Tora-Verschärfung im häretischen Spätjudentum" in ThLZ 79 (1954), 347—52; by the same author: *Spätjüdisch-häretischer und frühchristlicher Radikalismus*, 2 vols. (1957).

[25] Cf. W. G. Kümmel, "Jesus und der jüdische Traditionsgedanke" in ZNW 33 (1934), 105–30; W. Gutbrod in ThW IV, 1051–7; R. Schnackenburg, *op. cit.* 37–45; E. Käsemann in ZThK 51 (1954), 144 ff.

[26] Cf. K. Schubert, "Bergpredigt und Texte von En Fesha" in ThQ 135 (1955), 320—37; R. Schnackenburg, "Die Vollkommenheit des Christen nach den Evangelien" in *Geist und Leben* 32 (1959), 420–33.

[27] Cf. as well as the second volume of the work of H. Braun (see note 24 above), H. W. Huppenbauer, *Der Mensch zwischen zwei Welten* (1959); P. J. du Plessis, Τέλειος. *The Idea of Perfection in the New Testament* (1960), 104–15 (Qumran), 168 (gospels); F. Nötscher, "Heiligkeit in den Qumranschriften" in *Revue de Qumran* 2 (1960), 315–44, particularly pages 328–33; D. Barthélemy, "La sainteté selon la communauté de Qumran et selon l'Évangile" in *Recherches Bibliques* IV (1959), 203–16.

[28] Cf. above, Part Two, § 3.

[29] Cf. R. Schnackenburg in LThK II, 429–33 (bibliography).

[30] Cf. S. Schulz, "Zur Rechtfertigung aus Gnaden in Qumran und bei Paulus" in ZThK 56 (1959), 155—85.

[31] Cf. J. Gnilka in *Revue de Qumran* 3 (1961), 185–207.

[32] Cf. above, Part One, note 77, and Part Three, note 1.

[33] Cf. N. A. Dahl, *op. cit.* 142 f.; J. Jeremias, *Jesu Verheissung für die Völker* (1956), 9–15. English translation, *Jesus' Promise to the Nations* (Studies in Biblical Theology 24) (1958).

[34] Cf. E. Sjöberg, *Gott und die Sünder im Palästinischen Judentum* (1938), 72–94, 210 ff.

[35] Cf. A. Vögtle, *Das öffentliche Wirken Jesu auf dem Hintergrund der Qumranbewegung* (1958).

[36] N. A. Dahl, *op. cit.* 142 (both quotations).

[37] Cf. E. Neuhäusler, "Ruf Gottes und Stand der Christen" in BZ N. F. 3 (1959), 43–60.

[38] Cf. J. Jeremias, *op. cit.* 14.

[39] Cf. W. Thüsing, *Die Erhöhung und Verherrlichung Jesu im Johannesevangelium* (1960), 22–29, 101–7.

Part Four

[1] W. G. Kümmel in H. Lietzmann, *An die Korinther* (4th ed. 1949), appendix 166.

[2] Cf. A. Wikenhauser, *Die Kirche als der mystische Leib Christi nach dem Apostel Paulus* (1940), 77—81.

[3] Cf. H. Wendland, *Geschichtsanschauung und Geschichtsbewusstsein im Neuen Testament* (1938), 23–39; R. Bultmann, *Theology of the New Testament*, I, (1952), 274–9; M. Meinertz, *Theologie des Neuen Testamentes* (1950) II, 214 ff.

[4] Cf. O. Michel, "Die Lehre von der christlichen Vollkommenheit nach der Anschauung des Hebräerbriefes" in ThStKr 106 (1934–5), 333–55; E. Käsemann, *Das wandernde Gottesvolk,* 82–90; P. J. du Plessis, Τέλειος. *The Idea of Perfection in the New Testament* (1960), 212–33.

[5] Cf. F. J. Schierse in LThK III, 924.

[6] On the history of the idea in the Old Testament and its theology, cf. Dahl, *Das Volk Gottes* (1941), 2–50; H. Strathmann in ThW IV, 32–39 (significance of the Septuagint linguistic usage).

[7] N. A. Dahl, *op. cit.* 83.

[8] Cf. J. B. Bauer, "Könige und Priester, ein heiliges Volk (Ex 19, 6)" in BZ N. F. 2 (1958).

[9] *Op. cit.* 243.

[10] Cf. I. Hermann, *Kyrios und Pneuma. Studien zur Christologie der paulinischen Hauptbriefe* (1961), bibliography.

[11] Cf D. E. Holwerda, *The Holy Spirit and Eschatology in the Gospel of John* (1959).

[12] Cf. J. Jeremias in ThW IV, 278 f.; O. Michel, ibid. 892; H. Schlier, *Der Brief an die Epheser*, 142 and note 3 (bibliography).

[13] J. Blinzer, "'Ιεράτευμα Zur Exegese von 1 Petr 2 : 5 and 9" in *Episcopus* (Festschrift für M. Kardinal Faulhaber) (1949), 59.

[14] Cf. H. Wenschkewitz, "Die Spiritualisierung der Kultusbegriffe Tempel, Priester und Opfer im Neuen Testament" in *Angelos* 4 (1932).

[15] O. Michel in ThW V, 129, 133 ff.

[16] Cf. P. Seidensticker, *Lebendiges Opfer (Röm 12, 1)* (1954).

[17] Cf. J. Gewiess, *Die Urapostolische Heilsverkündigung nach der Apostelgeschichte* (1939), 94 f.

[18] Cf. A. Oepke, "Leib Christi oder Volk Gottes bei Paulus?" in ThLZ 79 (1954), 363–8; I. Backes, "Die Kirche ist das Volk Gottes im Neuen Bund" in TThZ 69 (1960), 111–17; J. Ratzinger, "Kirche" in LThK VI, 167–86.

[19] The whole set of questions is envisaged from the idea of the

"corporate personality" by E. Best, *One Body in Christ* (1955), see especially pages 20–30; similarly, in the sense of "representation", S. Hanson, *The Unity of the Church in the New Testament* (1946), *passim,* here 79–82.

[20] Out of the abundant literature the following may be mentioned: E. Mersch, *Le Corps mystique du Christ,* two volumes (2nd ed. 1936); A. Wikenhauser, *Die Kirche als der mystische Leib Christi nach dem Apostel Paulus* (1940); L. S. Thornton, *The Common Life in the Body of Christ* (2nd ed. 1944); E. Percy, *Der Leib Christi in den paulinischen Homologumena und Antilegomena* (1942); S. Hanson, *The Unity of the Church in the New Testament* (1946); L. Cerfaux, *The Church in the Theology of Saint Paul;* L. Malevez, "L'Église, Corps du Christ" in RSR 32 (1944), 27–94; H. Schlier, "Corpus Christi", RAC III, 437–53 (bibliography); J. Reuss, "Die Kirche als 'Leib Christi' und die Herkunft dieser Vorstellung bei dem Apostel Paulus" in BZ N. F. 2 (1958), 103–27 (bibliography). Further indications cf. notes 26 and 31 below.

[21] Cf. L. Cerfaux, *The Church in the Theology of Saint Paul* (1947), 277 f. note. J. Reuss, *op. cit.* 109 f.; J. Havet, "La doctrine paulinienne du 'Corps du Christ'" in *Recherches Bibliques* V (1960), 185–216.

[22] Cf. J. Reuss, *op. cit.* 106: Paul "probably means by πνεῦμα the σῶμα πνευματικόν of the risen and glorified Christ, of which the Christians have become members."

[23] Cf. P. Neuenzeit, *Das Herrenmahl. Studien zur paulinischen Eucharistieauffassung* (1960), 201 f. He rightly recognizes that v. 16b may not be drawn into the syllogism of verse 17. "Verse 17 gives the thought a new direction, which parts from the original trend of verse 16 as well as from the general argument" (p. 202).

[24] Cf. P. Neuenzeit, *op. cit.* 210 ff.

[25] Cf. H. Schlier in RAC II, 439; id. *Der Brief an die Epheser* (3rd ed. 1962), 90.

[26] Cf. Käsemann, *Leib und Leib Christi* (1933); E. Percy, *op. cit.* (note 20 above); J. A. T. Robinson, *The Body* (1952); P. Benoit, "Corps, Tête et Plérôme dans les Epîtres de la Captivité" in RB 63 (1956), 5–44; H. Schlier, *Der Brief an die Epheser* (3rd ed. 1962), Excursus 90–96.

[27] Cf J. Gewiess, "Die Begriffe πληροῦν and πλήρωμα im Kolosser- und Epheserbrief" in *Vom Wort des Lebens* (Festschrift für M. Meinertz) (1951), 128–41; H. Schlier, *op cit.* Excursus 96–99; G. Delling in ThW VI, 297–304.

[28] G. Delling in ThW VI, 291, 6 ff.

²⁹ Cf. H. Schlier, *op. cit.* 260 f.

³⁰ On the anthropos myth, cf. W. Staerk, *Die Erlösererwartung in den östlichen Religionen* (1938), 7–144; S. Schulz in ThR 26 (1960), 219–39 (account of research, in particular regarding C. Colpe).

³¹ Cf. P. Pokorný, "Σῶμα Χριστοῦ im Epheserbrief" in EvTh 20: (160), 456–64; H. Hegermann, "Zur Ableitung der Leib-Christi-Vorstellung" in ThLZ 85 (1960), 839–42; C. Colpe, "Zur Leib-Christi-Vorstellung im Epheserbrief" in *Judentum, Urchristentum, Kirche* (Festschrift für J. Jeremias) (1960), 172–87.

³² Cf. R. Löwe, *Kosmos und Aion* (1935); H. Sasse in ThW III, 867–96; R. Schnackenburg, *Die Johannesbriefe* (1953), 117–20; R. Bultmann, *op. cit.* I, 254–9; F. Mussner, "Kosmos" in LThK VI.

³³ At the most we might recall the clash with the pagan diabolically corrupted State in Apocalypse, chs. 13 and 17; yet that antithesis must be seen in relation to the anti-God and anti-Christian attitude of that State which had degenerated into emperor-worship. There is a more positive judgment as well (Rom 13). Cf. R. Schnackenburg, *The Moral Teaching of the New Testament* (1965), 235–44; O. Cullmann, *The State in the New Testament* (1957); H. Schlier, "Die Beurteilung des Staates im Neuen Testament" in *Die Zeit der Kirche*, 1—16.

³⁴ For the world as creation too, for example, ὁ κόσμος is used, especially in the expression "from the foundation of the world" (Mt 25 : 34; Lk 11 : 50 etc.); cf. H. Sasse in ThW III, 883 f. On the use of τὰ πάντα cf. O. Perels, "Kirche und Welt nach dem Epheser- und Kolosserbrief" in ThLZ 76 (1951), 391–400; F. Mussner, *Christus, das All und die Kirche, Studien zur Theologie des Epheserbriefes* (1955), 29–33; B. Reicke in ThW V, 892 f.

³⁵ Cf. H. M. Biedermann, *Die Erlösung der Schöpfung beim Apostel Paulus* (1940), especially 69–78, 100-4.

³⁶ Cf. B. Caird, *Principalities and Powers* (1956); H. Schlier, *Principalities and Powers in the New Testament* (Quaestiones Disputatae 3) the same author in LThK IV, 849 f.

³⁷ Cf. F. Mussner, *op. cit.* 64–8; he only admits this interpretation.

³⁸ Cf. H. Schlier in ThW III, 681 f.; *Der Brief an die Epheser* (3rd ed. 1962), 64 f.

³⁹ H. Schlier, *Der Brief an die Epheser*, 47.

⁴⁰ Cf. R. Schnackenburg, *God's Rule and Kingdom* (1963), 312–17.

⁴¹ Cf. V. Warnach, "Kirche und Kosmos" in *Enkainia*. Edited by H. Edmonds (1956), 170–205.

221

[42] As the Apostle in the Epistle to the Colossians takes up views of the false teachers and to a certain extent their terminology too, he could be thinking in Colossians 2 : 19 with the "whole body" of the "cosmos represented by the στοιχεῖα"; this is the view of M. Dibelius - H. Greeven, *An die Kolosser, Epheser und Philemon* (3rd ed. 1953), on the passage; but this interpretation remains open to doubt. The application to the Body of Christ-the Church, is retained by most commentators. H. Schlier would prefer to interpret the same expression in Eph 4 : 16 as referring to the "cosmic body" (cf. his commentary on the passage); but this is hardly likely in the context.

[43] *God's Rule and Kingdom* (1964), 302–8.

[44] R. Grosche, *Pilgernde Kirche* (1938), 42 f. rightly opposes such a thesis of A. Vonier, as he presented in three lectures given at Salzburg (*Das Mysterium der Kirche*, 1934).

[45] Cf. R. Grosche, *op. cit.* 66 f.

[46] Cf. H. Schlier, *op. cit.* on the passage (258 and note 4).

[47] *Retract.* 1, 7, 5 (PL 32, 539).

[48] O. Cullmann, *Petrus* (see above, Part One, note 28), 235.

[49] Cf. A. Vögtle in LThK II, 480–2.

[50] O. Cullmann, *op. cit.* 234.

[51] P. Neuenzeit, *op. cit.* 132.

[52] Cf. L. Michl in LThK II, 1085 f. (bibliography); R. Schnackenburg, *God's Rule and Kingdom*, 329–31.

[53] Cf. L. Cerfaux, *The Church in the Theology of Saint Paul* (1959), 348 ff. J. Schmidt in RAC II, 546 f.; J. Jeremias in ThW IV, 1097 f. Eph 5 : 22 ff. must be differently regarded; cf. H. Schlier, *op. cit.* 264 ff.